KOTA MAMA

FROM THE ANDES TO THE ATLANTIC — AN AMAZING JOURNEY OF ADVENTURE AND DISCOVERY

JOHN BLASHFORD-SNELL
AND
RICHARD SNAILHAM

HEADLINE

First published in 2000
by HEADLINE BOOK PUBLISHING

First published in paperback in 2001
by HEADLINE BOOK PUBLISHING

10 9 8 7 6 5 4 3 2 1

British Library Cataloguing in Publication Data
is available from the British Library

ISBN 0 7472 6138 5

Typeset by Palimpsest Book Production Limited
Polmont, Stirlingshire
Printed and bound in Great Britain by
Mackays of Chatham plc, Chatham, Kent

HEADLINE BOOK PUBLISHING
A division of Hodder Headline
338 Euston Road
London NW1 3BH

www.headline.co.uk
www.hodderheadline.com

JOHN BLASHFORD-SNELL, a Royal Engineer, is the veteran of many successful expeditions, including the Blue Nile, British Trans-Americas and Zaire River. In 1969 he and his colleagues formed the Scientific Exploration Society, and went on to launch Operations Drake and Raleigh. He was awarded the Segrave Trophy in 1974 and in 1993 the Royal Geographical Society presented him with their Patron's Medal for 'encouragement of exploration by young people'. He is the author of several bestselling books including *In the Steps of Stanley*, three books on *Operation Raleigh*, his autobiography *Something Lost Behind the Ranges* and *Mammoth Hunt*.

RICHARD SNAILHAM was for twenty-five years Senior Lecturer at the Royal Military Academy Sandhurst. He has taken part in expeditions to places as far apart as Mongolia, Honduras, Chile and Zaire and heads lecture tours in areas as diverse as China, Ethiopia, Bolivia and Brittany. He was educated at Oakham in Rutland and Keble College, Oxford, is married to a doctor and lives in Windsor, Berkshire. This is his fifth book.

This book is dedicated to Canning House, that unique institution in London's Belgrave Square, for its pivotal role over more than half a century in kindling and fostering a fascination with Latin America in so many British hearts.

CONTENTS

Acknowledgements

We are very grateful for the help received from the library staffs at the Royal Military Academy Sandhurst, the Royal Geographical Society, Canning House, Windsor public library, the Shaftesbury Library and the Scientific Exploration Society archives.

Thanks are also due to the Chairman, Richard Hodgson, and members of the Constitutional Club at Windsor for allowing Richard Snailham to work in its telephone-free peace; to Anne Carter for her excellent lunches; and to David Waters, Roy Thomas and Christopher Hotton for their various forms of help.

The great burden of the typing was borne by Darren Ward, whose work was unfailingly accurate and prompt, with considerable help from Judith Blashford-Snell and Anne Gilby at the Scientific Exploration Society's Expedition Base. The immeasurable support given by Jim Allen, Jim Masters, Peter Minter, Yolima Cipagauta and others members of the Kota Mama team was much appreciated. For the maps we are indebted to Ben Cartwright and Nick Hunt, while helpful medical advice came from doctors Christina March and Philippe Ribet.

The Army Training and Recruitment Agency at Upavon also deserve a word for putting up with Richard's Jack Russell terrier while in the care of his sister-in-law, Mrs Mary Newbery, during his absence in South America.

We are also most grateful to Simon Trewin, who while with Sheil Land Associates efficiently found us a publisher.

Finally, we acknowledge the steady encouragement from everyone at Headline, including Heather Holden-Brown, Lorraine Jerram and Jo Roberts-Miller, and the sensitive and painstaking editing of the text by Gillian Bromley.

John Blashford-Snell
Richard Snailham

LIST OF CHAPTER OPENING ILLUSTRATIONS

The Kota Mama Expedition, 1998 and 1999

THE JAGUAR COMES HOME

As the reed boats drifted down the tree-lined canal into the Buenos Aires suburb of Tigre it seemed that they had not just sailed across one continent but reached another. They had traversed the lower half of South America from Lake Titicaca to the Río de la Plata; but they were now in Europe. The trim gardens of the weekend homes of *Porteños* came down to the canal's edge. *Kota Mama 2* and *Viracocha Spirit of Bahamas* passed prestigious office blocks, boat-houses, shipbuilding yards . . .

They arrived at a busy T-junction of canals where smartly varnished wooden river ferries, roofed and glazed against intemperate weather, carried commuters in and out of the canal spur like taxis round Trafalgar Square, managing narrowly to avoid passing scullers. It was Venice with its *vaporetti*.

The green lawns of the Tigre Sailing Club sported a fine mainmast and spar from an old sailing ship, from which no doubt the club's burgee could be flown when members gathered for drinks after a regatta. It was St Mawes in Cornwall.

On the corner of the T-junction a roller-coaster swooped and climbed noisily through a *papier-mâché* mountain. A Ferris wheel circled lazily and there was a steady hum of dodgem cars and the piercing shrieks of the young people of Tigre enjoying their afternoon in the amusement park. It was Munich at the *Oktoberfest*.

Crisply uniformed officers of the Argentinian Prefectura Naval, with names like Bertolucci, Mannheim and Martinovic, bustled up and down outside their marble headquarters as support vessel *Puerto Quijarro* executed a five-point turn at her journey's end. Strolling couples stared at the bright Bolivian flag at her stern. It had every right to be flown in these international waters, but probably never had been before in this Río de la Plata backwater. Nor, perhaps, had the red ensigns worn by our reed boats been much seen here.

A heavy drizzle fell from a leaden sky. Only the twenty or so white heron sitting impassively on the pleasure-garden railings reminded the boats' crews of the bankside wildlife they had become so used to over two months.

Argentinians take readily to the water themselves. Tigre is full of oarsmen. Huatajata on Lake Titicaca, where we began our journey, has its yacht club, but there are more rowing clubs in Tigre than there are tea-shops in Torquay. Narrow-gauge railway lines cut across the asphalted esplanade on which the clubs' fours and eights are manoeuvred gingerly out of their hangars and down ramps into the canal. It was a world away from the torpor and squalor of the Bolivian frontier town of Desaguadero where we had begun our first trial run with the reed boats in March 1998.

Throughout our odyssey we had been in Latin America, but the people had exhibited subtle differences as we moved east and south: the Bolivians of the Altiplano, impoverished, inscrutable, wary; their smarter cousins in La Paz, slow-moving but supportive; their richer cousins in Santa Cruz de la Sierra, even more ready and able to help; then the Brazilians, who seemed on brief acquaintance accomodating, cosmopolitan, flashy; afterwards the delightful Paraguayans, insouciant, welcoming, corrupt, happy-go-lucky; finally the proud, neurotic, efficient, sophisticated Argentinians. A kaleidoscope of friends and supporters all the way.

Our flagship, *Kota Mama 2*, had successfully navigated 2,770 kilometres down the Paraguay and Paraná rivers to Tigre. This was, in a special way, an appropriate terminus, for 'tigre' was what the early Spanish conquistadors had called the jaguar, the native wild cat of South America; and perhaps the most arresting feature of our big reed boat was the massive jaguar head at its prow.

PHASE I

Lake Titicaca–Lake Poopó
1998

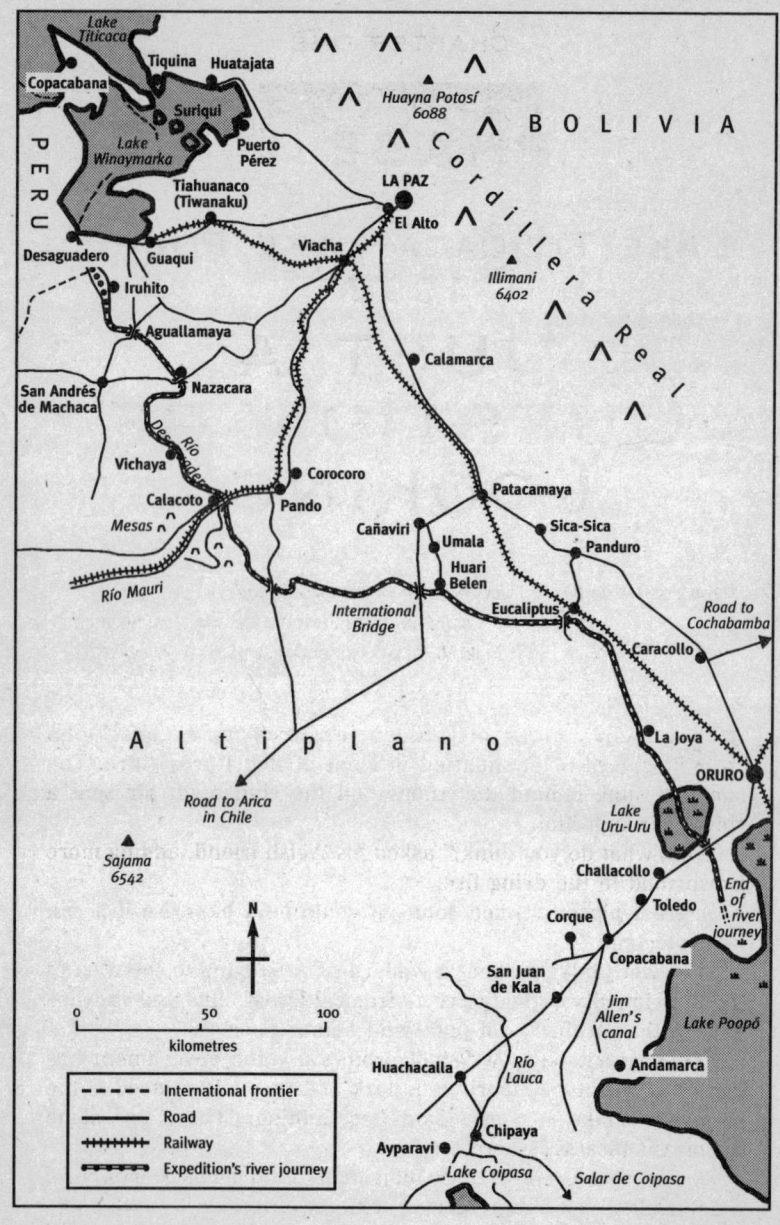

CHAPTER ONE

'JUST A QUESTION OF LOOKING'

You cannot do better than to go by Dover and Calais.
CHAIRMAN OF THE ROYAL GEOGRAPHICAL SOCIETY,
TO A FELLOW ASKING THE BEST ROUTE TO BOLIVIA, 1881

Gratefully pulling off sodden jungle boots, Colonel John Blashford-Snell squatted in front of Reg Hardy's fire. The sun had sunk behind the Andes and the chill night air sent a shiver through him.

'Well, what do you think?' asked his Welsh friend, adding more brushwood to the dying fire.

'A great place,' replied John. 'It could be a paradise if it can be protected.'

They were talking about a wilderness area lying to the west of the Bolivian city of Santa Cruz – tropical forest, hills and canyons alive with a profusion of plant and animal species.

'Don't worry, boyo, we shall protect it – the government has agreed to gazette Amboro as a park and now all we need is the money to make it work,' said Reg, adding: 'There are some important Inca sites here too.'

Reg Hardy was one of those individuals John meets everywhere: a determined, energetic idealist with an obsession to save some place, some fauna or flora or a people from the relentless march of progress and the destruction it can cause. Invariably such people all have the same problem – few or no funds. What they do is done for love, which usually means they spend their hard-won savings trying to achieve their aim. Some succeed, others fail, and throughout his life John has tried to help many in whom he has believed.

It was 1985 and, as the leader of the massive global youth enterprise, Operation Raleigh, John had sent a team of 'venturers' (as the participants were known) into a remote, drug-growing area of Bolivia to assist Reg in his quest. Continued support would be vital and, knowing the colonel would have to return to his flagship, the *Sir Walter Raleigh*, in Chile the next day, the conservationist talked far into the night.

'Tell me about the archaeology,' said John, pouring two fingers of whisky into his mug.

'There were people here long before the Incas, you know,' said Reg. 'I've seen their roads and their fortresses – and I believe they moved all over South America by foot and boat.'

John, a man noted for his exploration of rivers, pounced on this. 'By boat? What sort of boat?'

'Reed boats, I tell you,' said Reg. 'I'm sure these people navigated the rivers with craft built of reeds – like you see on Lake Titicaca today – and I think they also used balsa rafts and log canoes. It was for trade, you know. There are even legends that they crossed the Atlantic.'

John was looking thoughtful. Pulling out the black notebook that went everywhere with him, he started jotting.

The next morning, bidding Reg farewell at Santa Cruz airport, John brought the subject up again.

'I'd like to talk more about your theories on early river navigation,' he said. 'We must meet when you get home.'

'You have to come and look. This land is barely explored,' urged the Welshman. 'If you don't look, you can't expect to find.'

But although, thanks to Reg and the Raleigh venturers, the Amboro Park became a reality, the two friends were not to see each other again: for, shortly after his return home, Reg died.

Frank Dawson, Texan, Doctor of Law, amateur archaeologist and explorer of Central America, stood in front of his fireplace in Cambridge.

'I've asked a young man to join us,' he informed John. 'Jim

Allen was in the RAF and is one of the best photo interpreters around. He wants your help in South America.'

At that point the doorbell buzzed and a tall, thin, slightly academic-looking Scot in his late thirties entered. He had a rather sad expression but there was a twinkle in his eye and Jim Allen was soon outlining his hypothesis with undisguised passion. As a cartographer, having helped archaeologists to identify sites for many years, he had become deeply interested in the legend of Atlantis.

'I think it could be in the Bolivian Altiplano,' he said, unrolling a sheaf of maps and aerial photographs.

Jim talked non-stop, his long, artistic fingers waving across the maps as he described his theory with deep conviction. 'Thirty-two of the features Plato ascribes to Atlantis apply recognizably to the Bolivian Altiplano,' he said.

John drove straight to London and handed Jim's papers to Jan Spencer. A schoolteacher and the daughter of an archaeologist, she had a lively mind and an interest in history.

'Could you look at this theory and say if there might be some substance in it?' he asked. A month later she phoned: 'We can't say whether there is anything in this. You really need to go and look.'

The ocean was lapping gently on the golden beach of Panama's Bahía Caledonia as John Blashford-Snell and Yolima Cipagauta emerged from their sortie into the Darien jungle to see the ruins of the lost city of Acla that John and archaeologist Dr Mark Horton had discovered in 1978.

'Have you ever looked for other lost civilizations?' asked Yoli, as most of the Scientific Exploration Society's team now called this petite, well-groomed professor of economics at Colombia's military university. '—like Atlantis!' she added.

Munching bananas, they stared into the translucent blue waters; feeling he needed half an hour's rest, John told the tale of a search at the island of Bimini in the Bahamas.

'I've always been fascinated by the mystery of Atlantis – fact or fiction,' he admitted. 'Some years ago the idea that the legendary city existed in the Bahamas was put to me by the Institute of Underwater Archaeology [based in Miami], but all the evidence we discovered could be explained naturally – it wasn't Atlantis or indeed anything man-made.'

Yoli had not spoken a word but, seated on this isolated strand, she seemed, although dressed in US Army fatigues, to be part of history. John realized why. It was her unmistakably Inca profile. Her serious brown eyes sparkled as she said, 'South America is full of undiscovered old places. Have you ever been to Bolivia? They say it is the wilderness of archaeology. Perhaps you should go and look there.'

The Bolivian Altiplano, a huge plateau nestling in the high Andes over 12,000 feet above sea level, was in ancient times twice filled by a huge inland sea. Though the water level has dropped 200 feet, Lake Titicaca, at the northern end, remains a most impressive body of water. Among its vast beds of totora reeds live countless waterbirds; stocky Aymará Indians farm the shore very much as their ancestors did 3,000 years before, when the city of Tiwanaku was the capital of a great empire. Further south the plateau grows drier and at the shores of Lake Poopó, now rapidly disappearing, it is pure desert. Beyond the southern lake are enormous, virtually lifeless salt flats. The intense sunlight, searing wind, blistering heat and bitter cold do not encourage habitation; although hardy races once lived and prospered here, today it is indeed a wilderness.

Three years after their first meeting in Cambridge, Jim Allen had new aerial photos of the Altiplano for John to look at. These pictures appeared to show canals and tracks criss-crossing the desert.

'They seem to fit Plato's description but we need to examine them on the ground. Are you likely to be in Bolivia any time?' he asked. At that time, in the 1980s, John had no immediate plans to go to the region; but a few years later, as luck would have it, Bolivia did figure in his itinerary as one of the possible locations for expeditions to be run by the Scientific Exploration Society. Thus it was that in June 1995 he and Yoli, now the Society's South American representative and John's local PA, found themselves puffing up flights of office stairs in La Paz, at 12,500 feet the highest capital city in the world. One meeting led to another, and it emerged that an area which would benefit most from community aid projects and wildlife studies was that west of the large, shallow Lake Poopó. This was also the location of Jim's Atlantis 'canals'; so, boarding a comfortable bus, they set off for the city of Oruro where Yoli had an introduction to the Prefect.

The journey through a flat, barren landscape fringed by snow-capped peaks was broken only by stops at hamlets of square mud-brick cottages, where women boarded the bus to sell their basketfuls of tasty hot *empanadas* – snacks like small Cornish pasties, sometimes with cheese. The other passengers were Indians: the women in bowler hats, shawls and voluminous skirts and the men, sullen and silent, in trilbies, sweaters and jeans. They showed little interest in the *gringos*, preferring to concentrate on the sex and violence that appeared intermittently on the video screen suspended from the roof. John wondered what these poor, simple people made of Sylvester Stallone and mused that few were even old enough to remember the genuine horrors of Bolivia's war with Paraguay in the 1930s.

Oruro was even higher and colder than La Paz and their heads ached from the altitude. Some relief was afforded by gallons of *mate de coca*, an aromatic infusion of coca leaves, along with locally produced pills of aspirin and caffeine. They found shelter from the cold dry air in a modest hotel on the main square, donned their smartest clothes and walked over to the fortress-like block of offices where they were to meet the Prefecto y Commandante General del Departamento de Oruro. Here Yoli, immaculate and businesslike, took over; her Colombian military identity card had more impact than John's old British one. Crossing a cobbled courtyard, they were led past numerous pistol-packing *carabineros* in smart green uniforms and polished black boots. At 2.25 p.m. they were ushered into the Prefect's office. National flags flanked a portrait of the President behind an impressive antique desk. A settee and easy chairs were arranged around a coffee table and it was here that they were invited to sit by the besuited middle-ranking official who had brought them in. He then retired to the door and said no more.

'Do you know the Prefect?' John asked Yoli.

'No,' she replied, 'but she is a friend of the Bolivian Consul in Bogotá who speaks highly of her and has given me a letter of introduction.'

'She? Her?' John looked puzzled; he had been expecting a bemedalled general or at least a colonel. But there was no time to probe further. At precisely 2.30 p.m. the curtains at the far side of the room swished aside and, accompanied by the faintest aroma of a good perfume, Señora H. Mirtha Quevedo Acalinovic made her entry, advancing with hand outstretched. 'Good afternoon, Colonel; welcome to Oruro,' she smiled.

John tried to hide his surprise at being confronted by a beautiful, immaculately dressed lady. Tea was served in delicate china cups and the Prefect listened to the proposals for expeditions

in her region of the Altiplano. There was no need for Yoli to interpret; she spoke perfect English.

'You will need letters of authority which I shall give you,' said
the Prefect, clapping her hands. Instantly an official appeared
and was briefed in rapid Spanish. 'Sí, sí, Señora,' he muttered
and bowed out. 'The people of the Altiplano are very poor and
all help is welcome,' explained the Señora. 'You should also visit
our most respected archaeologist, Dr Luis Guerra, and see our
museum. I shall arrange this. Please let me know how you get
on and do not hesitate to say if I can be of further assistance.'

By the time the second cup of tea was finished the letters were
ready for the Prefect's signature and an official pick-up truck
whisked John and Yoli off to meet the legendary Luis Guerra,
Bolivia's first prominent archaeologist and former Director of the
museum in Oruro. The old gentleman was caught slightly off guard
by their sudden appearance and, although clearly amazed by the
aerial photos, appeared reluctant to divulge much information. He
told them of some ancient mines, but knew nothing about canals.

Slightly more fruitful was a later stop at the office of Estebán
Pinaya, an engineer responsible for the maintenance of the Río
Desaguadero as the main waterway of the Altiplano – a task that
involved its protection within high banks to prevent it spreading
over the flat countryside through which it runs between Lakes
Titicaca and Poopó. Pinaya produced a chart showing a matrix
of canals called Sukakollos, traditionally used by pre-Columbian
Indians for irrigation in the area, which looked almost identical
to Jim Allen's theoretical lattice of waterways. But it was at the
museum that John became quite excited. Showcases of mummies,
the elongated skulls of royal personages with the forehead flat-
tened by compression from birth, and artefacts of the Tiwanaku
and Inca cultures were fascinating, but just as they were leaving
he spotted something else. Tucked away in a corner was an
amphora – looking every bit like those he had found under the
sea when diving on Greek and Roman wrecks off Cyprus in the
1960s. Photography being forbidden, he made a quick sketch and
measured it. 'Tiwanaku,' shrugged the curator, who did not
consider it especially important.

Through the Prefect, Yoli procured a four-wheel-drive vehicle
with a rather reluctant driver who promised he would be ready
to depart at dawn the next day.

'That will be about nine-thirty,' said Yoli as they tucked into
their evening meal: thick asparagus soup and an enormous pepper

steak, washed down with some good Chilean claret, for $5 each. Clearly exploration here need not be expensive.

Early the next morning John woke with a thumping head from the altitude – not, he insisted, the claret! Worse still, a military band was playing rousing patriotic tunes right under his window. Unable to get back to sleep, he put on his warmest clothes and sallied forth with his camera to photograph this dawn chorus. In the street were hundreds of paramilitary *carabineros* forming up for a parade. As the band struck up again the ranks of grim-looking men marched off, arms swinging, towards the Prefecture. '*¿Con permiso?*' asked John. 'Sí, sí,' growled a sergeant in time for a platoon of fierce alsatians, rottweilers and weimaraners to be captured on film as their handlers led them past. Highly polished jeeps and motorcycles followed, all the occupants clutching matt black sub-machine guns. As they swung past the Prefecture, they saluted the general on the balcony. John raised his camera to record the scene and found himself looking beneath the peak of a Castro-style hat into the dark eyes of Señora H. Mirtha Quevedo Acalinovic. He could have sworn she smiled . . . 'She is the Commandant General of our Forces,' explained an old man in response to John's enquiry, 'and they are rehearsing for Armed Forces Day.' The colonel returned to his hotel with renewed respect for Bolivian women.

Eventually, at 10.40 a.m., the short, chubby Otto arrived with his old Toyota. Yoli was outraged by an increase in the fare, but there was little to be gained by objecting: few Oruro drivers fancied venturing into the desert in midwinter with a couple of crazy foreigners – even if they were friends of the Señora.

Driving westwards, past flocks of pink flamingo on the still waters of Lake Uru Uru, they entered a sparsely populated, windswept and mountainous landscape which reminded John of Tibet. Soon they were examining Jim Allen's sites. The aerial photos led them to remains of ancient bridges and depressions in the desert that might have been canals or irrigation ditches. John carefully photographed all these features and mapped the ground out on a blank sheet of paper using compass and Global Positioning System (GPS). However, as he told Yoli once they had resumed their journey, this time heading south, it would take an experienced archaeologist to say whether these features were natural or man-made.

Passing through the once thriving but now almost deserted village of Estancia Rosa Pata, they encountered giant cactus and saw ancient corrals and the walls of terraced fields dating back thousands of years. The few locals whom they met on the road could tell them little about the place, for the most part merely muttering 'Very old . . .'

'This is a land in the last throes of death,' grunted Otto. 'It is a dangerous place. We must be careful.'

'Of what?' asked John, but received no answer.

The sun was glowing red on the western horizon as they rolled into the small town of Andamarca, where they were considering carrying out an aid project. Several men in trilbies and ponchos came out of the shabby municipal building to greet them.

'We are expected,' said Yoli. 'The Prefect has sent a message by radio.'

As she spoke, the councillors were summoned by the blasts of a great curved cow-horn and the visitors were led into a bitterly cold council chamber where for two hours the Mayor, or *Alcalde*, explained the needs of the town: clean water, electricity and help with llama production were high on their list, but strangely the top priorities were a theatre and science laboratories for the schoolchildren. Of canals and ruins he knew little, but the basalt mines at Cerro Pucara, near the south-west corner of Lake Poopó, were recognized as being very old. 'There is also silver there,' he said.

The cloudless desert sky was alive with twinkling stars as John and Yoli moved into their quarters at the radio shack.

'We'd better go to see these mines,' yawned John as he crawled into his sleeping bag.

The next day they really did set off at dawn; but although Otto had crossed himself three times as they drove out, they were soon in trouble. Steam erupted from the bonnet, Otto swore and the car stopped. A herd of vicuña raised their graceful heads from breakfast to see what was up. 'Frozen radiator, I bet,' remarked John, and he was right.

'Minus six degrees Centigrade,' said Yoli, looking at her thermometer. Seizing an empty can, Otto set off towards some distant houses.

Having refilled the radiator, they drove on southwards through featureless sagebrush country, populated by small herds of the tawny-coloured vicuña and stately flightless birds like miniature ostrich that Otto called *ñandu*. The tracks bore no relation to the map and, seeing a small shepherdess with her flock, Yoli asked the way to Orinoca. The enchanting little girl was terribly shy and had to be coaxed with boiled sweets. Her name, she said, was María; she could have been no more than five and, clutching a lamb, she made a delightful picture. Then her uncle appeared and tried to persuade John to adopt her. 'She has no parents,' he said. They drove on, leaving the sad little orphan, with her sheep and her dog, looking somewhat bewildered.

The people of Orinoca, another run-down desert town, were celebrating something and most of them were drunk when the Toyota rolled in, but Yoli managed to hire a guide to take them to the basalt mines. Approaching a low ridge, they realized that it consisted very largely of huge mounds of basalt flakes left by the craftsmen who had fashioned millions of tools from the hard black rock. All around were ancient corrals which would have housed the thousands of llamas used to transport the tools throughout the continent. Jim Allen's aerial photos showed tracks as straight as Roman roads radiating out from the mines in all directions.

The shafts were there too, chiselled out of hillsides, but Otto and the guide declined to enter so Yoli and John went on alone. A narrow entrance forced them to stoop, but after a short way a cavern opened up. It was around 30 feet in diameter with smooth, almost polished walls and a rock-hewn table in the centre. Low side tunnels led off from this chamber, but without caving gear and good torches it would have been foolhardy to attempt further investigation.

'It's so clean and neat! Can it really be three thousand years old?' asked Yoli. John was examining some discarded, beautifully made cutters and axe-heads on the slag heap.

'If these were rejects, the tools were clearly of a very good quality,' he remarked. 'It must have been a highly developed civilization.'

By the time they left the mines the daylight hours were running out, and if they were to be back in Oruro by nightfall they could not afford to linger at many of Jim's locations. Passing an extinct volcano near Estancia Rosa Pata, they saw a long white line cutting through the brush.

'Another of Jim's sites,' said Yoli, who was studying the photos.

'It will be dark in an hour and the ground looks pretty marshy down there,' cautioned John. 'I don't fancy tackling that this late in the day with a single vehicle.'

They pressed on; but even so, night caught them winding along a mass of confusing trails, and it was slow work navigating by stars and compass, with shallow rivers to be forded. Eventually they reached the main road and the contrasting discomfort of the clouds of choking dust thrown up by the convoys of buses and trucks heading into the city.

Back in La Paz two days later they met Dr Carlos Ponce Sanjines, a leading authority on the Tiwanaku culture to whom they had been introduced by Dr Jaime Ponce García, a solicitor and Vice-President of the Central Bank of Bolivia; and it was with Dr Ponce and his wife that they visited the ruins of the great city some 45 miles from the Bolivian capital. The pyramids, temples and statues, and the massive stone blocks, some of which weighed over 100 tonnes, were certainly impressive. Carlos Ponce had played a leading role in the reconstruction of the site, much of which had been destroyed by the Spanish colonial armies, and was an extremely informative guide. He spoke enthusiastically about the navigation of rivers with reed boats and the possibility that early trade had been conducted by this method; but he had no views on Jim Allen's Atlantis theory and John, sensing a lack of interest in this line of enquiry, did not press the subject.

The report that John sent Jim was inconclusive and somewhat negative, but two items caught the cartographer's eye: the amphora in the Oruro museum and the site that John and Yoli had not had time to visit – the long white scar north-east of Estancia Rosa Pata. Jim drew out his last savings and took a plane to Bolivia.

A month later he was back in Britain, convinced that the amphora was an important clue. After all, had not a wreck containing Roman amphorae been discovered off the coast of Brazil – at a place now known as the Bay of Jars? But it was the white scar that had produced really outstanding evidence. He had visited the site and measured it with a surveyor's care. It was a narrow ribbon of water running for about five miles on a north–south axis. The channel was contained between what appeared to be low embankments. The dimensions were especially interesting, corresponding closely to those described by Plato. Could it have been one of Plato's canals?

'The Chaco is one of the least-known areas of South America, and its thorn forests are virtually impenetrable unless you go along on four feet,' remarked the wife of the Paraguayan

Ambassador in London over a glass of champagne. John was listening to every word.

'The wildlife is prolific,' went on Señora Diane Espinoza, 'but when the Paraguayan Army pulls back, settlers will move in and the habitat will be destroyed.' Diane, a trustee of the Fundación Moises Bertoni, was greatly concerned about the conservation of this wilderness, roughly the size of England and Wales. For sixty years, ever since the war with Bolivia, the Paraguayans had maintained a strong military presence in the Chaco; if this were reduced, as now seemed likely, land-hungry peasants would be able to clear the dense forest and raise cattle.

'Why don't you bring an expedition from your Society to help us to preserve this unique region?' Diane asked. 'There are little-known tribes of Indians there, and only a few years ago the giant peccary – a species quite new to science – was discovered.'

Next day, in the library at Canning House – the home of Latin American studies in Britain, named after the early nineteenth-century Foreign Secretary George Canning, who helped rebel movements in the region gain independence from Spain – the explorer scanned the few books available on the Chaco. The name, he discovered, meant 'hunting ground' in the Quechua language. From titles like *Green Hell* he learned what a little-known and under-explored region this was. Relatively little archaeological research had been done there. On the west the Río Pilcomayo flowed from the foothills of the Andes until it disappeared into a great swamp; on the east the Río Paraguay, a much larger waterway, ran from the Mato Grosso of Brazil to join the Río Paraná and eventually the Río de la Plata and the Atlantic. Several tributaries rising in Bolivia fed this river system. 'Perhaps Reg Hardy was right,' John thought, recalling his late friend's ideas about ancient riverine trade routes.

The summer heat had been chilled by a downpour, and the gutters were overflowing as Yoli and John drove into Asunción from the airport. The Gran Hotel Renacimiento produced a room with a large bed 'for a big colonel' at $36 per night and a tiny room with a smaller one for his PA, and the pair set off to meet Diane and Antonio Espinoza. Diane, though a Texan by birth, had a good understanding of the complex politics of Paraguay and her husband, as a former Ambassador to the Court of St James, had made many friends in Britain. Over a delicious steak they provided an excellent briefing; and at a meeting the next morning Graham

Pirnie, the British Ambassador to Paraguay, was keen to encourage a British expedition. 'However, there is one person you must see,' he told John, 'General Lino Oviedo, Commander of the Army – I have made an appointment for you.'

The taxi driver seemed uneasy when Yoli told him where they wanted to go; the general was much feared by certain sections of the community. At the gate of the barracks an officer climbed in and escorted them to a group of unpretentious married quarters where a Guaraní maid opened the door and the general, clad in an English sports jacket and cords, met them with a grin and a firm handshake. He was a small man with bright eyes that darted from one face to another as he spoke in Spanish and German. After generations of training by the German Army, Paraguay had recently started to send officer cadets to Sandhurst; clearly the general was delighted to have a visit from a British colonel who had once been on the staff at Sandhurst, albeit now retired, and was eager to help. The meeting went well and it was obvious that General Oviedo was much interested in the development of the Chaco and keen to assist its Indian population.

'I am told there are ancient ruins there,' he said. 'You should organize some of your scientific exploration expeditions to seek them.'

Next day the general's four-wheel-drive staff car arrived to convey John and Yoli north. The driver, Sergeant Gonzalez, spoke no English, but it was clear that he understood it well enough.

Flanked by the red earth, the tarmac highway ran straight through flat scrub and fields. There were few settlements, but at 2.00 p.m. they pulled in to an army camp where the Paraguayan colonel provided lunch and then showed them around the military farm where conscripts, who do a year's compulsory service, learn agricultural skills and animal management.

'I am sure there are many creatures awaiting discovery out there,' he remarked, with a wave at the thick forest.

Driving on through the afternoon, at sunset they reached Filadelfia, one of the Chaco's Mennonite towns. Many of the followers of Simon Menno, who originated in Germany, emigrated when their beliefs, which included adult baptism, separation of church and state, and pacifism, got them into difficulties in the early twentieth century. In 1927 a large number who had settled in Canada moved on southwards to the Chaco, where they were joined later by others from the Soviet Union, including in 1947 several Germans from the Ukraine. Settlements were founded at

Filadelfia, Loma Plata and Neuland, and there are now over 10,000 Mennonites in the Chaco, where they have made a successful way of life as farmers of fruit, sage and other crops.

Having checked in at Filadelfia's spotlessly clean hotel, John and Yoli met the Governor of the Chaco region and members of the Chaco Foundation, which seeks to conserve the region's fauna and flora. Its director, Wilfred Giesbrecht, had planned a bird sanctuary and John readily agreed to see whether some of the Society's younger members could set this up.

The Chaco war of 1932–5, fought over territory wrongly believed to contain oil, had cost the lives of over 60,000 Bolivians and 30,000 Paraguayans, and throughout the region there were carefully preserved memorials and battle sites. Even now, some men still carry rifles for fear of snakes, Argentinian cattle rustlers and Los Ayoreos, a tribe of Indians who had killed Mennonites in the early days of the settlement.

'We occasionally come home with arrows in the canvas sides of our pick-ups,' mentioned Wilfred casually. 'I think Los Ayoreos just want to be left alone. We rarely see them.'

Near Filadelfia was a compound in the forest where there was a herd of the recently discovered species of wild pig, the giant peccary, awaiting shipment to overseas zoos. They appeared very timid compared with the smaller white-lipped variety John had met in the Darien jungle of Panama in 1972.

At the military base of Mariscal Estigarribia, two hours' drive further on, Major General Guillermo Escobar and a guard of honour awaited them. Accommodation was provided in a spartan but comfortable single-storey officers' mess built around a small courtyard filled with shady trees – and dozens of fat toads which were said to eject poisonous urine.

Three generals, including the Corps Commander, General Torres, took them to dinner at the Hotel Alemán. The host had emigrated from Germany after the war and his son, a handsome, fair-haired Aryan, proudly produced a photo of his Leopard tank with its black cross. 'I was in NATO,' he smiled.

The army seemed keen to show their interest in the welfare of the Chaco Indians. Driving out from the base over the next few days, John and Yoli visited Indian settlements, watched a birth in the army hospital and penetrated far into the thick bush on the few narrow trails. The vegetation was extremely dense, and in the rains the ground would become a morass. Winter temperatures could drop below freezing, but in the summer they were in excess of 50° Celsius. It was obvious that wildlife was plentiful, and not only from the copious tracks left: driving along they saw foxes, hares, armadillos, deer, peccary and dozens of snakes. A night game drive took them to a wide tarmac road in the middle of nowhere. When John remarked on the lights set into the kerbs, Guillermo explained, 'This is an airfield.' It was 5 kilometres long and completely deserted. As they passed the darkened control tower he said, 'The Americans built it for emergency space shuttle landings.' Later it was suggested that it played a significant part in the smuggling of Scotch whisky into Argentina and Brazil.

When the subject of archaeology came up, the soldiers knew nothing.

'You will have to go and look,' was all they could say, though they added, 'there are rumours of stone buildings and strange inscriptions.' The problem would be how to get through this green hell where the thorns were four inches long. 'It is like concentrated barbed wire,' warned Guillermo Escobar. 'Make friends with the Indians, they have secret paths.'

The original idea had been to go on north into Bolivia by bus, but General Torres had advised against this – and he was right. A national strike in Bolivia forced John and Yoli to return to Asunción and fly to Santa Cruz. From the plane they looked down on the wide Río Paraguay.

'If we are to explore this area, that is the route,' thought John.

The strike was in full swing and the only way to get anywhere from Santa Cruz was by taxi. Yoli hired a battered Toyota and its equally tired Indian driver for $250 to take them the 500 miles to La Paz. Climbing aboard at 7.00 a.m. they found the front seat already occupied by an enormous lady, who obviously expected to be carried, together with her numerous packages, to the capital free of charge. John doubted whether the vehicle would make it up the long climb even without her weight. Yoli, bristling with indignation, unleashed a tirade of Spanish and ejected the hitch-hiker – and the trek began.

A long day of breakdowns, police checks and demonstrators' road blocks dragged on into darkness, heightened by an eclipse of the moon. Fernando, the driver, chewed coca leaf non-stop in the attempt to keep awake. Some miles out of Cochabamba, just over halfway through the journey, John awoke to find him driving on the wrong side of the road and navigating by the feeble light of the one headlamp that worked. When an oncoming truck appeared, Fernando swerved across to the side on which the majority of Bolivians drive and then resumed his snail's crawl on the left. The poor man was almost asleep at the wheel and, after about a kilo of coca leaf, seemed to be in a state of overdose. 'I'll drive,' ordered the colonel. Fernando crawled thankfully into the back seat, while Yoli moved into the front and talked continuously to keep John awake. He needed all his powers of concentration. The steering wheel made almost a full circle before it had any effect, none of the instruments worked and the footbrake required heavy pumping before it had any effect. There was no handbrake. In the back Fernando snored and farted loudly. The road ahead was illuminated by the single dim headlamp – one more than many of the vehicles they met possessed. When overtaking, John prayed nothing was coming through the swirling dust. Cows and dogs lay asleep in the road, and in villages inebriated peasants wandered aimlessly in front of the traffic. Yoli's flashlight, which she held out of the window, was little help. Miraculously, they reached the Sucre Palace Hotel in La Paz just after midnight. It was the Thursday before Easter, and they had twenty-four hours to get through many important meetings before the capital closed down.

The next day started well, with the British Ambassador, David Ridgway, offering his support for a project. Later Dr Carlos Ponce proposed that John launch an expedition by traditional reed boat down the Río Desaguadero to show that the Tiwanaku could have used this method of navigation. Over the holiday period Yoli and John visited Lake Titicaca and through a local tour operator, Darius Morgan, met several reed-boat builders. John was impressed by the Cataris: Máximo and his son Erik, who regularly built large reed craft in their yard at Huatajata beside the deep blue waters of the lake. Máximo Catari Cahuaya, an Aymará who had studied boat-building in Chicago, Philadelphia and New York (of all places), is one of only a few remaining Aymará who can construct traditional sailing craft made from tightly bound totora reeds. Thor Heyerdahl's *Ra II*, in which he successfully sailed from Morocco to Barbados in 1970, had been built of this reed by four men from Suriqui island in Lake Titicaca. In 1993 Máximo and his son, Erik Catari Gutierrez, built a monster reed boat called *Titi*, 14 metres long and 3.5 metres wide, which Erik skippered on a month-long circumnavigation of the lake, covering 613 kilometres. Erik, a student of engineering at La Paz University, exhibited the youthful vigour that has always appealed to John, and the silent Máximo had the experience and skills of the older man.

Furthermore, their prices were reasonable and they were enthusiastic about a voyage down the Desaguadero.

'If we do this, we'll get you to build the boats,' said John.

However, back in La Paz complications were appearing. Carlos Ponce wanted the Scientific Exploration Society to pay for most of the expenses of an expedition, including 1,000 copies of a 200-page report that he would write. There were other matters on which John and he did not see eye to eye. After a three-hour meeting and copious cups of *mate de coca* they agreed to disagree; Carlos said he would give John's arguments his consideration and be in touch. They never heard from him again. Meanwhile, another player had entered the scene.

Hugo Boero Rojo was regarded by many Bolivians as their leading historian. His knowledge of the country was legendary and his infectious enthusiasm soon won John's admiration. Hugo's English and John's Spanish were not the best, and it was a mutual misunderstanding, while Yoli was ordering more *mate de coca* in the Sucre Palace Hotel, that led to an extraordinary chain of events. John was trying to describe some of Jim Allen's sites that he had examined near Lake Poopó, and his visit to the basalt mines; but Hugo somehow got the impression that the British explorer had stumbled on a lost city that only he, his sons and a few close friends had seen. Knowing of John's discoveries elsewhere and his reputation for assembling scientific teams and finance, the historian decided to take him into his confidence. Yoli returned in time to interpret an account of how Hugo, with Oswaldo Rivera Sundt, the Director of National Archaeology, had come across an Argentinian artefact hunter with a magnificent, bejewelled basalt face mask, in which the nose had been bored out to produce a flute: the item was clearly of considerable interest and quite a rarity. Hugo did not reveal how they persuaded the Argentinian to part with his treasure, only that he did so and also gave them the name of the Indian who had sold it to him. Having tracked down the latter, they went to an isolated site which Hugo described as 'very old, many mounds, ruins, walls one metre high, over an area of about five hundred square kilometres. I think it is a parallel culture to the Tiwanaku.' His eyes twinkled and he added, 'It is covered by cactus and thornbush, a difficult place and there are many snakes. But we need much help to explore it thoroughly.'

John's interest was aroused; but, having heard tales of lost cities before, he was naturally cautious.

'Come to my home for tea tomorrow,' said Hugo. 'You will see the mask and other important artefacts that we have found. I will ask Oswaldo Rivera to come too.'

Arriving at Hugo's house in a well-to-do suburb the next day, John and Yoli found that a full-scale English tea complete with muffins had been laid on by Hugo's wife, Sonia. Oswaldo shook hands, his dark eyes seeming to be summing up all that the visitors said. His English was good and there was no doubt that he was an expert archaeologist. The conversation as Sonia passed round the muffins was lively. Hugo told them of 40 kilometres of caves and tunnels in southern Bolivia that were filled with amazing rock paintings. 'They are unexplored – waiting to be photographed and documented.' John talked of the discovery of Acla in Panama. Yoli described her visits to ancient gold mines at Fallan in Colombia. There was no mention of the mask, nor of the lost city. It was almost time to go when Hugo and Oswaldo stood up and said, 'Now we shall show you what has been found so far.'

Climbing the stairs to an upper room, the visitors were confronted by a large bookcase. Daylight was fading and Hugo switched on the lights. Facing them were a dozen black basalt masks, the eyes surrounded with turquoise and precious stones, the noses hollowed out to produce flutes.

'Good heavens!' exclaimed John as he examined one. 'What a find!'

'They are to become part of the National Collection,' said Oswaldo seriously, 'but there are thousands of sites all over Bolivia awaiting exploration and we do not have the resources to explore more than a few. You could help us.'

Presenting John with his book on Tiwanaku, Hugo said, 'We need an expedition that will focus attention on Bolivia's great archaeological resources.' Thus was formed the alliance that led to the Kota Mama project.

Seated in Robert Rose's London drawing room, John outlined the results of his recce to the officers of the British Chapter of the Explorers' Club. A ripple of excitement ran round the group as he said, 'It will need another recce to finalize details and I propose that we do this in March next year. Who can come?' Robert, a tall, fit American former insurance company chairman, and Barry Moss, a director of HSBC Gibbs, had both been with John on several previous expeditions and readily agreed to take part. Planning began at once. The greatest problem was to get Hugo to respond to letters or faxes, and eventually the reason became apparent: he was seriously ill with cancer. Nevertheless, Oswaldo was enthusiastic and plans for the final recce pressed ahead.

On Easter Monday 1997, the team – John and Yoli, Robert Rose and Barry Moss – watched the first light of dawn striking the snow-covered peaks as the American Airlines flight from Miami descended at La Paz. A large Bolivian in military uniform travelling in first class was rumoured to be the President; certainly he held some status as a couple of dozen army officers awaited him on the tarmac. Whoever he was, it seemed to speed up customs formalities and the recce party was soon breathing deeply as they hauled their bags into a taxi at the world's highest international airport. At the Sucre Palace Hotel they were met by Oswaldo and Hugo's son, who brought sad news: Hugo was not expected to live. He was in a private clinic and had asked to see John and Yoli. After this sombre beginning the conversation turned to archaeological sites. There was a problem: those concerned now wanted $20,000 to take the team to the locations. Yoli was furious; Oswaldo looked embarrassed; Hugo's son appeared to be representing a particular faction. John was adamant that they had come to assist the Bolivians and would not indulge in any horse-trading. This enterprise was intended to be for the benefit of Bolivia, not to line the pockets of certain individuals. Oswaldo pointed out that there was a great deal awaiting discovery along the Río Desaguadero; consequently the expedition need not be held to ransom in this way and could instead concentrate on focusing attention on the importance of Bolivian archaeology by navigating the river with a fleet of traditionally built reed boats and seeking new sites en route.

From this uncomfortable discussion John and Yoli hastened to the clinic where Hugo was being cared for. They found him propped up on a pile of pillows. The cancer was closing its grip, but he managed to hold their hands and say a few words. 'I don't know about Atlantis,' he whispered, 'but there is much to discover in my country. Work with Oswaldo Rivera and keep looking.' He went on to speak of a man called Werner who wanted $10,000 to guide the team, but his voice weakened and his words became unintelligible. Within a few days this great historian had passed away.

The day after the initial discussion, Hugo's sons called to say that they had sold the 'right of exploitation' of the sites to an Italian foundation. Yoli made no comment, and the project proceeded without further reference to the lost city or the tunnels filled with petroglyphs. As Hugo had said, there remained much to discover in Bolivia.

Hiring an Hyundai four-wheel-drive, John, Yoli, Robert, Barry and Oswaldo set off for Huatajata on Lake Titicaca, where Máximo and Erik Catari confirmed the arrangements made on the previous visit. John agreed to pay 9,000 bolivianos for the construction of three reed boats and stayed the night at the Crillon Hotel, where an excellent dinner of lake trout was marred only by the accompanying sound effects: the pipes, drums and guitar of an Inca band in direct competition with the loud voices of a large group of German tourists.

Next morning a three-man Bolivian Navy hydrographic party arrived to join them, sent by the Commander of the Navy to lend their expertise in studying the flow rates, depth and width of the river, and their knowledge of the facilities available along its length, to help the team's reconnaissance of the Desaguadero. However, the Hyundai could not take more than two others, and then only at a squeeze; so the lieutenant, seemingly undismayed, returned to La Paz with a massive echo sounder, leaving behind the slim Sergeant Freddie Ramos and Francisco, the driver. As the recce team drove on south to the Río Desaguadero Freddie's ability to speak Aymará was immensely useful, enabling them to seek guidance and information from the local people as they proceeded by rough tracks and often cross-country along the river. Initially up to three miles wide and flowing sluggishly, the Desaguadero looked like a long, shallow lake filled with reeds. As they went further south they found the river narrowed dramatically, and, knowing that 1998 would be an El Niño year, they became concerned about depth, conscious that this climatic phenomenon could cause the river to dry up and boats to run aground. The team motored about, finding suitable landing places, examining archaeological sites and checking routes. Robert operated the GPS, while Barry, Francisco and John shared the driving. Yoli interpreted and Oswaldo, well used to the altitude, bounded around with incredible energy.

At Iruhito they found a great mound littered with potsherds.

'Some of this is 1600 BC,' Oswaldo announced. 'This is a place we must visit next year.'

Vicuña, hare and fox appeared in the brush; at Nazacara they met Mateo Hinojosa Lauri, the local game warden, who was devoted to the conservation of the vicuña. In 1988 there had been barely 300 left. Now, he told us with pride, there were 7,000, but tragically these beautiful long-necked creatures were still poached for their fine wool. Mateo knew the river well, for the pink flamingos, *ñandu* and numerous duck came under his care too, and he assured them that in April there would be sufficient water to float the reed boats.

At Corocoro, once the site of an enormous copper mine, they found lodgings for $2 per head. Yoli bought a huge piece of beef to cook for their dinner and arranged the loan of a kitchen to cook it in; John and Barry pounded away at the meat in an effort to soften it, and mashed potatoes and salad were produced to accompany it; but even so, when they came to eat it was pretty tough. Indeed, it comprehensively upset Robert's stomach, which was now rebelling against the local diet.

'Tomorrow we go to Calacoto,' said Oswaldo, finishing his last mouthful of leathery steak. 'Fifteen years ago I visited a flat mountain. It was surrounded by stone walls. It is high and we shall need all our strength to climb up.'

An old suspension bridge built in colonial times near Calacoto is still used for people and animals although a modern bridge now carries the dusty road across the river into the town. The expedition's boats would need to negotiate both. 'We must be able to drop the masts to pass under these,' remarked Barry as they headed west towards three *mesetas* silhouetted against the deep blue sky.

The car was left at the base of the centre mountain where Robert reported the altitude as 12,750 feet. The plateau seemed at least 1,000 feet higher so the team took it gently as they puffed and panted upwards. Leaping from boulder to boulder like a mountain goat, Oswaldo gave a running commentary on the plants, potsherds and ancient field systems that covered the slope. As they drew closer to the top, the well-constructed defences became visible. Three concentric dry stone walls up to 20 feet in height surrounded the table top. Oswaldo and Freddie found a narrow entrance passage only wide enough for one person to pass at a time. It wound between massive rocks and would have been easily defended. They followed one another through; then they were on top.

'Where are the houses?' asked Barry, for, apart from masses of broken pottery on the flat surface, there was no sign of human occupation. Oswaldo shook his head. 'I don't know. It's a mystery.'

John was scanning the horizon with his powerful binoculars.

'There are some strange buildings on the next *meseta*,' he said. 'They are like pepper pots; and the mountain is surrounded by even more impressive walls than this one.'

Sure enough, a mile away across a steep valley there appeared to be a walled city of conical buildings with small square doorways. Their hearts leapt. But storm clouds were gathering over the plains and lightning was flickering over the Río Desaguadero. It was four o'clock and no one fancied a night on the mountain. 'We must go back,' said Oswaldo, 'but we have a prime objective for the expedition.' As a chill wind sprang up, they hastened down to the car. Behind them a striking sunset glowed, with the flat-topped mountains silhouetted against a sky that turned from salmon pink to gold while to the east, thunder growled and lightning flashed.

The drive back should have been uneventful, but the storms had swollen the rivers and although Oswaldo was sure of the way to the main La Paz–Oruro highway, the night was black and the tracks confusing. It was 9.30 p.m. when they approached yet another ford across a small river. The track was firm as the vehicle entered the swirling water; but suddenly John yelled, 'Stop! Back out quickly.'

Luckily Francisco wasted no time. In the faint glow of the mud-spattered headlights they could see that the torrent had completely swept away the road and the ford now ran into a six-foot vertical bank. Going forward on foot Barry, Freddie and John sought a safer way across, but still they were not safe, for the car was halfway over when the wheels began to sink into the riverbed. They were now in the middle of the watercourse; rain was falling and lightning indicated more to come. Digging feverishly, they hardly noticed that the temperature had dropped below zero.

It was Freddie who solved the problem. Somewhere in the darkened valley he had found two Indian boys and, shoeless, they came to help. So it was that the car was got on to solid ground and, with the youngsters running barefoot in the headlights for over a mile through the sodden terrain, back to the track. Yoli produced biscuits and a handsome tip and the youngsters disappeared into the night. It was 2 a.m. when the weary group rolled into Patacamaya on the highway.

In the days that followed the team examined points downstream and right to the edge of Lake Poopó. Although the river was rarely more than 3 feet deep and flowing at a couple of miles an hour, it seemed that navigation should be possible all the way, provided El Niño did not produce exceptionally severe effects.

At this point Oswaldo, Robert and Freddie had to return to La Paz; but before he left the area, John wanted to meet the Chipaya. This tribe lives on the northern edge of the great salt pans that occupy much of the southern Altiplano and is believed by some anthropologists to be the last remnant of the lost Tiwanaku civilization. Others think their unique language has links with Arabic or Hebrew. It was also believed that the Chipaya still used a system of irrigation canals that had been dug in the distant past. John felt a visit might produce some useful information. These people had a reputation for resenting outsiders, but John had a good reason for approaching them. The previous December a dam had burst, flooding their town. The British Embassy had given aid to help the Chipaya and said that they would appreciate an update from John and his team.

Rainstorms were still sweeping the desert as the depleted party of John, Yoli, Barry and Francisco drove to the west of Lake Poopó, and the Río Caquiza was flowing fast when they reached the crossing. While they were checking the depth a lorry arrived, laden to the top with local people.

'Let's see how he does,' said Barry as it ploughed into the current. In midstream the lorry seemed to drop into a hole and stopped dead. As the driver revved the engine, the rear wheels dug in and it sank lower, tilting upstream.

'My God, it's going over,' said John.

Francisco seized a rope and ran to the water's edge. The passengers, many of whom were mothers with babies and small children, were screaming with terror. But now the stricken vehicle had stopped rocking and a ladder was used to get the people down into the river. Luckily the bed to one side was firm and shallow and, forming a chain, the adult passengers passed the babies to safety and then waded knee-deep through the swirling brown flood to the bank. The team helped them ashore, where the women calmly made a fire of brushwood and started to dry themselves as if this were an everyday event. Perhaps it was.

A few miles away, Yoli found a village school for the team to camp in, and the next day they returned to the river. The lorry remained stuck, but the passengers seemed quite unperturbed by having spent a bitterly cold night in the open. Eventually a tractor arrived and hauled out the stricken lorry, everyone climbed back on and it headed off to Oruro. However, the ford still looked too deep for the team's vehicle, so they took a longer route to Chipaya.

It was mid-afternoon when they saw the camp. 'I don't believe it!' exclaimed Barry, but, sure enough, there were rows of green tents looking for all the world like a Bedouin settlement. As they approached, men in ten-gallon hats and ponchos emerged with sullen looks on their dark, weatherbeaten faces. Behind them appeared Mongolian-featured women, clad in strange chocolate-coloured hooded robes. They looked quite unlike other Indians of the Altiplano. 'Chipaya,' whispered Francisco uneasily. Yoli explained that they had come to offer help and the atmosphere became more friendly. The people knew nothing of the aid sent by the British Embassy but the headman described how the Río Lauca had burst its banks and flooded the village; now they lived under wretched conditions, in need of medical help, food and clothes. Tents had been provided by the Defensa Civil, but now winter was coming on. Rather than rebuilding their village in the same place, the Chipaya suggested that it be relocated away from the recurrent danger of flood.

John, who had once spoken some Arabic, noticed a similarity to it in their language but could not identify any particular words. However, the Chipayas' looks, dress and, by chance, the tents certainly gave an impression of a Bedouin encampment. The visitors did not have sufficient food to be able to share it with the Indians, who were already casting envious glances at the sleeping bags. Francisco was distinctly unhappy about spending the night there so, having inspected the broken dam, the team returned to a nearby village. Here they bought as much rice and other foodstuffs as possible and took all this to the Chipaya as a gift in the morning. As a precaution they left Francisco in the town to alert the local army post if they did not come back; however, the reception was perfectly cordial. Three senior chiefs had arrived in ceremonial dress, wearing llama wool bags of coca leaf around their necks and carrying silver-topped sticks of office. They produced a letter for the British Embassy which John would deliver in La Paz. Then they presented the team with llama wool wallets and invited them to take photographs, a very rare privilege. 'Come back to help us,' they pleaded and John promised that he would return. Yoli learnt that there was indeed a system of ancient canals further east beyond the flooded river.

Back in La Paz the Bolivian Navy continued to cooperate and agreed to provide two hydrographers for the expedition, one of whom would be Freddie. David Ridgway and the staff at the Embassy also offered encouraging support for the project. Oswaldo became the expedition's Archaeological Director and recruited other archaeologists to join him from the National Institute of Archaeology and Anthropology (DINAAR). Erik and Máximo Catari finalized the designs for the three reed boats, the largest of them to be named *Kota Mama*, Aymará for 'Mother of the Lake' – which was also the title given to the whole project.

Things seemed to be taking shape pretty well; so, the reconnaissance being complete and the team being happy with the cooperation and support promised by the Bolivians, John returned to Britain and Yoli to Bogotá.

The Kota Mama project now consisted of two, possibly three, phases. In 1998 the expedition would take its fleet down the Río Desaguadero from Lake Titicaca to Lake Poopó, investigating archaeological sites en route, examining Jim Allen's theories and also giving assistance to the Chipaya community. The following year new boats would sail from southern Bolivia via the Río Paraguay and Río Paraná to Buenos Aires, carrying out further archaeological and anthropological studies as well as wildlife conservation and community aid projects in Paraguay and Argentina. The final phase, which at this stage was a possibility rather than a definite plan, involved building a *balsa* craft and allowing the wind and sea currents to carry her from Buenos Aires to southern Africa: the reverse of Thor Heyerdahl's voyage in *Ra II*. John felt this voyage needed a fair amount of research before a reasonable assessment of its feasibility could be made, and to this end he had consulted his old friend Colonel Frank Esson, and his wife, Joanna, both of whom were experienced ocean sailors and navigators; they were to examine current trends in wind and weather and offer suggestions on a possible route.

As the outlines of the project took shape, the tempo accelerated at Expedition Base in the quiet Dorset village of Motcombe. Jim Masters, who was to be fleet commander of the expedition, recruited members, assembled stores and tried to forecast the effect of El Niño on the Río Desaguadero. Yoli joined them for some of the time, as well as doing much to ensure backing for the expedition in Bolivia. One of their greatest allies there now was Admiral Jorge Zabala Ossio, Commander of the Bolivian Navy; and an even more illustrious supporter was acquired through an introduction arranged by John's old friend, Michael Sheppard, a British expatriate living in Santiago, Chile, in the person of the newly elected President of Bolivia, General Hugo Banzer Suárez, who became Patron of the expedition.

Good publicity management would be a key element of the project, and the task of handling the press, along with organizing the all-important search for sponsorship, fell to the energetic Chrysoulla Kyprianou. Although the media tended to concentrate on the search for Atlantis, no one ridiculed the expedition, whose line had become, 'If you don't look, you can't expect to find, and there are a great many sites to be located in Bolivia.' Faanya Rose, Robert's wife, joined the quest for sponsors and a visit by her husband and John to the UK office of American Airlines paid dividends in bringing the company on board as the expedition's major sponsor. Many backers of the Scientific Exploration Society assisted with equipment. Avon Inflatables provided a boat, and E. P. Barrus supplied a Mariner outboard motor at a very good discount, while Motorola and London Communications lent vital radios.

Communications would, of course, be vital. A website was set up through Peter Monson, former Master of the Worshipful Company of Information Technologists, and a satellite phone link was planned with Brixham Community College in Devon, where Spanish was taught.

Meanwhile, El Niño was creating havoc worldwide.

At the final briefing at Expedition Base in January 1998, Jim Allen outlined his theory, Jim Masters warned the members that it would be no picnic for them and John said, 'I don't know if we'll discover Atlantis, but I'm damned sure we shall find something. It's just a question of looking.'

CHAPTER TWO

UNDER
STARTER'S
ORDERS

Bolivia emerged in practice as a non-maritime Pacific state . . . a remote,
mid-continental hinterland of extreme physical difficulty, its core
secluded to the point of isolation within the lofty Andean cordilleras . . .
It has never been easy to find many Bolivians who have seen the sea.

J. VALERIE FIFER,
Bolivia: Land, Location and Politics since 1825 (1972)

Blashford-Snell's geriatrics he called us, jestingly, and it's true
that we were a touch on the senior side. John himself was
sixty-one, and his right-hand man Jim Masters was the doyen of
the team at sixty-nine. Jim, together with Richard Snailham, had
been with John on the famous navigation of the Ethiopian Blue
Nile in 1968 and again on the Zaire River expedition in 1974–5;
the shared experiences of this trio were considerable and their
camaraderie over thirty years of expeditioning together played a
big part in pulling the Kota Mama team together. Maybe advancing
years made us all keener; after the sad death of his much-loved
wife Joan the previous year Jim Masters had been at a low ebb,
and when John invited him to lead another boat party down
another river the news perked him up visibly. Richard Snailham,
who was sixty-seven, had been equally cheered to be enrolled on
this venture, if somewhat apprehensive of the effects of the
passage of three decades since his first exciting Blue Nile days.

'Don't worry,' John had reassured him, 'there'll be some slots on the foredeck for your Zimmerframe.'

The oldest member of the team, though only with us for a short time, was seventy-six-year-old Robert Rose, a retired American insurance chief domiciled in London. Tall, rangy, immaculately suited, he had the broad smile and vice-like handshake of a much younger man. His resilient English wife Faanya accompanied him. Born in South Africa and given a distinctive Ukrainian first name, she was raised in Rhodesia, where her first husband, a member of Ian Smith's government, had been killed by terrorists in 1979. She had married Robert in 1993.

A vital member of any large expedition is the doctor, and Noel Burrell, another senior citizen at sixty-eight, kept a calm professional eye on us all. Some of us he already knew well: Jim Masters and his brother Gerry were both his patients in Ilchester, Somerset. Noel had spent a lifetime in general practice, and although he had worked in Paris for four years this was his first expedition. A family man, married with three children, there was an unflappability about him which steadied us throughout.

The last member of the contingent that the younger members tended to call 'seriously old' was Gerry Masters, Jim's younger brother and a mere sixty-two, for whom this was also a first expedition and who, though a builder by trade and a specialist in restoring old churches, made a very good fist of being quartermaster and cook – two of the most taxing and unrewarding roles on any expedition.

Although he seemed naturally to gravitate towards the senior citizens' group John Lyons, an international business consultant and engineer from New York, was in fact only fifty-two. He played a star part as one of our computer and satellite telephone wizards, but, like the Roses, was unable to be with the expedition for very long.

Barry Moss was, with Jim Masters, John's right-hand man and had probably been involved with the planning of this venture for longer than anyone except John himself. A youngster at thirty-nine and an Essex man in the insurance business, he and his indistinguishable twin brother Trevor – the 'Moss Bros' – had both been keen members of the Scientific Exploration Society (SES) for a very long time. Since Richard Snailham had first met him in an RAF Hercules when they were both on their way to Nairobi to take part in John's first youth venture, Operation Drake, in 1980, Barry had graduated to lead three phases of Operation Raleigh (some of the first, to the Turks and Caicos Islands in 1985–6), so it was clear that John had great faith in his abilities. He had been on the Council of the SES for three years and Secretary of the British Chapter of the Explorers' Club for four. It was natural, then, that John should ask Barry to go with him to Bolivia on the reconnaissance of March–April 1997 and then make him deputy leader of the ensuing expedition. Richard Snailham was recruited as historian, and to assist him a twenty-five-year-old Oxford graduate in archaeology and anthropology from Leicestershire, Elsbeth Turnbull. She had worked in Hong Kong but had always had a yearning for South American archaeology. Unfortunately, as will be related later, she spent most of her time in a La Paz hospital.

All this wisdom and experience had to be bolstered by some raw muscle and verve. We had, after all, to paddle, punt, drag or pull three heavy reed boats down a long river and climb and survey many of the plateaux which rise above the central Altiplano to heights of over 4,000 metres (13,000 feet). Mindful of the physical demands of all this, John had recruited a four-strong service, or recently ex-service, element. Prominent in this group was Sebastian Sheppard, until not long ago a lieutenant in the Fleet Air Arm. He had been a helicopter pilot in the Adriatic and an interpreter in the tuna-fishing 'wars' with Spain. The son of an English couple resident in Santiago – it was his father, Michael, who had laid the ground for the expedition's acquisition of the Bolivian President as Patron – Seb had been brought up in Chile for eighteen of his twenty-nine years. He had been a venturer on Operation Raleigh and a staff member for them in Chile. John had employed him on recces in Chile and Bolivia, and his linguistic skill and expertise in dealing with our Bolivian colleagues in 1998 were invaluable.

The boat team depended very heavily on the strengths and skills of two young army officers: Captain Lee Smart (Royal Signals; thirty-three) and Lieutenant Luke Cox (Royal Engineers; twenty-three). Lee, born in Benghazi, Libya, had read architecture at Dundee University before embarking on a military career which had taken him, after Sandhurst, to Germany, Sardinia, Milan, Ulster and twice to Bosnia. He spoke to the Bolivians in Italian, which seemed to work surprisingly well. He was an accomplished watercolourist and one of his paintings adorns these pages. Luke Cox, then serving at Quebec barracks, Osnabrück, was a head taller than Lee, ten years younger and equally fit. A graduate of Manchester University from Hornsea in east

Yorkshire, his abilities as a rock climber and yachtsman both came into play in Bolivia.

As tough as either of these was Lance-Corporal Jason Joyce of the Royal Logistical Corps. A twenty-six-year-old Brummie, he was currently at the Post and Courier Depot at Mill Hill and came to the expedition as boat crew member and postman. Thanks to Lieutenant Colonel Howard Hughes, who had been John's PR officer at Fort George near Inverness in 1982, on a tri-service government scheme for training unemployed young people, we had arranged a British Forces Post Office facility (BFPO 747), but responsibility for this did not weigh too heavily upon Jason because traffic was fairly light – we preferred to trust to the diplomatic bag or the vagaries of Correos Bolivianos. What we did need was Jason as a tower of strength on the reed boats.

John prefers, where he can, to invite tried and trusted friends to join him on his expeditions: a solid bedrock of people of known abilities on which to set unknown quantities, in the hope that all will gel into a team. Ben Cartwright, like Jim Masters, Barry Moss and Richard Snailham, fell into this category. An engineering and computer lecturer, now fifty-two, Ben had slogged with John and Jim through the Panamanian jungle on the Darien expedition of 1972 and served on Operations Drake and Raleigh in Panama, Sulawesi and across the Atlantic to the Bahamas. At home in Over Wallop, Hampshire, he specializes in repairing and servicing old aircraft – which is more or less what he was doing as a sergeant with the Royal Electrical and Mechanical Engineers when Richard Snailham first met him on the Zaire River expedition in 1974.

Some of our luckier expedition colleagues had simply to get fit, pack, and turn up on the appointed day of departure for Bolivia. Others, like Yorkshire-born PR queen Chrysoulla Kyprianou, had a string of difficult tasks to complete before we could set off.

On the Blue Nile in 1968 our two Royal Signallers would tap out their morse for another signaller at base camp in the Ethiopian highlands, who would later relay it slowly to an army station in Bulford, Wiltshire. In this way Chris Bonington's news reports were passed on to the *Daily Telegraph* in Fleet Street and the expedition's other requirements met. Things have changed dramatically: Christopher Beale, twenty-six, a computer wizard from Bournemouth, administered Kota Mama's telephone satellite links and maintained a daily input of news for our website on the Internet. Every so often John, Richard and two or three young schoolchildren spoke live by telephone from some remote village

on the Altiplano to staff and children at Brixham Community
College in Devon; and each day our news was transmitted by
computer to the PR staff at the SES base in Dorset. Chris, who
ran all these communication channels, was fearful of strong
sunlight and remained clothed in black, his pale features and
pony-tail reminiscent of Nigel Planer in *The Young Ones*. But,
unlike Nigel's character, he was a fount of wit, good cheer and
optimism and always succeeded in winkling glitches out of our
sophisticated equipment.

The last of the British contingent to be signed up, and at
eighteen the youngest member of the party, was Mark Lobel. A
chance meeting between his mother and John led to swift preparations and his flight out with the main group on 9 March 1998.
Mark had just left St Paul's School in London where he had coxed
the Second Eight on the Thames, an experience which qualified
him for instant membership of our boat team. He also did much
useful video recording and proved one of the most dedicated and
loyal among us.

Mark was signed up just after John had held the last of his
many presentations to potential sponsors and been interviewed
on Channel Four, and just before he and the Roses flew out to
Bolivia on 8 March. Medic Noel Burrell, quartermaster Gerry
Masters and interpreter Seb Sheppard were already there, having
gone over on 4 March to buy food and camp gear. John Lyons,
too, had made his own way. And so, in dribs and drabs, we all
arrived in Bolivia – most travelling from Heathrow via Miami to
La Paz courtesy of American Airlines. Some loyally sported an
AA baseball cap; others wore the expedition fleece with American
Airlines on the right breast. All were very well looked after by
ground and flight staff; but it felt odd to be flying in a Boeing
757 over the Amazonian rain forest at 30,000 feet and watching
The Full Monty.

A fierce dawn broke over the Bolivian Andes as La Paz came
nearer. La Paz . . . a magical name and surely one of the world's
most exotic capital cities. La Ciudad de Nuestra Señora de La Paz,
founded by a Spanish conquistador, Alonzo de Mendoza, in 1548,
occupies an astonishing position. It fills all sides of a deep valley
which falls abruptly away from the eastern flank of the bleak,
flat Altiplano. One can imagine a few Spaniards huddled on the
edge of the cold, windswept plain saying to each other as they
looked down the sheer cliffs to where a stream ran away

eastwards in the valley bottom, 'We'd be better off down there: shelter, good water, a bit warmer maybe, and there's gold in the river.'

La Paz is known as Chuquiago to the Aymará people of the Altiplano (after the Choqueyapu, the river which courses down its valley), so there was probably something there when the conquistadors came down from the heights. The city, amoeba-like, has now crept up the side valleys, trickled down the main valley to lower ground and climbed back up on to the Altiplano which it had shunned – in the shape of a vast, unlovely suburb called El Alto, now home to half a million people and the airport. The one fact the proverbial schoolboy knows is that La Paz is the highest capital in the world at 3,636 metres. Its airport at El Alto is the highest commercial destination in the world at 4,018 metres. If an American Airlines Boeing 757 were to take off with full fuel tanks it could only carry ten passengers, so outgoing flights to Miami make a fifty-three-minute run with almost empty tanks to Santa Cruz de la Sierra in Bolivia's eastern lowlands and refuel there. Incoming passengers often suffer from *seroche* or altitude sickness. Anoxia struck down some of our party for two or three days and was relieved only by rest, the passage of time, Diamox and regular infusions of *mate de coca*. Not all of us took to this strange, bitter refreshment – though John ordered it at every opportunity. It was a novel experience having an expedition leader permanently high on coca!

The La Paz people are attuned to the altitude. Of *los Paceños*, well over a million of them, half are *cholos* or Indians, living in the upper terraces under the rim of the Altiplano and scratching some sort of a living down in the centre. The smarter Bolivians of Spanish descent live in the lower, eastern purlieus of the city, like La Florida or Calacoto. In the middle a long arterial throughway runs down, down, down along the line of the now mainly subterranean river, its name, like Bayswater Road, Oxford Street, New Oxford Street, High Holborn, changing every few hundred metres – Avenida Ismael Montes, Avenida Mariscal Santa Cruz, Avenida 16 de Julio, Avenida Villazón, Avenida 6 de Agosto. Over it all, to the east, looms the snow-shrouded, 6,402 metre extinct volcano Illimani.

Thanks to some careful preparations by the advance party and our good friend Lita Kushner, owner of the Sucre Palace Hotel where we were to stay, the main party cleared immigration and customs easily, to be welcomed by Seb Sheppard and John Lyons and ushered to waiting vehicles. Nobody was quite ready for the double whammy which lay ahead. First, the dreary awfulness of El Alto, the brick sprawl on the Altiplano's edge: wide avenues choked with taxis, lorries and the characteristic multicoloured, long-bonneted buses; on each side abysmally designed blocks of flats, offices, gas stations; potholed side streets full of standing sewage, tatty little market stalls, car repair shops and scrapyards. But then, past a police checkpoint, the *autopista* ran over the edge of the canyon, and we saw the city of La Paz filling the 5 kilometre wide bowl below us: pink brick houses amid a scattering of eucalyptus and, in the bottom, a mini-Manhattan of high-rise towers in the city's commercial centre. It ranked alongside one's first view of Hong Kong, Istanbul or New York.

The Sucre Palace Hotel was on the Avenida Mariscal Santa Cruz section of La Paz's main drag, just downhill from the fine equestrian statue of the country's founder, Simón Bolívar. John was in the hotel foyer, resplendent in his new green Savile Row explorers' suit: cut by Norton & Sons (Tailors and Breeches Makers), grateful for the publicity it would attract, it was said to be embellished with thirty-five pockets, several of them secret and at least one capable of taking a game-bird or two. Dashing from John to the hotel manageress and back was Yoli, who despite her diminutive stature was a force to be reckoned with throughout the expedition, tirelessly liaising with Bolivians, ironing out difficulties, introducing VIPs, conjuring up meals in restaurantless villages.

Trays of *mate de coca* came round and so, slowly, did the members of the main party. With most of his medical kit still stored in grips in what Jason Joyce called the hotel suppository, Dr Noel Burrell did his best to treat the sufferers from *seroche*. One by one Chrysoulla, Ben and the others groggily emerged from an all-too-brief rest in their rooms and ate a tentative breakfast in the downstairs café. The last meetings had taken place. John had seen David Ridgway, the Ambassador. Lita had been fully briefed. The final provisions had been bought – crucial items like plastic bins and bowls for food preparation and storage, mops and scourers for washing up. We were ready to go.

Or so we thought. Then an Embassy aide told us he had had a call from DINAAR saying that the Kota Mama expedition did not have the necessary permissions which Oswaldo Rivera was understood to have obtained. This was ominously reminiscent of 1968, when John and the Blue Nile expedition had flown off to Ethiopia without having yet secured official authorization. So, on our final day in La Paz a meeting was arranged and an agreement was drawn up and signed by three top Bolivians and John. *Now* we could go.

How major expeditions get about in remote countries is a constant source of amazement. In the Congo John moved the stores for the Zaire River expedition (165 people) up-country by hiring a train from Kolwezi to Kongolo. In Mongolia with Operation Raleigh (120 people) it had been a convoy of eight massive Russian Kamaz lorries. For Kota Mama I (28 people) we had a series of hired minibuses, two Range Rovers and one large Mercedes truck loaned to us by the Bolivian Navy. (Bolivia has no coastline now, but it does have part of the world's highest navigable lake, Lake Titicaca, and it has a lot of big rivers flowing away north and east into Brazil, Paraguay and Argentina. So it has retained its navy, still 5,000 strong.) The camouflage green lorry duly arrived, driven by lean, wiry, forty-two-year-old German (pronounced 'Hair-Marn') Villarroelalba (which no one ever tried to pronounce). He and his dark, barrel-bodied colleague, Rodolfo Quispe Chura, forty, loaded our assorted gear in the back and soon the Mercedes was grinding its way up the seemingly endless hill out of La Paz towards Lake Titicaca, followed by the expedition personnel in the smaller vehicles.

We all knew that Lake Titicaca was where it was. It is perhaps the most famous of Bolivia's geographical wonders. Yet there was a communal intake of breath when we first saw its shimmering blue expanse. Shared more or less equally between Bolivia and Peru, Titicaca (sometimes spelt Titikaka) is the size of Crete, or of Delaware and Rhode Island put together. Twice in ancient times inland seas covered much of the Altiplano. It may have been the latter of these inundations that occurred 12,000 years ago and flooded an ancient city in the south which some, including our expedition member Jim Allen, equate with the lost city and civilization of Atlantis. Since then the water has receded to form Lake Titicaca, whose fluctuations over the last century or so have been of the order of only 6 metres, giving it a height above sea level of between 3,806 and 3,812 metres. There are many tributaries that feed the lake, most of them (72 per cent) flowing down out of the Peruvian Andes, but there is only one outlet: the Río Desaguadero, which the Kota Mama expedition was to try to navigate. For a thousand years and perhaps more, boats made from the local totora reeds and known as *balsas* have sailed this river, and we wanted to see if it was still possible to do so.

Aymará-speaking Indians settled on the southern shores of the lake about 1400 BC and developed what has become known as the Tiahuanaco (Tiwanaku) civilization. These people built an elaborate city of that name, now one of Bolivia's greatest heritage sites, and are known to have traded on the lake and down the Desaguadero as far south as Lake Poopó and maybe further.

Despite the bleakness of the Altiplano the land around Titicaca has, from Tiwanaku through Inca and Spanish times, always been an area of relatively dense population and today 700,000 people live around it, some 150 per square kilometre. There was dismay among them when in 1986 the lake levels rose and for three years remained at a height unprecedented since measurements began in 1912. This led to a study of the lake carried out jointly by Peru and Bolivia. Titicaca and the Desaguadero had to be monitored. What water came into the lake? How much evaporated? How much flowed out? All the previous studies (456 of them) were re-examined. It turned out that 95 per cent of the water which flows into Titicaca or falls on it as rain evaporates; only 5 per cent runs out at the two towns of Desaguadero, one on each side of the Peru–Bolivia border, where the river debouches.

Various plans were proposed to regulate the use of the lake waters. It would be an environmental tragedy if Titicaca suffered the fate of the Aral Sea, reduced to salt desert by water extraction to irrigate the cotton fields of Uzbekistan. Both nations therefore undertook not to take off water irresponsibly in the way that the Russians had done in Central Asia. Specifically, there would be no deal between Bolivia and Chile whereby sweet water from Titicaca could be piped off to the Atacama desert in return for the restitution of a slice of Bolivia's former Pacific littoral.

As we bowled along north-westwards to the little lakeside settlement of Huatajata the cloud-enshrouded Cordillera Real de los Andes lay to our right. Peak followed peak, like the spines on a stegosaurus, Huayna Potosí at 6,088 metres prominent among them. Huatajata turned out to be a string of eateries and lodging-houses along the lake's edge, with all the dynamism of a Scottish seaside resort in March. Apparently it comes to life in the season and at weekends, but this was a Wednesday. We were aiming for the Catari family's establishment, the Hostal Inti Karka, which features, not very flatteringly, in the Lonely Planet guide and is also listed in the *South American Handbook*.

For several months Máximo Catari and his son Erik had been building three reed boats to John's specifications. These were the vessels which we hoped would carry us down the Desaguadero to Lake Poopó. We had all seen drawings of these fine-looking *balsas*, their prows made fearsome by large detachable heads of puma and condor, but the moment of conviction that the Kota Mama expedition was a going concern came when we drove down into the yard by the Hostal Inti Karka and saw these three boats side by side on the hard.

The flagship, *Kota Mama* ('Mother of the Lake'), was 7 metres long. The totora reeds for it had been cut the previous December, tied into bundles with prairie grass rope (*ichu*) and left to dry. Some weeks later the bundles were bound into two long, tapering, cigar-shaped cylinders which were lashed together and pounded into a shallow crescent. More bundles were added to trap air and increase buoyancy. A light mast was stepped in, carrying an orange gaff mainsail decorated with the face of Kota Mama herself. The head of a puma, the local mountain lion, with dangerous-looking wooden teeth, adorned its bows. Our other two boats, *Viracocha* and *Pacha Kutec*, named after local gods, were smaller, had purple sails and sported condors' heads. A Somerset friend of Jim Masters had asked him, 'What are you doing going down a river on a straw bale?' The reality could not have failed to impress him.

It was an idyllic setting for the start of an expedition. The dawn's light struck the hills on the four Bolivian islands in Lake Winaymarka, the southern extension of Lake Titicaca, ducks and moorhens bobbed on the water and tiny fishing boats were setting out from Puerto Pérez. A ginger kitten jumped up on to the *balsas*: Titicatcat, Richard called it; John preferred Titipusspuss. Throughout the day fitting out work went on on the boats. Máximo sat and carved a wooden throat for the gaff boom; expedition members tried manoeuvring a reed boat on the lake or practised loading one into our navy Mercedes. At night we tucked into the standard meal of *quinua* soup, protein-rich and made from a local form of sorghum, pink trout from the lake with potato and rice, fruit salad and coffee.

John had hired an extra lorry to help carry our boats to Desaguadero and had arranged for some cadets from a marines unit at nearby Tiquina to help us lift *Kota Mama*, the heaviest of the three, into it. In our first four days we had already suffered from what we came to call the BLF, and now, on this final afternoon at Huatajata, the Bolivian Lateness Factor manifested itself again. At the appointed hour neither lorry nor cadets had appeared. Some of us with wider South American experience were forming the view that the *mañana* syndrome was more pronounced here than in other Latin countries. Of course, they turned up eventually – only to cause us some initial consternation, for as a people Bolivians are small in stature, and this was borne in on us with particular force when the twenty marine cadets impassively marched down into the yard in their neat blue uniforms and flip-flops. They were tiny. However, they lent their collective weight to the task and together we humped our flagship into the hired lorry. How would we fare downriver, some of us pondered, when we didn't have these tough little men to help us?

The loading of our three boats was much photographed and videoed, and it was as a result of this normally unhazardous activity that the expedition suffered its first casualty. There was a scream from an upper room and Elsbeth Turnbull, Richard Snailham's archaeological assistant, came rushing on to the balcony clutching her right wrist, which was bleeding profusely. After taking pictures she had shut a window and inadvertently pushed her hand through a pane. A new Medical Law began now to manifest itself: 'An accident always happens when the medical kit has been packed and loaded on the lorry.' Noel Burrell found that Elsbeth had severed the tendons of her wrist and one of our Range Rovers had to drive her fast to the German Clinic in La Paz. It was Friday the 13th.

Before we left Huatajata there was another hiccup, which reminded us of the existence of an old Bolivian fly in the ointment. We were not sure whether Máximo Catari would be joining the expedition but felt confident that his son Erik was keen to take part. There now came a suggestion that neither would be coming along. Erik was translating a book from Aymará into Spanish for the archaeologist Carlos Ponce Sanjines. As related in Chapter 1, in 1995 John had discussed the possibility of a joint expedition with Ponce, but the Bolivian had produced a plan which John did not much care for: it seemed to him to lack practicality and to be simply a vehicle for Ponce and his friends which John was being expected to fund. John had come up with his own plan and the two men had drifted apart. Now Erik was afraid that if he and his father joined up with us they might damage their opportunities for future cooperation with Ponce, with whom they had worked on the 1993 *Titi* voyage round Lake Titicaca. Ponce was President of his own Fundación Tiahuanaco and gave the impression of regarding all investigations of archaeological sites

in the area as his own intellectual property. Other Bolivian archaeologists saw this as a preposterous assumption; nevertheless,
there was a report that Ponce would sue us if the Kota Mama
expedition proceeded. The grey clouds which massed every afternoon over the lake and brought torrential rain were not the only
ones louring over us.

Fortunately, not only had we secured the agreement signed by
John, the Vice-Minister of Culture, the Director General of the
Cultural Patrimony and the National Director of Archaeology and
Anthropology, but no less a person than the President of Bolivia
himself had agreed to be our Patron. This, and the lure of another
sailing expedition, eventually overcame the fears of the Cataris.
The loyalty of two such experienced reed-boat handlers was
reassuring to us all.

John invited the *Commandante* of the marines base at Tiquina
to our final dinner at the Hostal Inti Karka. Candles lit up the
Explorers' Club pennants on the tables. More *quinua* soup and
pink trout were consumed. Glasses of Kohlberg, a perfectly drink-
able Bolivian red wine, were raised in toasts to Señor Presidente
de la República, General Hugo Banzer Suárez, Padrino de la
Expedición; Her Majesty the Queen; the President of the United
States; and the Armada Boliviana. A local band, Rumis Nueva
Renovación, bowler-hatted and ponchoed, bobbed and wove as
they puffed into their pan-pipes to the beating of a drum.

'A glass of J & B at night and a *mate de coca* in the morning and
I'm all right,' said John as he sipped his hot infusion at the break-
fast table. It was the day the expedition was to set off to
Desaguadero for the launching of the boats.

The road there first ran all the way back to the featureless
urbanizaciones of El Alto, wastelands of brick and adobe,
depressing even under a hot sun. As we arrived the municipal
band were oompahing away, inaugurating a new abattoir. A
Japanese Zero fighter in Bolivian colours reared up on a pedestal
outside the Bolivian Air Force station. We turned and headed west
for Tiahuanaco.

It was important for us all to understand the Bolivian past,
vestiges of which our archaeologists might turn up. Accordingly,
John had allowed for a day's visit to this, the ancient world's
highest urban centre at 3,850 metres (13,000 feet) above sea
level. A pre-Inca civilization flourished south of Lake Titicaca for
twenty-six centuries – from about 1400 BC to about AD 1200 –

leaving behind impressive stone monuments, pottery, metalwork and textiles. In a fenced enclosure there is a large mound, inside which is a (not yet fully excavated) stepped pyramid. North of this is a large, walled platform 3 metres high, with entrance steps leading up to a restored portico through which at the summer solstice the sun, as at Stonehenge, casts its rays on a large monolith. The surrounding wall of the platform had conical perforations in places, perhaps to amplify the incantations of the priests in the centre. We tried these out with reasonable success.

The finest structure is another stone archway cut from a single block of andesite: the Gate of the Sun, moved from its original site by the Spanish conquistadors and defiled by them as a relic of paganism. Its central feature, a masked figure holding two long vertical staves in either hand, may be the bearded white god Viracocha, after whom we named one of our boats. Or it might be Thunupa, a weather deity and sky god, who brought rain, thunder and lightning. East of the platform is a sunken quadrangle with a representation of Kontiki, the main deity, at its centre and carved heads set in its walls. All this was probably built in the heyday of the Tiahuanaco empire around AD 900 by the descendants of the Aymará-speaking Indians who swept down from Peru some time after 1400 BC.

A Polish archaeologist, Arthur Posnansky (1874–1946), spent most of his life working at Tiahuanaco, and though he misdated it badly he put it on the map as one of the finest pre-Inca sites in South America. His work was carried on by Carlos Ponce Sanjines and Hugo Boero Rojo, who wrote the definitive book *Discovering Tiwanaku*, published in 1980. Our own archaeologist, Oswaldo Rivera Sundt, has continued to study the place since 1978. While Ponce only really looked at the monuments, Rivera's approach has been multidisciplinary: specialists in up to twenty-one different fields have researched Tiahuanaco. He had a small museum there, outside the southern perimeter fence by the single-track railway line from La Paz to Lake Titicaca, but now there is a splendid large one, achieved by Rivera's assiduous fund-raising and with help from the British Embassy: Queen Sophia of Spain, herself an archaeologist, gave $17,500 and the Bolivian Ambassador to Spain, presenting her cheque, doubled it. Rivera's banker doubled the resultant sum yet again to make it $70,000. In the end the new museum cost $135,000, but he plans another one, for the sacred rather than the domestic artefacts, for which he is seeking state help.

Aerial photographs show that the metropolis at its apogee spread over almost 8 square kilometres and, although once thought to have been home to some 25,000 people, may have held upwards of 90,000. 'Only 1.2 per cent of the Tiahuanaco site has been excavated,' Oswaldo told Richard Snailham, 'so there is plenty of work to do.'

Just as at Stonehenge the Blue Stones came by sea and river from the Preseli Hills in west Wales, so here the grey andesite was brought in reed boats across Lake Titicaca from Kajaphia, a volcano near Copacabana. It was intriguing to us that *balsas* like our three, though no doubt bigger, were capable of ferrying monolithic structures as huge and unwieldy as the Gate of the Sun across 40 kilometres of frequently stormy lake. What other cargoes might they have carried, we wondered, along what other rivers?

In our time in Bolivia we were to consume a fair few kilos of potatoes, so it was interesting to us to see the Tiahuanaco people's agricultural arrangements. They had built on an area of perhaps 65 square kilometres a series of rectangular raised fields 6 metres wide and up to 200 metres long, separated by 3 metre wide canals. When Titicaca was full its fish-laden waters filled these canals. During the day they were warmed by the sun and during the freezing nights their heat passed into the earth plots.

We drove on westwards, parallel to the railway, through the old town of Guaqui (pronounced 'Whacky') with its fine colonial church and rail terminal near the lake's edge (steamers from Puno in Peru once docked here to link with the railway to La Paz, now unoperative), and came eventually to the deeply grim town of Desaguadero. Frontier towns are always a mess, with queues of lorries waiting to cross, cheap flophouses and ugly checkpoints; but this place was needlessly awful. One becomes used to uncollected rubbish and undispersed effluvia in many Third World countries, but nowhere (except perhaps in Mombasa) had we seen such filth and degradation as in Bolivian Desaguadero (the identically named town on the Peruvian side is tidier). The stench of human faeces hung heavy in the evening air. Houses and shops seemed half-built or derelict. Plastic bags and bottles were strewn over the large tracts of open ground in which pools of green water festered. The only decent building in the place was the Gobierno Municipal where, presumably, languished the officials who should have been doing something about the problem.

We unloaded our boats on a sand spit just out of town and

found billets in the main street in the Avaroa II, a dismal lodging-house just short of the International Bridge over the river and a large banner saying 'Welcome to Peru'. The Desaguadero river has been dammed up a little way downstream of the bridge, as part of the new control systems being implemented after the bilateral studies undertaken by Bolivia and Peru had led to the setting up of PELT, the Special Lake Titicaca Project, in 1993. The river is very narrow here, and near the dam rowboats ferry townsfolk from one country to the other for 50 centavos. Seb Sheppard and a Bolivian friend crossed over to Peru in the evening to buy wine (unavailable on the Bolivian side) and pushed a few cases in a borrowed handcart across the International Bridge in full view of both sets of customs and immigration officers without any let or hindrance. It must be a haven for *contrabandistas*. During the night some Peruvian youths, seeing three desirable reed boats newly arrived on the opposite bank, rowed over and ransacked them, stealing some of our spars and cordage. Our three guards alerted the police and much was later recovered.

The following day, Sunday 15 March, we had planned a launching ceremony at noon to which several eminent person-ages had been invited. Happily, the sun shone. Expedition members dressed the boats overall, John donned his Norton & Sons suit, Richard tacked up direction signs to help VIPs find the launch site, Yoli organized the Mayor (*Alcalde*) and a priest to bless the fleet. The expatriate contingent rolled up in their Range Rovers and Landcruisers in good time but some Bolivian VIPs had still not arrived when the proceedings were due to begin. Rain clouds were already massing and John knew we couldn't hold things up indefinitely for the BLF.

Bolivians love ceremonies and John is good at laying them on. He had appointed as compère our senior Bolivian naval officer, the portly Lieutenant Vladimir Terrazas Montesinos, now head of security for the naval hydrographic service in La Paz. (At John's insistence he had been roused from his bed the previous night and sent out into the dark, pistol in hand, in a vain attempt to apprehend the Peruvian robbers.)

Vladimir welcomed the guests and a sound amplifier blasted out several verses of the Bolivian National Anthem. We followed, quaveringly and unaccompanied, with verse one of 'God Save the Queen'. It is probably as well that no one knew the other verses: Bolivian politics are complex enough not to need further confounding and there had so far been no knavish tricks to have to frustrate. The *Alcalde* was called forward and welcomed. He read out a long declaration which was handed over to the British Ambassador with a friendly bear-hug. John then made a speech which was translated by Marcia Paz Campeo from the Embassy. With seconds to spare the stubby, bespectacled Vice-Admiral Lozada pushed his way in through the crowd of townsfolk who were watching these unusual proceedings with open-mouthed incredulity. He was just in time to be welcomed, pull out his speech and read it. At its conclusion he introduced the Vice-Minister of Culture, Dr Ramón Rocha Monroy, who spoke next. Sergeant Freddie Ramos, our Bolivian Navy hydrographer, then marched out with a Bolivian flag on a cushion and handed it to Luke Cox, who hoisted it almost to the top of the flagship's mast. A local priest, in full canonicals, then stepped forward, made a speech of benediction culminating in the Lord's Prayer in Spanish, dipped a bundle of reeds in the river and sprinkled some drops on all three boats. The *Alcalde* and two other ministers were next invited to christen them. Three bottles of white wine were simultaneously smashed on three rocks, thoughtfully placed nearby, and John wrapped up the proceedings with three rousing cheers for Bolivia. Plastic cups of fizzy wine and some buns were passed round. To the astonishment of the Bolivians, Ben Cartwright spoke to his wife Ruth in England by satellite phone. All in all, it was quite a pleasant way of spending a fine, if blustery, afternoon.

'When are you going to launch the boats?' asked Fiona Adams, the *Sunday Times* stringer in Bolivia and Paraguay. 'Not while you lot are all here,' said Jim Masters. 'Anything could go wrong.'

Soon the guests dispersed and in a freshening breeze we pushed the boats into the murky waters. The crews hoisted sail; cameras and video recorders clicked and whirred. It was a great moment. In some chaos the boats drifted across the river and entangled themselves in Peruvian reeds on the other side. Our expedition had begun.

CHAPTER THREE

'DOWN A RIVER ON A STRAW BALE'

The people of Tiwanaku often founded sites in sparsely occupied areas, probably settled by Altiplano colonists from the vicinity of Tiwanaku itself.

ADRIANA VON HAGEN AND CRAIG MORRIS,
The Cities of the Ancient Andes, 1998

On comprend que le peuple de l'Altiplano ne soit ni communicatif ni aimable.

PAULE BERNARD, 'A TRAVERS LA BOLIVIE',
Connaissance du Monde, October 1962

Our fleet had extricated itself from the Peruvian reeds at Desaguadero by mid-afternoon on that first day, and with a following wind they made good progress. For a long time the Support Group in the Range Rovers – John, Yoli, Richard, Chris Beale, Noel and our Americans – could see the orange sail of *Kota Mama* in the lead and the two purple sails following. Towards the end of the afternoon Erik Catari, with all his experience in *balsas* on Lake Titicaca, had edged *Viracocha* in front. He led the fleet in to a mud bank on the Bolivian side where some local boats were moored and the Support Group were waiting. Progress for our Avon recce boat – a small inflatable which acted as support craft to the reed boats for most of the way – had been very slow as its engine was playing up. 'I'll be able to fix it tomorrow,' said Ben Cartwright as he and Jim Masters, both seriously sodden by the afternoon's rain, coaxed the Avon in.

That first camp site was the most miserable of the whole voyage. We were on flat, spongy ground. Torrential rain fell before our tents were up. Darkness fell unhelpfully rapidly. The local country people, the *campesinos*, were drunk and surly. Our kitchen was a squalid adobe hut. The first meal in the field is often a bit of a shambles, and this one was no exception. We slept damply and uncomfortably.

On the second day the Support Group drove southwards on a track parallel to the river and on its eastern side. The Inca had built a road here from Titicaca to Lake Poopó and it was probably better in their day than it was now. We made our way to a village on the river called Iruhito, at the last-minute having to leave the road altogether: the approach to the village was being improved and spoil heaps blocked the way. We were led into Iruhito across open country by Elias Panu Chacon, a local missionary, who took us through to a solid-looking building standing on rising ground which turned out to be a museum. John had been here on a previous recce and he now made it his HQ.

Iruhito is a village of a minority people known as the *nación Urus* with its own language and style of dress, a white gown and white cap with ear-flaps (*chullo*) for the men. There are Urus in the city of Oruro and further south near Chile. Their former territory was called Umasuyo, 'water-realm', and there was a great deal of information about it on posters in the museum. Their collection also had stuffed birds, fishing nets, hunting implements and pottery shards, but the prize possessions were two *chacha-pumas*, 'man-pumas', dug up by one of our hosts, Lorenzo Inta, formerly Sub-*Alcalde* and now the museum's curator. A *chacha-puma* is a stone figurine of a kneeling man with the head of a puma, carved in andesite and about the size of a rugby ball. The man's right hand, cut in relief down the side of the figurine, holds an axe; the left hand holds a severed head. Two others had been previously found in the pyramid at Tiahuanaco, and these were of the same period.

We were welcomed on arrival by the village chief, Damaso Inta, the *máximo autoridad* and a relative of Lorenzo. However mean the mudhole over which they preside, the Bolivians of the countryside, the *campesinos*, love titles and Damaso was also styled Secretario-General. He was quite happy for us to have a look at the field where the *chachapumas* had been found, adjacent to his house and until recently producing coca.

Next day we were joined by Oswaldo Rivera and his two colleagues from DINAAR: Adrian Alvarez, a young archaeologist, bear-like and moustachioed, and the smaller, even younger Danilo Villamor, an anthropologist currently working on a thesis on health, ageing and disease in early Bolivian peoples at the Universidad Mayor de San Andrés in La Paz. We all went over to the coca field, where Richard fell into conversation with one of the group of interested women who had come out to take a look at the strangers in their midst. One of them, María Inta, who was married to Damaso Inta's nephew, told him that when they had ploughed the field in the past they had from time to time struck rock. She waved her arm in the general direction of the place and, needing no further encouragement, Richard started probing the ground with a metal spike, albeit more in hope than expectation. Suddenly he hit something solid. Further prodding established that whatever it was seemed to stretch a fair way in all directions. He and Lee Smart began scrabbling away at the earth and, 7–8 centimetres down, revealed part of a flat stone. They and others tore at the soil over it like demented Jack Russells. It turned out to be a rectangular slab, some 50 centimetres by 42. It was a supreme moment. Richard had dabbled in archaeology before, in the unlikely setting of the Blue Mountains in Jamaica, and hours of back-straining toil there had produced only a few broken eighteenth-century claret bottles. Now with almost the first stab he had found what looked like being a significant discovery. He was exultant. 'I was Schliemann at Troy,' he said afterwards, tongue in cheek; 'I was Layard at Nineveh.'

Oswaldo pegged out a 2 square metre plot with string and all day the DINAAR team, Richard and Lee dug, sifted, dug, sifted with shovels and entrenching tools, examining every likely-looking stone and shard they turned up. The slab went down for 10 centimetres but it did not end there – it receded a centimetre or two and then went down again. After 10 centimetres there was another recession; then on it went down further. It was in fact a pedestal, some 1.5 metres deep, in the style of an altar – for ceremonial purposes, Oswaldo thought, perhaps sacrificial.

Near its foot a stone emerged, leaning against the shaft. Painstaking scraping and dusting revealed it as a *chachapuma* and beneath it a second, somewhat damaged. The Spanish desecrated all these images as a matter of course. But it was clear that we now had two more. Oswaldo's feline features beamed; he almost purred. He pointed out to us the standard characteristics of the kneeling man, the axe, the trophy-head, the puma mask, worn perhaps so that the warrior might be imbued with the agility, strength and ferocity of the animal itself.

The inevitable rain drove us off, but the next day we finished the job. The villagers' impassive faces had shown no flicker of interest at first, but as time went on they came in increasing numbers, and shy smiles appeared among the stares. A ceremony was deemed appropriate. Lorenzo Inta put on a poncho and a knitted *chullo*, knelt on the western side of the excavation and conducted an Aymará service of blessing. Water and 'wine of the earth' (wine with coloured soil added) in little phials were sprinkled from coca leaves on to the stones. John was invited to follow him, and then the rest of us. Next, John had to take a handful of something sticky and of animal origin that Lorenzo had just unwrapped and ceremonially pass it over his arms and body. This, I later discovered, was *mesa con sullo*, the chopped-up remains of an aborted llama foetus smeared with fat. Luckily he wasn't wearing his smart Norton exploring suit. All the women stood around reverentially as prayers and blessings were offered; Lorenzo then buried the remaining bits of foetus in the ground to the east of the excavation. All a mite spooky.

Oswaldo carefully washed the *chachapumas* and we gave them to the Urus museum to add to its collection.

'Do you think there's more stuff in the ground around the pedestal?' Richard asked Oswaldo.

'Oh, sure. This was a little city with two parts. Where we are now, by the river, was the domestic site. They could fish from here and trade could come in from upstream. Over there, where we find the *chachapumas*, was the ceremonial site. This mound, on which the museum stands, is called Karakontu, and it is from the Chiripa time.'

The Chiripa lived at the same period as the early Tiahuanaco people, a village culture flourishing in what we call pre-Christian times.

'The ceremonial mound over there, known as Lakotkontu, we found to be different,' Oswaldo went on. 'From the third, fourth and fifth periods of Tiahuanaco, 33 BC to AD 1172, when they developed towns. It is a fairly flat mound, but maybe was a pyramid once.'

He felt certain that there would not be just the one isolated pedestal, with its two *chachapumas*, struck down and defaced by incoming Spanish priests. There would most probably be more pedestals, on a floor, perhaps, of stone flags. It will need the time and energy of succeeding Bolivian archaeologists to uncover it all.

Meanwhile, on their second day afloat the boats had got away at 10.00 a.m. on their way to Iruhito. The weather was cloudy and drizzly; there were light winds from the north and the fleet made 2 knots. The border with Peru soon marched inland westwards, leaving both banks of the river to Bolivia. The waterway then broadened alarmingly but became choked with vast reed beds. The rain settled in and mists hung over the far bank. Visibility was poor, but at 11.30 a.m. the crews spotted a local who had come out from Iruhito in a rowing boat to look for them – a brave effort against the wind and current. He tried to lead them into the main channel, but all four boats at various times became entangled in the tall reeds and/or grounded in a shallow lagoon. Everyone aboard was now wet and miserable. There is nowhere to hide on a *balsa*; the narrow deck of slippery totora is exposed to all the elements. You get wet on the boat, sitting there and poling along; or you get wet off the boat, by jumping in the river and pushing – in this broad reach the water was often only knee deep.

By the early afternoon they could see the headlights of John's Range Rover drawn up on the mound at Iruhito about 2 miles away, and with binoculars he could see their distinctive sails. He had given them a bearing over the radio, but it was impossible to move along it in a direct line. The wind was inconsistent, gusting unhelpfully this way and that, so they lowered their sails. A storm brewed up: lightning knifed into the flat fields beyond and hailstones as big as quail's eggs soon began to drum down. Máximo Catari said that they should just sit it out – and he, with all the resilience and stoicism of an Altiplano Aymará, could probably have done so; but Barry was very worried about how cold everyone else was getting. They had no hot drinks or food or dry clothing, and if they had to stay out overnight hypothermia could set in. Periodically the entire crew of *Kota Mama* would drop into the river and try to bulldoze their *balsa* through the reeds. At least it stopped the limbs from seizing up. Slowly they inched nearer the broad eastern channel; but the wind had turned contrary in the storm and it was exhausting work, even with the Avon acting as tug-cum-shepherd, alternately pulling and pushing the boats through the reed beds.

Ashore, John, too, was growing concerned. As he peered through the squalls Jim's Somerset tones, calm and collected as ever, came over the radio. 'People are getting very cold,' he warned. 'We may be better off to leave the boats here and wade ashore. Can you meet us on the beach?'

John despatched a recce party to see how far a vehicle could move along the river bank; but they soon radioed back to say a swamp made the route impassable. If Jim's crews were to wade to the shore they would have to struggle through this morass for 2 miles to reach Iruhito. Furthermore, Yoli had been talking to the Urus and learned that a deep channel lay between the stranded craft and the bank. The prospect of cold, weakened people having to swim, even wearing lifejackets, did not seem a good one.

'Hold on where you are,' John told Jim, 'I'm trying to find someone who can guide you into the deep channel that leads directly to us.'

Now the lightning was striking the water near the boats.

'Do you think the masts will attract it, John?' asked Robert.

John nodded and sent Yoli off into the driving rain to find Damaso Inta, the chief. By the time the Urus leader arrived Jim was beginning to sound a little less calm, and from the top of the mound John pointed out the problem to the *campesino*, who looked grave and then turned and strode back to his house.

'Where on earth is he going?' demanded John.

'To collect his raincoat,' replied Yoli. 'Then he will take his boat out.'

By the time the chief had returned, resplendent in trilby hat and a yellow lifeboatman's poncho, the weather had worsened, and so had John Lyons, who was showing symptoms of exhaustion.

'What are you going to do about Lyons?' asked Robert.

'Right now I'm concentrating on getting the fleet off the river,' snapped John, peering upstream again through his powerful binoculars.

The rain was coming down like stair rods and even those ashore were shivering. The chief pushed his skiff out and was soon pulling through the deluge towards our boats. As luck would have it the wind veered again; Jim had found deeper water and the crews were inching their *balsas* forward as the chief came up to them out of the storm. Dusk was falling when they raised sails and came towards Iruhito. 'They are racing for home now,' said John, a distinct note of joy in his voice, 'and the light's improving all the time.' *Viracocha* came in first, with Erik Catari, a Bolivian crew and Seb Sheppard – obviously a Spanish-speaking boat. The flagship followed close behind, and then there was a long wait for a tired *Pacha Kutec*. Chrysoulla, blue with cold, managed a grin as she staggered ashore.

'Wow, what an experience!' she said through chattering teeth. Last of all came Jim and Ben with the Avon.

Everyone was played out, but it was amazing how morale zoomed up after the landfall. Seb Sheppard and Luke Cox bounded up and down the muddy strand with boat gear, emulated by the members of the Support Group. Even the rain eased off to a gentle drizzle during the disembarkation, though later it bucketed down again for a further twelve hours. And there was welcome hot food: Gerry Masters and Noel Burrell had toiled all afternoon making soup and a potato and onion mash with corned beef.

Iruhito had provided us with a surprise early success, but it was not a happy place for everyone. Noel Burrell examined John Lyons and diagnosed a recurrent heart problem; Jason Joyce had developed a testicular infection. We ferried them both off to the German Clinic in La Paz. The next day, sadly, we had to bid farewell to Seb Sheppard: one of our key boat's captains and a fluent Spanish-speaker, he had seemed indispensable. But his work, as a designer of pilot training courses for the new Royal Navy helicopter at Lockheed Martin, called him back to Britain. With him went the Roses: Bob to take a look at Paraguay (though he didn't in the end get there, being put off by the threat of malaria, for which he had not been taking the necessary preventive medication), and Faanya to a meeting in London. The day after that Chris Beale, who had been recumbent in his sleeping bag for several days with a persistent dizziness, was also carted off to the German Clinic. We now had four members in the La Paz hospital, including Elsbeth Turnbull who had had an operation on her wrist. Would they have enough beds for us all, some wondered?

The next leg would take us to Aguallamaya, where a track forded the river and a fine modern suspension bridge spanned it for pedestrians and cyclists in time of spate. The fleet left at 8.30 a.m. with the Iruhito chief as guide. The crews had a hard time of it: there was no wind after the night's storms and they had to pole the boats along until past noon. It was a tedious run: despite all the rain the river seemed low in its banks, and as time went on there was more pulling and pushing than poling, with the *balsas* constantly running aground. It was the first time that Jim had done a river journey with John where the problem was not the river's ferocity and volume but its sluggishness and shallowness. Towards the end of the day mounting frustration with this uncooperative watercourse led to a little *contretemps* over the walkie-talkies:

> JOHN *(on the bank by his Range Rover on the edge of a vast pool just upstream of the suspension bridge)*: Avon, this is Rover One, over.
>
> JIM *(a good distance away in the middle of the pool and leading the fleet)*: Send, over.
>
> JOHN: If you go to your left there is a deep channel which leads round to the take-out point where we are, over.
>
> JIM: Yes, but it looks to be full of weed.
>
> JOHN: Avon, it may seem to be but there is a good channel through it.
>
> JIM: Rover One, we can see what you can't, over.
>
> JOHN: Avon, when I was here the other day I saw cattle there with water up to their bellies.
>
> JIM: Roger, out.
>
> JOHN: Avon, why don't you follow the channel round to this location and take out here?
>
> JIM *(rather testily)*: Next time I come this way I'll take that route out.

It turned out that the cattle were themselves standing knee-deep in mud.

In the event, the boats all landed easily on the far side of the pool. John drove our guide, the chief, who for all his helpful intentions had proved quite deficient in his knowledge of the river and, indeed, largely unnecessary, back to Iruhito. The Desaguadero was at this time only a thin dribble of a stream for several hundred metres under the suspension bridge, and a recce on foot by Barry Moss had suggested to John that a considerable portage of the boats was now inevitable, perhaps as far as Nazacara – about 25 kilometres off. This might involve hazards of its own: Barry thought he had seen a puma, though it turned out to be only a *zorro* or fox.

Spot on 4.30 p.m. the rains came and a terrific storm blasted the tin roof of our borrowed hut. Gerry Masters and Noel Burrell had again taken on the task of preparing meals for us all – not an easy one, but at least there was one problem they didn't have here: whenever they wanted water they simply pushed a pan outside the door and within moments the rain had filled it.

In the morning the river was at last running full after all the storms; but its new-found vitality was short-lived, and it soon became clear that a portage was the only answer. We were always astonished that in the middle of a thinly populated Altiplano, where even scattered homesteads rather than villages were few and far between, and many of these were deserted, it was always possible to hire a lorry. Whenever we came across one and could flush out its owner, the prospect of a few unexpected bolivianos was too enticing to be turned down. Even when we had to unbolt its back gates and sometimes take down the central ridgepole the owner looked on with equanimity, and in most cases happily joined in the destruction of his own vehicle.

So, with his large American International and our navy Mercedes we reckoned we could run an effective shuttle service to Nazacara – provided, that is, we could lift the boats into the back of the lorries unaided. Gerry Masters took charge. No doubt he had had practice harnessing the energies of squads of Somerset labourers, but even so this was a new challenge. Everyone had his own theory about how it should be done and generally gave voice to it. Calls for silence fell on uncomprehending Bolivian ears. It was, Jim said, 'like an Arab market'. Eventually both national-ities got the significance of his 'Hands on! – One, two, three, LIFT!' The boats themselves couldn't have been less accommodating; one and a half tons of wet reed, a slippery cylinder with no hand-holds. We managed *Viracocha* well enough, but the larger *Kota Mama* nearly defeated us. The Avon was deflated, folded and thrown in with a *balsa* but we had no room for *Pacha Kutec*. So it had to be left on the bank to be fetched subsequently.

Nazacara, our next destination on the river, was something of a one-llama town on a road from La Paz to Chile. The Support Group had left Aguallamaya first and taken an L-shaped route south and east towards it. The two lorries, with a *balsa* each, followed. Luke Cox, Lee Smart and Freddie Ramos decided to walk down the river bank. It took them five hours; and although Luke considered the Desaguadero might have been navigable, Freddie thought not.

Our pattern of progress through Bolivia was that John and Yoli would go ahead a few days before the team's due arrival date and meet the local *responsables*. This usually led to the temporary assignment to the expedition of the school buildings as sleeping quarters. (The children, fortunately, were on holiday at this time.) Apart from schools, and the museum at Iruhito, we were often allocated the *Alcalde*'s office. Otherwise we were *al fresco* in tents; and after the rain of the first nights the hard classroom floor of the Nucleo Escolar Rural 'Loa' Nazacara 23 de Marzo 1979 had its attractions. Simón Bolívar's lean and saturnine features stared down at us from the wall, as did the arms of Bolivia, a wonderfully triumphal assemblage of cannons, lances, banners, llamas and snow-capped peaks. Moral precepts in Spanish, like *La ociosidad es madre de todos los vicios*, were pasted up all around. If idleness was the mother of all vices, then, Richard thought, he had better get off his butt and help unload the two lorries, which had just rolled in at noon.

The river level had risen 8 centimetres in the few days since John and Yoli's recce trip, so everyone was hopeful of good progress for the boats downriver.

'How deep do you reckon it is here in midstream?' Jim Masters asked John.

'Only about forty-three centimetres when I first came, so just over fifty now, I guess.'

'Out of curiosity, how do you actually measure it?' Jim went on, never having actually seen John with his boots wet.

'I do it by sending a small boy in and then measuring his legs.'

The Mercedes, with eight boat-lifters and two drivers, went back to Aguallamaya to pick up the remaining *balsa*; at dusk, when the party had still not returned to Nazacara, concern began to mount. Jim drove off west in the direction from which they should be coming, and 10 kilometres along the undulating way he came upon Rubén, one of our Range Rover drivers, running towards him.

'The Armada lorry is broken. Rodolfo has taken off the drive shaft. The gear box is gone,' said Rubén as they headed back to the school for some tools. Jim Masters then took to the road again, reached the stricken vehicle which had broken down a kilometre short of Aguallamaya, and managed to get everybody back to Nazacara for a late evening meal.

There is no fourth emergency service in Bolivia: if you break down you fix it yourself, and every driver has also to be a mechanic. At this point John showed his ability to pull chestnuts out of the fire. The Commander of the Navy in La Paz, Admiral

Zabala, was notified of the expedition's plight by the British Ambassador and hinted that he might be able to provide a new gear box. Before dawn the next day Rubén drove off with Lieutenant Vladimir Terrazas and Rodolfo to collect either the gear box or a new lorry.

This setback gave us an extra day at Nazacara. John, who is punctilious about PR, wrote sixty postcards to our supporters and sponsors, something along the lines of:

'Everyone fit and well, the natives friendly. We have found a lost city already and there are rumours of more in the vicinity. Your waterproof socks/Tirfor jack/magic marker pens/dehydrated apple flakes are proving invaluable. Bless you for your help. On to Lake Poopó!'

Oswaldo Rivera, with the archaeologist's eye for ground, saw the steepish hill behind Nazacara as an obvious old settlement site. It was not long before he had found half a bronze axe-head, masses of pottery, a burial ground, about fifty flint arrowheads in what was clearly a weapons factory and, best of all, vestiges of a glyptodont, a three- or four-million-year-old armadillo-like creature with carapace and horns. Fragments of it lay below strata of volcanic ash and so were older than an earlier time of severe eruptions – the very ones that had destroyed Atlantis, perhaps?

In the evening we heard gunfire in the town. Were the natives all that friendly? It was suggested that the locals were firing maroons into the clouds to induce rain, as some of us had seen being done in Mongolia. But the truth was more prosaic: the town, though tiny, was divided, like Buda and Pest, by the river. The people of Naza were at odds with those of Cara over a disputed boundary, and the guns were being fired to summon supporters of one side to a meeting.

Richard lay in his sleeping bag between the school desks, staring up at the only picture on the walls – a rather gruesome medical chart entitled *El Aparato Urinario*, with a diagram of kidneys, ureter, bladder and so on. He was reminded that the evening's usual two or three glasses of Kohlberg would probably make their presence felt in the small hours.

After midnight the restored Mercedes rolled in with the third *balsa*. In what had been an unconscionably long day for Rubén, Rodolfo, German, Vladimir, Máximo Catari and his seventeen-year-old cousin, the medical student Alexander Huañapaco, they had picked up a gear box in La Paz, driven out to Aguallamaya, fitted it and brought the truck, plus *Pacha Kutec*, back to Nazacara. The fleet was reunited.

The next leg, a 30 kilometre run from sleepy Nazacara to the very similar riverside town of Vichaya, began at 8.30 on a windless Sunday morning. It was soon necessary for the crews to slip into the ochre waters and push. The Avon recce boat got stuck as often as the *balsas*, so Lee Smart and Luke Cox tended to walk or wade ahead as pathfinders. Sometimes they found themselves swimming in mud as they dragged a boat along. It had been hoped that tributaries like the Kollpajahuira and the Quillhuiri, bringing in water from the distant mountains on the Altiplano's rim to the east and west, would raise the river's level; but they seemed only to have brought in more silt, which banked up and checked the river's flow. Every morning John looked anxiously at the sky. Would it rain? In our first days it had bucketed down in the late afternoon, evening and night, but at Nazacara this pattern changed, the days and nights alike were becoming mostly rain-free. Was this the effect of El Niño? The world's weather was awry because of the dreaded Child, who, thanks to the unusual warming of the Pacific Ocean surface waters, had brought climatic abnormalities as far away as Africa and Asia: drought in some instances, rain in others (for example, in Kenya, where Richard in January had seen unparalleled deluges in Nairobi and road bridges washed away). Through all the months that the *balsas* were being constructed John had prayed for Bolivian rain and had warned us all in Britain that El Niño could play havoc with our plans. It now looked as if our task of navigating the Desaguadero would be extremely difficult to accomplish, impossible without a fair amount of portage. Would we perhaps be the last fleet to make this passage?

The Support Group again followed the boats, this time down the western bank. On high ground John was able to speak to them by radio.

Jim had said, 'Progress is very slow. I don't think we can make Vichaya this day.'

This was confirmed when John reached Vichaya and then drove over the bridge and out in a wide arc to try to reach the river from the eastern side. After 30 kilometres he was within sight of the fleet, which had covered only 18 kilometres and had had to stop to camp while still 12 kilometres short of its destination. The crews – wet, muddy and exhausted, having spent the entire day hauling their craft over sandbanks – cut *tola*, the ubiquitous tough brushwood, made a fire and ate a scratch meal. The night was perishingly cold and few slept well. Next morning Jim roused them at 5.00. Another day of the same toil loomed, and morale was at its lowest ebb so far.

'What the hell am I doing this for?' thought Mark Lobel. 'At least the Thames has water in it when we put the St Paul's eights in.'

The Support Group lorry had made its way to Vichaya on rarely used tracks, crossing dry tributaries, cutting *tola* to provide firmer purchase on the spongy bits and asking ragged *campesinos* the way whenever one was sighted. Pleasant *estancias* were dotted about, dry stone walling ran up the hillsides and there were glimpses of an occasional adobe church. In Vichaya we were welcomed by a policeman who showed us to a smart, glazed building with a promising-looking stack of palliasses in the corner. Our evening meal in the little town's only bar was typical: a fried egg on a bed of rice, potatoes, salad and plantains (none of it very warm); then a bowl of good mutton soup and a piece of cheese. No Altiplano bar had furnished us (and none ever did) with a meal that would win even half a star in any food guide, but this one, for nine people, was less than five bolivianos, or 60p, each, so criticism was muted.

The next morning a miserable-looking old lady, presumably the caretaker, came into our smart building and snooped about a bit while the Support Group prepared to support. The fleet was expected at noon and so Gerry and Noel began to make ready a cauldron of *sopa de quinua* to warm the crews through. John, Richard and Yoli went down to the bridge to make a 10.00 a.m. telephone call to the pupils of the Brixham Community College. The ease with which we placed the O'Gara telephone on the Range Rover bonnet, lined up the antenna towards the nearest satellite, dialled and spoke never ceased to astonish. Every three or four days we sent a news bulletin to the school and later on began to run interviews in Spanish between Bolivian and Devon children, which must have been amazing for the local *chicos* and *chicas*, many of whom had never seen a telephone before. We told our Brixham audience how our boats were having problems with the shallow, slow-moving river and how ironic it was that the name Desaguadero means 'where all the waters gather'; and that we had yesterday eaten a kind of fish called pejerrey. Any sort of information seemed to go down well. The questions that came back were mainly about how we lived, what we ate and what wildlife we had seen.

Then it was time to go and help the boats. The Range Rovers drove upriver as far as they could get across the riparian flats. Five kilometres north of Vichaya Richard spotted the three sails in an east–west line, far away. They seemed at first to be static, but after a few minutes of observation some movement was just discernible. John had time to go back to Vichaya for some human reinforcements before the four boats were pushed and heaved round a long bend and came distantly into sight. The crews were all in the river, which came up to the mid-calf and occasionally just over the knee. We heard their far-off cries. Lee and Luke, like eager dolphins, leapt and thrashed forward, finding the best route.

'Take fifteen minutes,' came a shout from Jim. They had been at it for eight hours already and were tired and dehydrated.

John and four locals help Rubén to pay out his Range Rover winch cable and attach a longer rope to it. This is carried forward to *Viracocha*, which has run aground again, and tied on. There is a hiccup when the rope snaps and whips back dangerously, but a knot is quickly tied; expertly the Rover edges back and the *balsa* is drawn easily over the bar. This is one moment's help in one and a half days' worth of struggle; a token morale boost only. The other two reed boats are similarly assisted, bottles of fresh water passed around and news exchanged. Then the slog goes on.

It was not until 4.00 p.m. that the flagship sailed slowly down the last reach to the bridge at Vichaya. The other two were hauled along by lines from the bank even later. At the bridge a substantial crowd of villagers had gathered and jolly Bolivian music was blaring from a hastily rigged-up amplifier. After some mutual back-slapping the boats' crews were lined up by John for a civic ceremony of welcome. It was the last thing they wanted. Most minds were set on a cup of tea or a bottle of Paceña, a change of clothing and a rest. But the town band had turned out, a bevy of schoolchildren was drawn up, and the *Alcalde* and the *Corregidor* had ominous-looking sheaves of speech notes in their gnarled hands.

First the Bolivian National Anthem. Then 'The Queen', rendered even less assuredly than at Desaguadero. The pan pipes played to the beat of a drum. The *Alcalde*, in broad-brimmed straw hat and with one trouser leg masonically reefed, began his peroration:

'Coronel [long pause] John [another pause before obvious forthcoming difficulty] Blashyfordy [pause] Eznell. . .'

As his speech unfolded, much was made of the *integración* between Lakes Titicaca and Poopó. Even the children were subdued as his ringing tones spelled out our achievements, his free arm waving theatrically.

'It must be Laurence Bolivia,' said Noel.

The children sang, the *Corregidor* spoke, the pan pipes piped again. Then a large, voluminously skirted lady proceeded down the line of expedition members and sprinkled a handful of blue confetti on top of each one's head. The *Alcalde* followed her, shaking hands and thanking us. The band struck up anew and a very wide-hipped lady came up to John and asked him to dance. Crates of pop were brought forward and bottles distributed. Gradually the boats' crews, their boots still full of river gravel and their sodden clothes steaming gently in the late afternoon sun, were inveigled on to the floor by village girls to join John in a lively salsa. It was all very affecting.

When we walked back up to our building the *sopa de quinua* had been bubbling away for seven hours.

'Probably done now,' said Gerry, ladling some out.

After the warmth of the villagers' welcome it was sad to find that the miserable old caretaker had locked our building and gone far off into the country with the key. Perhaps we should not have been surprised; her sour expression and protruding lower lip had earlier hinted that she was not pleased with our arrival, which had obviously disturbed her quiet days. The *Alcalde* was livid and cycled off to hunt her down.

'My daughter has the key,' she told him.

He cycled back to find that it was not so. The wretched evening dragged on as we waited outside the building, furious. 'Quartermaster,' asked John, 'do we have a ducking-stool?' In the end the *Alcalde* offered us other accommodation and we never did enjoy those palliasses again. The old woman was called Benigna, which means 'kindly'. She was the only curmudgeonly Aymará we ever met.

A big decision was made the following day: we would portage our fleet to Calacoto where the Desaguadero's biggest tributary, the Mauri, comes in from the west. Surely this big feeder would make for easier navigation southwards?

Portage presents its own problems. By dint of stopping every lorry she saw on the road, Yoli eventually managed to hire one. Unfortunately it followed the usual Bolivian pattern and had a ridgepole and two doors astern, both very firmly bolted on. This meant spending over an hour ripping away great pieces of lorry to get a good clear entry for our flagship. We had loaded a smaller boat on to the Mercedes by hand, but Jim and Gerry thought we should bring to bear a bit of engineering savvy on the loading of the big one. Accordingly, two sheerlegs were lashed together in an inverted V and mounted on the hired lorry over its rear wheels. A pulley hung from them, one end of a rope being secured to the Merc as an anchor point, the other trained over the stern of *Kota Mama* and secured. This was going to be easy. Let the crane take the strain. A highly geared Tirfor jack, a vital piece of engineering equipment, was cranked by two stalwarts along the rope and the flagship was inched forwards and upwards. But somehow it never quite made it. The sheerlegs occasionally canted backwards with a sickening shudder. After three hours we had the bow end of the flagship on the lorry's tailgate, but all efforts to get it to slide on further failed. In the end we had to urge the menfolk in the crowd watching all these antics to come forward to help us; and, by passing a pole under the boat's keel, manned four-a-side by eight of the most ox-like individuals, we were able by the time-honoured application of main force to heave it in.

The Support Group took a cross-country route west and south to Calacoto. Elegant vicuña trotted across our path. These brown and white, slender-necked creatures are close relatives of the llama. *Vicugna vicugna*, 'a cud-chewing Andean artiodactyl mammal' as encyclopaedias more prosaically term it, had dropped dangerously in numbers on the Altiplano until a census showed the need for a conservation programme. In 1986 a count showed 12,047 vicuña. In ten years they had risen to 33,844. But the vicuña carry their danger on their backs. The finest merino sheep wool measures 30 microns; but that from the tuft below the neck of the vicuña is only 10 microns. So they are once again being poached and slaughtered for this fine wool. We had talked to Mateo Hinojosa, *guardafauna* in the Nazacara area, who had about 5,700 vicuña in his care. The *guardafauna* around Vichaya was Hilarion Quisber Chura, and we reckoned he would be one of the most dedicated, spending all his days outdoors, tramping along through the *tola* protecting his flocks and communing with nature – for his wife was the dreaded Benigna, enemy of river-borne *gringos*, hider of the key and doubtless an accomplished nag.

Calacoto, like all Bolivian towns and villages that we entered, had a vast, empty, unpaved central plaza, with an ornately roofed bandstand over it. Lying in its shade were Chris Beale, Jason Joyce and Elsbeth Turnbull, all now discharged from the German Clinic (albeit only temporarily in Elsbeth's case) and Fiona Adams, the sparky *Sunday Times* stringer. We were back up to strength for the next phase.

CHAPTER FOUR

CITIES OF THE EAGLE MEN

*Events in the highlands between 1200 and 1400 are less well docu-
mented. This is partly because the people living there on the eve of the
Inca conquests never developed the monumental architecture or the art
to rival their coastal counterparts or their . . . Tiwanaku predecessors.*

ADRIANA VON HAGEN AND CRAIG MORRIS,
The Cities of the Ancient Andes, 1998

U p the Mauri river, to the west of Calacoto, the horizon is
dominated by a series of flat-topped tablelands or *mesas*,
features which had intrigued John when he was taken there by
archaeologist Oswaldo Rivera in 1997. They had climbed one of
them, Thia Phasa, which in Aymará means 'small mountain', and
found impressive stone walls and hut circles. At the end of the
day, as the sky darkened with a coming storm, John had trained
his binoculars across the valley to another *mesa*.

'It looks like a town on the top there. Pity we haven't time to
have a look at it. Perhaps on some other occasion,' he had said,
carefully recording the location with his GPS.

That other occasion now presented itself, as on the tenth day
out of Desaguadero John and Oswaldo led Luke Cox, Elsbeth
Turnbull, Fiona Adams and Richard Snailham on an investigative
expedition to Taypi Phasa, the 'medium mountain'.

A road to Chile snakes between two of the *mesas*, and here the
party left Rubén's Range Rover to follow a contour line up through
ancient abandoned terrace plots, passing under the sheer cliffs

of the *mesa* John and Oswaldo had climbed the previous year and dropping down to a windy col. John and Richard were amazed that after only two weeks in the High Andes they were able to plod along quite easily at over 13,500 feet. 'Must be the effect of the *mate de coca*,' remarked John.

From the col the views eastwards across the Altiplano were staggering. Under blue skies a distant plume of smoke from Calacoto hung like the pipe of a tornado. The broad, braided streams of the Mauri glinted in the sun. The Altiplano itself, which in fact undulates considerably, seemed flat. The tiny figures of *campesinos* tending their potato plots and patches of *quinua*, or riding horses, seemed to crawl over the land far below us.

A broken ridge led to the tableland of Taypi Phasa.

'Hey, look at that wall,' cried Luke.

Blending beautifully with the natural stone ramparts ringing the *mesa* were massive sections of dry stone walling, creating a virtually impregnable fortress. We followed the line of the wall around, looking for a gateway. There was none to be seen.

'I reckon even today a small force of good infantrymen could hold off a strong enemy for a long time from behind those defences,' said John.

Soon, however, a small aperture – little more than a cat-flap with no flap – appeared in the lower part of the wall; Fiona contrived to squeeze through this, and later we found another well-defended break in the wall, approached up two sides of a large boulder, where John and Richard could make a more decorous entry.

From afar we had seen, skylined on the top of the *mesa*, the stone houses which had intrigued John in 1997. Now they were all in front of us, dotted about on the extensive tableland. Shaped like old-fashioned beehives, built up from irregularly cut stones held together by rough mortar into a roughly conical shape, each had a small door but no windows or chimneys. It was clear from the narrowness of the doorways that these were not dwellings. Richard stuck his head through the first door slit.

'Come and look at this, Elsbeth,' he said. 'They're full of bones.'

In the darkness, scattered over the dusty floor, were whitened radii, femurs, ulnas, ribs and spinal vertebrae – but no skulls. Too many, too intact, too obviously human for this to be an animal lair; it was clearly a burial chamber. Fiona and Luke were despatched to survey the surrounding wall while Elsbeth, John and Richard investigated the forty or fifty more funerary structures dispersed among the natural outcrops of rock on the tableland. Each one revealed the same sort of assemblage of bones.

'Whose graves are these?' we asked Oswaldo.

'They are called *chulpas*,' he said. 'They are from the Pakajes people, which means the Eagle Men. *Paka* is Aymará for eagle and *kaje* is man. Some call them Lupaca. They were here between the fall of the Tiwanaku empire around 1175 and the coming of the Inca in 1420.'

'Why are there no skulls, do you think?'

'People have been here before.' He paused. 'And skulls are very necessary for medical students today. Maybe the locals sell them.'

John and Richard wandered through the vast necropolis.

'Do you think people lived here?' John asked Oswaldo.

'Maybe they lived over on Thia Phasa.'

'Well, why would they trouble to build such elaborate defences up here? It must have taken hundreds of men and months of work.'

'They held the dead in such reverence that they wanted to protect them well,' replied Oswaldo. But, he added, 'some of them did live here some of the time.' And indeed, though at first sight there was little evidence of domestic activity, John and Richard did find some broken grinding stones and traces of a few hut circles, as well as one larger building that Oswaldo thought might have been a temple. There were also cuboid recesses in among the outcropping rocks which might have harboured families or their animals, with what seemed like holes for beams to hold up a roof of dried *tola* or cactus wood. We also found a pattern of lines on a rock floor which looked like a witch's pentacle, filled with vegetation, but it turned out to be a natural feature.

The distribution of the *chulpas* seemed to be random, though several were perched on the edge of the *mesa*, their narrow doors aligned to catch the rising sun's first rays.

'I think they may have been arranged in clan groups, so that two or three charnel-houses together were occupied by the same extended family,' Richard mused. There seemed to be no internal walls or streets to separate one group from another, however.

Oswaldo, who had been studying this area intermittently for

fifteen years, said that there were probably some thirty *mesas* that had been occupied by the Pakajes in the triangle of land between the Mauri and Desaguadero rivers. John and Richard were reminded of similar *mesas* in Ethiopia, where they are called *ambas* – like the one at Magdala, the final bolt-hole of the Emperor Theodore, who took his own life there after having his European hostages forcibly freed by the invading Anglo-Indian forces of Sir Robert Napier in 1868. Had some great leader of the Eagle Men ever presided over Taypi Phasa, we wondered? These *mesas* made marvellous vantage points from which to sight an enemy advancing over the Altiplano, and were an obvious refuge. But there were inherent problems. Where did the Eagle People get their food and water? Some crops could be grown on the surrounding fields and foothills and we had already seen evidence of terracing, but there were no wells or cisterns and the only streams were far distant.

At the northern end of the tableland were two larger structures, not conical this time but rectangular, and made from dressed blocks of stone twice the size of those in the other *chulpas*. Oswaldo thought they might have been late Lupaca or early Inca.

'The Inca buried their dead in *chulpas*, too,' he said, 'but more elaborate ones.'

It was less easy to see inside these larger burial towers, so John suggested that Richard might crawl into one, which with some difficulty he did.

'I can just manage to stand up. There's a portion of skull in this one, loads of bones and one still fleshed but very desiccated foot,' was his report.

Meanwhile, Oswaldo, Luke and Fiona had discovered five main entrances and, more intriguingly, the mouth of a tunnel in the eastward-facing cliff. The entrances were larger than the hole Fiona had first crawled through – indeed, they were merely gaps in the wall with no elaborate defences. As for the tunnel, Luke managed to get into it, but only with some difficulty, by abseiling down the cliff face. It ran under the *mesa* across its whole width, right to the other side; but, given the inaccessibility of its entrance, it was hard to see what use the Pakajes might have made of it.

John's briefing that night was a memorable affair. Not only did he have the discovery of a second 'lost city' to announce, just days after the emergence of the *chachapumas* at Iruhito, but we were lodged in by far the most salubrious quarters we had yet seen. A new school had been completed at Calacoto and was now ready to open. Its three contiguous hexagonal class-rooms had not yet seen any children and its blackboards were unchalked when the authorities permitted us to move in. On the expectation of a visit from the British Ambassador and other dignitaries, the *Alcalde* lent us a conference table and six chairs upholstered in a splendidly rich mock velvet, somewhat anomalous amid the mud and squalor of the rest of Calacoto. True, we still slept on a dusty floor; but a chair is a rare pleasure on an expedition and the table gave John several square feet on which to spread out his various accoutrements and draw his maps.

This luxury was the more appreciated because we were to be in Calacoto for some while. As an operational base it showed initial promise, though in some respects this was sadly unfulfilled. On the plus side, it had an ENTEL telephone office for our regular calls to La Paz, which was very useful given that calls on the satellite phone cost $3 a minute, and a bus service to and from the capital. On the minus side, the fine adobe church with its imposing bell tower that adorned one side of the plaza remained locked and unused all the days we were there, including a Sunday (the nearest priest was said to be in Corocoro and a rare visitor here); and the small bar next to it which declared itself willing to make us an evening meal – a pretty sporting offer considering that there were over twenty of us – raised our hopes with bottles of beer at 50p and a good soup, but dashed them again with the impenetrable repast that followed: fatty, leathery wing of chicken on a mound of lukewarm potatoes, rice and salad. The railway line which passed through Calacoto from La Paz to Arica on Chile's Pacific coast excited the schoolboy in some of us; but the station was a ruin, and its rare trains passed mostly in the early morning darkness.

Calacoto's best feature was in fact its position on the Altiplano and the view to the west. Beyond the *mesas*, almost on the Chilean border, was the perfect snow cone of Sajama, a dormant volcano whose awe-inspiring height and symmetry roused us to new admiration every day. At over 6,500 metres, Sajama is one of the candidates for the accolade of highest mountain in Bolivia. Which of the four contenders actually takes the honours rather depends on which authority you consult, as the table overleaf shows.

Which is Bolivia's highest mountain?	Illimani	Ancohuma	Illampu	Sajama
Times Atlas of the World	6,402	6,388	6,385	6,542
The University Atlas (Philip)	6,462	6,550		6,520
Penguin Atlas	6,402		6,362	6,542
Philips Great World Atlas 1995	6,882	6,550		6,520
South American Handbook	6,402/6,460*	6,420	6,380	6,530
Lonely Planet	6,439	6,427	6,362	6,542
Bradt		6,420/6,427*	6,380/6,362*	
*Where two heights in metres are given maps and text differ.				

On our way back to Calacoto from the *mesas* we stopped to take photographs of the western view. The ground was covered in blue-green chunks of what looked like copper ore. We knew this was a mineral-rich country. The Inca emperor Atahualpa had rooms stacked high with silver and gold which dazzled Pizarro and his men on their arrival in Cuzco in 1532, and the conquistadors themselves had very quickly found their way to Potosí in Upper Peru (now Bolivia), where for several subsequent centuries they mined silver from a mountain almost solely composed of it. Simón Patiño, whose daughter Isabel eloped with the late James Goldsmith, was the head of just one of several families which made their money from Bolivian tin.

Oswaldo picked up some of the chunks.

'Cooper, cooper, everywhere is cooper,' he said.

We were told there were more *mesas* with *chulpas* to be found south of the Mauri river, and were keen to go and see them for ourselves, though getting to them was clearly going to be a little tricky. A reconnaissance trip showed that it was possible to ford the Mauri but, even so, both our cross-country vehicles and the Mercedes truck became stuck in it several times, often while returning late at night. However, the relative inaccessibility of the area had its own attractions: the *chulpas* here, we reckoned, might be less disturbed. So it was with some anticipation that on 27 March the whole team set off to explore a piece of land which geography has made it very difficult to get to. Cut off from Calacoto and Corocoro by the Mauri and Desaguadero rivers, there was no approach for vehicles other than a rather chancy ford. There is no marked way over the streams and sand-bars; just a point where the track goes into the river and another, 500 metres away, where it comes out again. Negotiating this crossing successfully was to take a bit of practice.

We made good progress south and west. There are few roads hereabouts, but plenty of tracks and open grassland – and, where necessary, a path can generally be bulldozed through the *tola*. Tough and unappetizing though it looked, parts of the *tola* plant were eaten in extremis by the resourceful Aymará. Doña 'Nelly', a rotund (but surprisingly nimble), rosy-cheeked *campesina* who had first guided us into these parts, showed us how she could dig below the bush and about half a metre down find strange phallus-shaped bulbs speckled, like some exotic condom, with pink buds. Eaten raw, the 'fruit of the *tola*' was said to be efficacious for complaints of the kidneys, lungs or liver.

One of our 4 × 4s, driven with some panache by Juan Carlos for the first fortnight of the expedition, had gone back with him to La Paz, and we now had what John was apt to call a Mitsibushi. At the steering wheel Antonio, a slow-moving, darkly handsome man with expensively golden teeth, was careful enough, but it was difficult not to become a back-seat driver. When Richard saw a depression coming up in the track he searched for the word. 'Bumpo!' was all he could dredge up, and the term caught on. When a serious rift was seen ahead the cry became 'Bumpissimo!' (One bumpissimo had us all out with shovels filling in a deep gash, where erosion had eaten away half the road, so that our lorry could squeeze through.) Yoli coined one for a more modest pothole: 'Bumpito!' Antonio seemed to understand all this; he probably had them all in his sights anyway.

Our local guide was of limited use: his instructions, given *sotto voce*, always came after we had passed the turning point. But somehow we found our way to the remote settlement of Anantuco and another set of school buildings, painted, as they all were round here, in bold blue and white stripes. Its fifty pupils were all on holiday, and we lunched in the playground. Here John divided the team into three groups. Jim, Gerry and Noel went off up the valley to look for petrified wood; Ben, Freddie Ramos, Danilo Villamor (our Bolivian anthropologist) and Richard were despatched to an imposing *mesa* to the north, Chosi Kani, under the leadership of a newly arrived member of the expedition, Captain Toby Marriner of the Royal Engineers, later to carry out some important recces for Kota Mama Phase II; and John himself, armed with a sketch-map drawn by Oswaldo, took the remainder on a longer route to search for some painted tombs in caves in a *mesa* wall.

The tombs proved elusive. The *Alcalde* was uncooperative and it took all Yoli's charm to induce him to say even approximately where they were. He went only a kilometre along the way with John: his people would be angry, he said, if he showed the visitors this 'place of spirits'. Instead the team found in the valley bottom a remarkable survival which he had not told them about: a tiny chapel from Inca times, now Christianized and full of colonial period artefacts. The interior walls were whitewashed and covered with Lowry-like sketches of companies of Spanish soldiers in shakos, their tricorn-hatted officers on horseback urging them towards the Inca foe. Two brass bells on a small table caught the eye of Adrian Alvarez, our archaeologist. A crudely designed one was Inca, he said; the other, more elaborate, was Christian. Yoli, herself part-Inca, was clearly moved by her visit to this humble chapel. Further across the valley there was a cluster of square *chulpas* and a great roofless hall, 34 metres by 9, its gable ends and window still intact.

'It is an Inca temple and treasure hunters have recently been here,' Adrian said, indicating some signs of digging at the southern end.

Meanwhile, at the top of Chosi Kani the second group emerged through a steep tunnel entrance on to a tableland the same size as Taypi Phasa where, to their delight, they found themselves looking on the same panorama of stone *chulpas* – fifty-two in all. The flat top was tilted slightly, rising gently for 2 kilometres or so towards the north. Ben and Toby began a survey where several *chulpas* were perched on the beetling cliff edge. Freddie, Richard and Danilo ambled up the slope inspecting others and noting their contents.

The first impression they had was that there were more bodies in each *chulpa* here than at Taypi Phasa. Here, too, for the first time there were skulls: up to six or seven in each, their eyeless sockets staring out eerily from the dark interiors. Most *chulpas* also contained rolls of brown basketwork, stained and folded. Danilo recognized these as *canastas*, woven containers in which the corpses were interred in a foetal position, knees to chin, limbs securely tied. Soon we found skeletons, fairly complete, still in situ in their grass *canastas*. Others had burst out of the rotting baskets and were spilled all over the floor.

'Sometimes they bury a chief with his wife and concubines,' said Danilo, 'and sometimes another *canasta* is placed over the top with a little hole cut for the face.'

Most of the *chulpas*, like those we had seen on Taypi Phasa, were shaped like old beehives, but others were a chubby bottle shape and two or three were cubic. At least two, much eroded, were of adobe. Many had a protruding course of stones as a foundation and another close to the tops. Clearly these were Lupaca structures, the work of the Eagle Men, though here too there was one very large structure, built with well-dressed stones and very little use of mortar, which Danilo thought to be Inca. Again all their narrow doors faced east. On this bright day the cone of Sajama stood clear on the horizon; it probably played a big part in the Lupaca belief system.

In the late afternoon, taking a route back to Calacoto which we hoped would be quicker but which would have necessitated fording the Mauri further upriver, we ran into trouble before we even got that far, becoming severely bogged while crossing the Achuto, a tributary. It seemed passable – crystal clear water, a foot deep or so, ran over small pebbles which felt firm enough underfoot, if a mite spongy – but the heavy Mercedes plunged in and sank to its axles. We emptied it of bodies and gear; still its wheels spun hopelessly, mud now around its engine casing. There was no stone or wood nearby to shove underneath, and (surprisingly) no *tola*. German and Rodolfo sweated away below their cab, shovelling silt and fruitlessly trying to find a firm base for their jack. To attempt a tow would have endangered the Range Rover and the Mitsubishi which had already crossed successfully. Rubén went back in the Range Rover and tried to haul out the Mercedes by his winch – to no avail. A moment for reflection reminded us that we were on our own: this was uninhabited country, miles from anywhere on unused tracks. Ironically, a pipeline carrying oil from Bolivia on its way to the Pacific crossed the tributary near us – but, maddeningly, just too far away for us to use its stanchions as an anchor point. Somehow, with all of us applying our muscle to the bodywork, after several almost superhuman efforts and with both the Range Rover and the Mitsubishi pulling, we heaved the Mercedes back up on to the bank and took the original route home.

Even then, we were not to get to the end of the day without a few more 'bumpitos'. The Mercedes became stuck again, crossing the Mauri in darkness; back at the school, in our tiredness we somehow managed to spill drops of candle fat on the *Alcalde*'s smart velveteen chair covers, Richard knocked John's whisky over and John himself later knocked over another one. Nevertheless, we counted the day a success, enthralled by our fascinating if macabre discoveries.

John has always said that one of his strongest motives for exploration is curiosity. He was curious now about the painted tombs Oswaldo had described to him. Where could they be? So far we had drawn blanks, but the hunt was still on; so the next day we approached the Mauri again. We were getting cleverer at crossing the ford now, and reached the far bank without mishap. Some time later we reached the pipeline (*oleoducto* on our maps) and crossed that too. By lunchtime we had found a quite large but abandoned settlement – Villa Utavi. Its blue and white school buildings had been built by none other than General Hugo Banzer Suárez, our Patron, when he was Commander of the Bolivian Armed Forces in 1976.

Next we struck eastwards across country, bypassing deeply eroded gullies and pushing through the *tola* as near as possible to another *mesa* called Pucara. This name rang a bell for many of us, for it was also the name of the ground-attack aircraft the Argentinians had used in their 1982 occupation of the Falklands. We remembered how several had been blown up by the SAS at Pebble Island. Toby Marriner led a group to the top of the *mesa* where he and Adrian Alvarez found twenty-seven *chulpas*, many half-ruined. Meanwhile, John's group and a newly arrived BBC film crew whom we had arranged to meet (Peter Getzels, a fast-talking BBC film-maker and producer, and Wolfgang Schüler, his German sound man, domiciled in La Paz) circled the sheer cliffs of the *mesa* looking for overhangs which might conceal the 'painted houses'.

Pucara is roughly crescent-shaped and we laboriously followed the outline of its longer outer side. It was hot work for those of us toting tripods, cameras, boxes of film. Then, as we reached the crescent's horn and rounded it, a loud cry came from John: 'There they are!' His binoculars had picked out small white structures far off at the foot of the cliff on the inner side of the crescent.

'Another lost city,' said Jim.

'Right on cue,' said Ben; 'we haven't had one for about three days.'

We skittled down into the valley and hacked up the other side through the brush, the film crew having a hard time with their heavy gear. When we caught up with them, John and Yoli were climbing around and inspecting a spectacular stone cube, just over 2 metres in all directions, whose walls were plastered over and painted in pale pink. Right under its flat, projecting roof a frieze of interlocking red and green triangles ran around the three exposed faces; the fourth, rear, wall was blank and faced into the overhang. Inside were four skulls, numerous ribs and femurs, and a grinding stone. Behind it, a natural cave with smoke-blackened roof was filled with more bones and skulls. Some time was spent measuring, sketching and filming this rarely visited charnel-house. Peter dashed about excitedly to get the best shots while Wolfgang recorded our commentaries.

'Now at last we have something,' said Peter, his lean frame crouched over the camera. Wolfgang, a big, moustachioed teddy-bear of a man, his long, blond wisps of hair blowing in the breeze, nodded approvingly.

John spoke to camera: 'This is another burial site of the Eagle Men, dating from probably the thirteenth century AD – pre-Columbian, pre-Inca, but only just.'

Nearby was a second house with a symbolic design in black on the massive dressed stones of its facade; and 200 metres further along under the overhang was a small white-painted tomb with exotic designs: five or six many-stepped ziggurat profiles inside circles, snake-like undulations, many-spiked crowns – or could they be animals, or even ships? These images tempted us to think of possible pre-Inca links with ancient Egypt. The Mayans and Aztecs, of course, also built step pyramids. Was theirs a spontaneous, non-derivative development, or had they had connections with the old Mediterranean world? Or were pre-Columbians in Central and South America and ancient Egyptians both influenced by Atlanteans?

Pondering on these possibilities we climbed to the top of Pucara at 13,084 feet and crossed it. No *chulpas* here, just enormous rock outcrops – with more *mesas* all around and, as always, Sajama in the distance.

For the 4 × 4s it was an easy run back to Calacoto – for most of us; but German deviated from the straight line across the Mauri and sank in up to his axles. Heroic attempts in darkness to tow him out failed. All the other lorry drivers in the town who might have been prevailed on to lend a hand were deeply drunk, and so we had to leave the Mercedes in the river overnight, along with the Mitsubishi, which Antonio had managed to mire while trying a rescue.

We dined in Calacoto in a shop owned by a local entrepreneur called Porfirio. On this occasion he and his wife laid on a buffet in his back yard, and while waiting for the soup to appear

John and Richard inspected the shop. In a glass case below the counter were cheap plastic torches (Calacoto was not yet on mains electricity), baby's teats, Chinese bicycle pedals and lamps – and, in among all this paraphernalia, what looked like brown candles.

'I wouldn't light them if I were you,' said John. 'They're sticks of dynamite.'

We found that most shops on the Altiplano stocked dynamite, together with the necessary fuses and detonators. The sticks sold for about 30p each and were used for quarrying, road construction and the like.

Back at the school after the meal, John put the O'Gara satellite telephone on the bonnet of the Mitsubishi and punched in a New York number. Moments later he was speaking to Robert and Faanya Rose, John Lyons and Barry Moss, all now back in the USA and attending the Explorers' Club Annual Dinner. John spoke to several other guests and members of the press, most of whom did not seem to know where Bolivia was.

Then – as every evening – we had our *conferencia*. John had always adopted this sensible practice on expeditions. In the Army it was called an O Group, where people got their orders; in Kenya it was a Baraza, from the Swahili for a meeting; in less exotic and more democratic circles it would be called a briefing. Ours was an excellent example of Anglo-Bolivian collaboration. John explained what we had seen and done, sought advice here and there, and then told us what we were going to do next. Every sentence was translated very thoroughly into Spanish by Yoli, including the important subtle nuances. It was a triumph of communication.

Many of us spoke some Spanish already, or had made an effort to learn some.

'*Repollitas*?' Jim Masters asked the young girl as she gave him his plate of rice, potatoes and chicken. She stared blankly.

'What's that?' said Gerry.

'Brussels sprouts. It's the only vegetable I can remember. I had a go at a phrase-book before I came out, but there's only one that stuck and I haven't had the chance to use it yet.'

'And what's that then?'

'"Please show me the way to the tennis court."'

'I get quite a lot of mileage from "*Dios da nueces al que no tiene muelas*,"' Richard said.

'Astonish us.'

'Well, it's a rather pathetic little saying: "God gives nuts to those that have no molars."'

'I know nothing,' said Jason Joyce. 'I am from Barcelona.'

Richard travelled frequently with the BBC team and their driver Don René, a Bud Flanagan look-alike with much experience of cross-country travel. This was a Spanish-speaking vehicle, and Richard was heartened to find he could understand about half of what was said. Indeed, at the end of the expedition (after two or three glasses of Kohlberg) he even gave an interview in Spanish to a journalist from *Provincia*.

The next day – Wednesday 1 April, eighteen days since we had left Desaguadero – it was time to take to the water again. Reconnaissances had indicated to John that the river below Calacoto was still very low, and so we should have to leave *Kota Mama* and *Viracocha* there for later collection while we took *Pacha Kutec* in the Mercedes the 60 kilometres or so to the International Bridge and put her in downstream of it. The water looked more promising from the bridge, at least as far as Eucaliptus – about another 60 kilometres away. Our camp site just south of the International Bridge was comparable to one on the Brocus by the Thames at Eton, a grassy field by a broad river with articulated lorries bombing along the nearby local M4: in this case, a smart new dual carriageway bringing Bolivia's imports up from Arica on the Pacific coast to La Paz. As we performed our morning ablutions, two old ladies came up to stand and stare. All *campesinas* are decked out in the same attire: woolly stockings, layers of voluminous skirts, woolly cardigans, black hair centrally parted with two long plaits linked at the bottom with woolly tassels, and a cheekily tilted bowler hat. Apparently, an early president of Bolivia visited London and saw all the affluent businessmen in bowlers; when he got home he decreed that they should be *de rigueur* in Bolivia. We were camping on land which belonged to these two, so we gave them a large bag of rice.

Pacha Kutec pushed off into liquid mud of no known depth and ran aground. The Avon, now crewed by Ben Cartwright and Lee Smart, nosed the *balsa* off and the two boats slowly drifted away. In the absence of any bankside tracks, it was difficult for the Support Group to give them much immediate help. The 4 × 4s had to go inland and then approach the river again at a little backwater settlement called Huari Belen. This detour took them through a fair number of Altiplano towns and villages, most of which conformed to a pattern – and not a very cheerful one. There was an air of dereliction and abandonment. The dismal adobe suburbs would lead along deeply pot-holed lanes to a vast plaza with a tiny central bandstand. On the four sides of the plaza were ranged a church, generally dilapidated; an *alcaldía*, with an oval metal plaque above its door; and shops, shuttered and padlocked or, if not, seemingly untenanted. 'There's a man!' someone would cry, and we would home in on him to ask the right route out of town. A shop might be nudged into life and a bottle of pop, a disposable razor or some chewing gum bought.

It is at about this time during one of his expeditions that John has traditionally started working on the next one. Richard recalls being invited to crawl under his bivouac on the banks of the Blue Nile in Ethiopia in 1968 to listen to him explaining the doodles on the back of an envelope which were the genesis of plans for another river-running expedition. In the present case, the seeds of the next project were already sown. In addition to our aims of carrying out archaeological, community aid and hydrographic projects on and around the Desaguadero, and looking into the likelihood of the Bolivian Altiplano as a site for Atlantis, there was the idea of investigating possible ancient trading links between central South America and Africa. This, John had explained, would mean launching a second phase of the expedition in 1999 to test out the feasibility of these links by running rivers from the foothills of the Andes to their junction with the Atlantic at the mouth of the Río de la Plata.

The idea of such a transatlantic trade route was not such a lunatic concept as it might at first seem. Traces of both cocaine and nicotine, unknown in Africa and the old world, had been detected in authentically ancient Egyptian mummies. Tests had been run and re-run. It was indisputable. Yet these are native South American substances. How had they got to the Nile valley in early times? The Spaniards had traded along routes from the Lake Titicaca region eastwards overland to Buenos Aires, so it was entirely possible that earlier civilizations could have done so. A shipwreck full of Roman amphorae is said to have been found on the Brazilian coast in what is still today called the Bay of Jars. Its cargo may have been bound for Mauretania on Africa's west coast and been blown severely off course, but it could equally be evidence of an intentional trading venture. Academics such as Professor Alice Kehoe of the University of Marquette, Wisconsin, are increasingly coming to believe that the great oceans were crossed much earlier than we have hitherto supposed.

Considerations like these had prompted John to plan a journey in reed boats, similar to those constructed on Lake Titicaca before the conquistadors came, down rivers from Bolivia to the Atlantic. He had even sounded out Máximo and Erik Catari on the prospects of their being able to build another, bigger *balsa* for this project. The Río Pilcomayo was a possible contender for the most likely way down, or the Río Paraguay, both of which run into the Río Paraná and to the Atlantic.

So it was no surprise that John's attention was suddenly arrested, as we bowled along the excellent road south from La Paz, via Patacamaya to Eucaliptus, by the sight of a Bolivian Army low-loader parked by the roadside. 'Just the thing for getting our big *balsa* from the Cataris' boatyard to the launch point,' he said.

True, the early coca exporters would not have had the benefit of an army low-loader; but time and money constraints mean that re-enactment trials like ours have to cut a few corners. Maybe we could borrow a low-loader from the Bolivian Army? Our Patron, President Banzer, was, after all, a retired general. We had had great help so far from the Navy, and a journey on Bolivia's eastern rivers would require more. Admiral Zabala had seconded several of his people to our expedition, but now it was perhaps time to enlist the support of the Army as well.

Since Bolivia's independence in 1825, its army has not had much luck. It did quite well against the Peruvians in the 1830s and 1840s, but has lost all the six or seven major conflicts in which it has subsequently been embroiled. Jim Masters put this down to the BLF – they never got to the battlefield in time, he reckoned, and the territory was lost before the troops had arrived. But there must be more to it than that. Can the armies of Argentina, Brazil, Chile, Peru and Paraguay have been so much more expeditious? The Bolivian flag has three horizontal bands: the lower one, green, symbolizes agriculture; the central yellow one indicates Bolivia's gold and other mineral wealth; the uppermost band of red stands for the valour of her armies. And yet they have been seen off every time by all their neighbours between 1862 and 1938 and lost half their original territory. Perhaps their armies have been badly led? General Mariano Malgarejo, head of state from 1865 to 1871, heard of the outbreak of the Franco–Prussian war in 1870 and, the balance of his mind confused by drink, set off at the head of his army to support Napoleon III. One of his generals asked what arrangements had been made for crossing the Atlantic Ocean; it is said that a timely shower of rain sobered him up, and the long march was abandoned.

Bolivia once rivalled Brazil in size, its broad swathe of territory, running north-west to south-east, the second largest in South America. Much of it, of course, was unexplored and its boundaries were ill defined. In the nineteenth century the vast hinterland of the southern continent seemed to attract few of those bold spirits whose 'manifest destiny' it was to pioneer the routes across North America. Argentina had taken the Chaco Central, a broad belt of land between the Ríos Pilcomayo and Teuco, before 1862. Brazil next took a quarter of a million square kilometres of little-visited rain forest in 1867: the middle reaches of the Ríos Juruá, Purus and Madeira, in Bolivia's far north, as well as parts of the Mato Grosso in the east (this last not recognized until 1928). But by far the most grievous loss, lamented since 1880 and still not a closed book today, was the outcome of the War of the Pacific fought with Chile from 1879 to 1884. The nitrate and saltpetre found along the Atacama desert's Pacific edge was being extracted by Chileans under licence from Bolivia and Peru when Alfred Nobel's development of dynamite in 1867 suddenly gave these minerals vital importance. Bolivia and Peru refused to renew the licences; Chile, with British support, attacked. Bolivia quickly lost her Litoral province and the port of Antofagasta; Peru forfeited the port of Arica. Bolivia was now land-locked, and the body blow has not been forgotten. In 1979 the centenary of the loss was marked by postage stamps showing Bolivia's nine provinces as links in a chain, with the tenth link, Litoral, hanging brokenly. Letters bearing these stamps were returned undelivered by the Chilean post office. Bolivia even has a war flag: a blue field represents the Pacific; the Bolivian red, yellow and green, in a canton in the top left corner, is ringed by the nine gold stars of the provinces; and one larger gold star for the lost province sits in the middle of the blue. Bolivia has free port facilities in Antofagasta, and Chile has built railways from the Pacific to La Paz. But the wound in the national psyche has not healed. In the way that Argentinian leaders, when the ecomomy was in trouble, diverted popular attention by claiming their sovereignty over the Falklands, so Bolivians, in difficulties, beat the drum for lost Litoral.

There were more defeats to come. During the War of the Pacific, in 1883, Argentina took advantage of Bolivia's preoccupation and seized Puna de Atacama, a windswept, stony, treeless southern extension of the Altiplano. In 1903 Brazil annexed the hillier part of the Acre region, in exchange for Bolivia's free use of its rivers for the export of smoked latex from its rubber trees to the Amazon and the sea. Six years later Peru's claim to Purus was grudgingly recognized by Bolivia. The final humiliation came in 1932 when the Chaco war with Paraguay began. Over the next three years 65,000 soldiers' lives were lost and another quarter-million kilometres of land – this time thorn scrub and swamp, but with the tantalizing prospect of oil – surrendered.

Bolivia's neighbours have often tried to compensate her for losses of land by building railways: Chile from Arica to La Paz; Argentina from Jujuy to Villazón and Embarcación to Yacuiba in Bolivia's far south; and Brazil from Guajará Mirim to Pôrto Velho, bypassing nineteen dangerous rapids on the Ríos Mamoré and Madeira and giving Bolivian rubber exports another route to Manaus and the Atlantic – completed with poor timing in 1912, the year before the market in natural rubber collapsed in the face of cheaper south-east Asian competition. This track ran only until 1919 and was finally abandoned in 1971.

John and Richard mulled over these tragic Bolivian military failures as they drove along. 'Well, they still have a country as big as France, Belgium and Spain together, and that's pretty vast,' said Richard.

John's thoughts were more practical: 'And they've got low-loaders now.'

CHAPTER FIVE

CHIPAYA

The llama is a woolly sort of fleecy hairy goat
With an indolent expression and an undulating throat
  Like an unsuccessful literary man.
And I know the place he lives in (or at least I think I do)
It is Ecuador, Brazil or Chile – possibly Peru
  You must find it in the atlas if you can.

HILAIRE BELLOC,
More Beasts for Worse Children, 1897

Towards the southern border of Bolivia, on the Chilean side, are two extraordinary geographical features: the flat, vast, dazzling white salt pans of Coipasa and Uyuni. At the north end of the top one, Coipasa, is a unique town – the town of the Chipaya people. Like the El Molo on the shores of Lake Turkana in Kenya, the Chipaya are a people with their own history, dress, language and culture, but minuscule numbers: some 1,500 in Chipaya town, another 400 in nearby Ayparavi. They live in beehive-shaped adobe huts and herd sheep, pigs and llama on the flat marges of the Río Lauca, which drains slowly into the salt pan, the Salar de Coipasa. Again like the El Molo, their uniqueness and small numbers have caused them to be much studied by anthropologists and philologists, and occasionally visited by tourists. As a result they are somewhat reserved and inhibited and dislike photography; but some members of our expedition were well known to them, and so we had a good welcome.

John, Barry and Yoli had sought out the Chipaya in 1997, but had not been able to reach the town itself. As described in the first chapter, some way to the north they had come upon a tented camp to which the townsfolk had fled after a disastrous flooding of the Lauca that had left their own houses a metre deep in river water. John felt that here was a clear need for help, and so in 1998 we determined, even though they lived a long way south of Challacollo, where we had set up our base on 8 April, to bring them some goodies, however token. Quartermaster Gerry Masters gave us a bag of flour, several of rice and some lentils. We also took a saw, a pick, a shovel and some British newspapers – which was not so crazy as it seems, for a medically trained missionary from Birmingham lives and works with the Chipaya. Sister Sylvia Sherwood of the Mission of Mary among the Poor, based in Chile, has been with them for four years.

John, Yoli and Richard, and their driver Antonio, knew they would not get to Chipaya in one day; so they were cheered to arrive in the afternoon of 8 April, after a long flog across *tola*-covered hills, at the small town of Huachacalla, site of a vast, castellated military garrison, guarding the passes against the old enemy, Chile. By the road was a sign proclaiming *Camas Matrimoniales, Dobles, Simples, Duchas* . . . at the Hotel Pacha. The idea of showers appealed greatly, although our days in Bolivia had already shown that what was advertised was often not available, and John could perhaps spread himself in one of the matrimonial beds. But where was the Hotel Pacha? After numerous enquiries it turned out, like most small shops in Bolivian villages, not to have even a nameboard outside. There was a large lorry park occupied by a mechanical digger and a solitary llama. This was it. A tiny lady in filthy garments, with an equally grubby baby slung at her back, came up and showed us into contrastingly clean, spacious, multi-bedded rooms. We took three. Best of all, the showers had hot water. Food was found at the Bar Restaurant Martinez on the main road. If there is ever a *Good Food Guide to Bolivia*, which we doubt, the Martinez might just creep in. The scrambled eggs and *salchichas* were excellent. 'I've had worse sausages in hotels in Britain,' said John. This may not be typical, however: Yoli had managed to ensure at least one-star service by upgrading John to General and claiming that he was a personal friend of President Banzer. Other diners, neglected, stared lugubriously at the snowstorm television screen as the patroness fussed over us.

The Chipaya people, whose town we reached mid-morning the next day, are said to be descended from the Tiwanaku, though none of the townspeople we met were able to confirm this.

Puquina, the Chipaya language, though not taught in the school, flourishes in the homes of the 1,900 people. It is said to have connections with Hebrew and Arabic, as well as Mayan. Try these opening verses of 1 Corinthians, Chapter 13: 'Jalla tužučha juc'ant zuma kamañaqui, zuma munaziz kamañaqui juc'ant zumacha tjapa kumañanacquiztanaqui. Tsjii žoñiqui ani pajta žoñž takunacami m'žaza anjilz takunacami chiyisačha.' The language may have few words, but they are certainly of a respectable length. Does it perhaps also have some links with the language of the Basques – who, according to some Atlantologists, are among the descendants of those who survived the sinking of Atlantis?

Chipaya houses, traditionally shaped like old beehives, are now only seen dotting the surrounding countryside; most of their town houses, damaged in recent floods, have been rebuilt of adobe in rectangular form. The most recent inundation had left a discernible tidemark on the walls a little way above the ground, as well as dunes of sand in the streets carried in by the waters. Hearing of all this from Sylvia Sherwood and her Chilean colleague, Marcella Valenzuela, and seeing the evidence, John reacted in characteristic Royal Engineer fashion: there must be some way of diverting the waters of the Lauca which cause such havoc more or less every ten years. He armed himself with compass, rangefinder, GPS, clinometer and measuring tapes and set off into the countryside north of the town. Here he found a series of canals dug by the Chipaya long ago – 'before the time of our grandfathers' was the closest he could get to their age – perhaps to lessen the force of the flooding, perhaps to irrigate their fields, perhaps both. He also found a dam across the Lauca itself which the force of the waters had burst in 1996, and saw traces of the various subsequent local attempts to shore it up. The trouble was that all the land around was unrelievedly flat. He felt like saying, 'Why don't you move the town away to higher ground somewhere?'

It was certainly difficult to see why the town was where it was. The grazing round about was no doubt an attraction, but the Río Lauca was a false friend. No question but that the Chipaya had once spread over a bigger area: in 1582 there were reported to be 80,000 of them. Now, outside the town, their conical houses and pigsties were scattered over a desolate plain which sloped imperceptibly into the salty wastes of the Salar de Coipasa. Only a couple of churches in the town gave it some three-dimensionality. The Chipaya, like the rest of the Bolivians, were for the most part Roman Catholic, but there were some Pentecostalists and some United Christian Unionists. They also worship their ancestors, the distant but visible volcano Sajama and, inexplicably, the Río Lauca, a malevolent god if ever there was one. The Catholic priest, Father Mario Malendrez, was an absentee, living in Oruro. He turns up about once a year but even then doesn't always sing Mass. A modern church with a splendid tower is maintained by the laity; *los fieles* run a great many churches in Bolivia which appear to have no priest.

After persistent questioning and close examination in the field, John came up with a plan. In the evening, in the house we had been lent (the resident and her four children having been temporarily dispossessed), John drafted a colourful map of the town and its environs, showing what the community could itself do to solve the problem. Possible British government or military assistance was discussed, but essentially, he patiently explained, this was a self-help exercise. There was some talk of an Irish bridge on the Lauca: this was RE-speak for a bridge which does not actually rise above the water but over which the water will run. The Chipaya authorities seemed quite pleased with our efforts. They brought a tureen of filling soup to our house that evening and next morning provided a good breakfast of *mate de coca* and *sopaipillas* (a sort of flat doughnut) in a local shop.

We decided to go back to Challacollo by a different route, which involved a long swing south and east along the edges of the shimmering white expanse of the salt lake of Coipasa. Navigation proceeded by fits and starts. Our first objective was the town of Andamarca, about ten miles off. The local man whom we had persuaded to guide us on the first stage of the trip pointed out roughly where it lay beyond the distant hills – 90° to the left of our course. But, he assured us, the road would turn north, and indeed it did. Then, after we had dropped our guide and his bicycle at a village, we proceeded by stopping to ask every *campesino* we met along the way. Gnarled old shepherdesses in their bowler hats, standing lonely all day by their flocks, were questioned in Spanish, or by Antonio, our driver, in Aymará. Often, they knew little beyond their immediate surroundings: Challacollo meant nothing to them, and even Andamarca, ten miles off, they seemed vague about.

At a farmstead we find two men and four very pretty little girls in their ribboned bonnets who pose obediently for photographs. One of the men says he'll come with us and show us the right

track. Can we take his bicycle? Of course. Then he brings to the
car door a large hobbled ram. He gets in and hauls the ram,
nearly a year old, on to his lap where it remains, very docile,
even asleep, for the next hour. Suddenly, in the middle of an open
plain, he asks to be set down. There is a little heap of droppings
on the Mitsubishi's floor. He takes a rope and lashes the young
ram on to his bicycle rack, its head lolling over the saddle. Several
times the bicycle falls over, landing the still unprotesting ram in
the dust. Eventually he lifts the head, sits astride and pedals off
– God knows where.

As he wobbles off, a motorcycle comes weaving through the
scrub. It is a low-powered machine with, astonishingly, six up: a
husband, his wife and four children. He knows the way to
Andamarca and will lead us. We take his wife and three children
with Yoli and me in the back of the car. Margarita, the eldest,
sits on Yoli's knee. Marlene slides to the floor and hides. Remy,
the youngest, attends to his mother's breast. They are quiet and
well-behaved. John sits impassively in front.

John's formidable capacity for concentrating on the matter in
hand, i.e. the expedition (or the next one) is well demonstrated
as we bounce along with this shy family party crammed in the
back:

YOLI *(in Spanish, holding Margarita's hand)*: This little finger
    got an egg, this finger put it in to boil, this finger put
    some salt in . . .
JOHN: You know that Operation Raleigh stable belt, Yoli? Do
    you think Admiral Zabala would like it?
YOLI: Yes, I think he would, John . . . *(in Spanish)* This little
    finger stirred it up, and this one gobbled it all.
RICHARD *(to Remy)*: Google, google, google.
JOHN: That's Jim Allen's canal somewhere over there . . . We
    must phone Peter Getzels when we get to Challacollo . . .
    Dick, how much more time have we on the O'Gara phone?
RICHARD: I don't know, John. I'll get Lee Smart to check . . .
    (to Margarita in Spanish) Can you say one, two, three in
    English?

At that moment, as we rolled northwards, Jim Allen may have
been measuring his canal, an extraordinary feature whose dimensions accord exactly with those given by Plato for the main feeder
canal which serviced a grid-iron pattern of smaller ones to the

Lake Titicaca, where the expedition's reed boats were built

José Limachi, the Aymará Indian who helped to build Thor Heyerdahl's boat, *Ra II*, also on Lake Titicaca

The El Niño storm strikes the Río Desaguadero

One of the fleet caught in the storm at Iruhito

Discovery of the pedestal at Iruhito. (Standing, left to right) Jim Masters, Oswaldo Rivera and Richard Snailham look on as the local shaman blesses the site

The expedition's two newly found *chachapumas* with one (on left) already in the museum at Iruhito

Kota Mama in full sail on the Río Desaguadero

The fleet making its way down the Río Desaguadero as interested locals watch from the banks. The river is getting more and more shallow

The gateway to one of the Cities of the Eagle Men, with its guardian 'lizard'

Major Lee Smart's illustration depicting how women were buried in the *chulpas*. It also shows a prisoner about to be sacrificed (*Lee Smart*)

Bones and mummified remains were found inside almost all the *chulpas*

Yolima Cipagauta standing beside one of the tombs located south-west of Calacoto, Bolivia, and, right, elongated skulls found inside the tombs

Richard Snailham examining the paintings on a tomb as he stands at the mouth of the tunnel leading into the mountain. Note the step pyramids at Richard's eye level

Further decoration on the tomb. It was suggested by some that this section showed boats on a wavy sea

Jim Allen's Atlantis map (*Jim Allen*)

At one of our camps on the banks of the Desaguadero: brewing a welcome cup of tea using a volcano kettle

Model boat in La Paz museum believed to be the type used by the Tiwanaku (*Peter Minter*)

west of the supposed site of Atlantis. But our thoughts were still on the Chipaya, whose women still dress in chocolate brown clothes held together by large safety pins, their heads covered with chocolate brown wimples. How long could they retain their distinctive identity in this modern age, so intrusive on the lives of remote peoples?

CHAPTER SIX

TO ATLANTIS?

The Support Group had had to stop in the small waterside town of Huari Belen for a few days while *Pacha Kutec* and the Avon made their way from the International Bridge to Eucaliptus; and Huari Belen was a dump. Our kitchen was in an unspeakable hole, insult being added to injury by an awkward entrance which gave every arrival a crack on the head. Many of us slept in a damp potato storeroom across the yard from this uninviting spot. John and Richard, Yoli and Chrissie – our PR wizard Chrysoulla Kyprianou – were more fortunately quartered in a nearby shack with a corrugated iron roof and false ceilings of cheesecloth – and walls on which someone with a curious taste in interior decoration had pasted pictures of Switzerland. Working conditions too left something to be desired: John had to show his skills as an engineer at one point when the single naked light bulb above his head suddenly exploded as he was busy at the table, showering him with shards of glass. There was no visible switch. How to unscrew the live element without touching it? Two wooden rulers didn't work – but he did the trick with a plastic clothes peg.

Eucaliptus, our next base, was cheerier: a well-ordered little town with a railway station, an impressive bridge over the Desaguadero and Bolivia's only sulphuric acid factory. Here the Support Group lodged on two floors of the sub-*prefectura*, where the only sign of life was a morning crèche upstairs attended by townswomen and their curious children. We had ample dormitory and cooking space in empty rooms. Many of us wondered whether a bunch of Bolivians, arriving in our home towns, would find the municipal offices vacated and available for them to doss in.

Easter was approaching, and on Palm Sunday we joined the congregation packed sardine-fashion into the church next door to our quarters – *campesinos* in the left-hand pews and *campesinas* in the right. (Noel Burrell and Richard caused some concern by sitting among the women: rows of heavily skirted mothers with bundles of children at their backs and others squirming around their knees, black heads with the universal centre parting all reverentially bowed.) An Argentinian missionary lady took the service, and we all emerged with a palm cross apiece.

In Eucaliptus we met the boats again. *Pacha Kutec* and the Avon had done well: 17 kilometres the first day and 24 the second, 17 again on the third and fourth day and 7 on the last. The crews had been cold and wet as usual but, making good progress, were understandably pleased with themselves.

'We know how to read the river now,' said Lee Smart; 'little ripples often indicate a deeper bit.'

The dehydrated rations had been excellent and now there was even an inexpensive hot shower to be had in the town. Morale was high.

After a day or two's rest, on 18 April the boats set off again. The next leg would take them to Lake Uru-Uru and then to Lake Poopó, our destination. On their right hand a vast conical hill loomed: La Joya ('the jewel') – not a volcano, but full of copper mines. The nearby little town of La Joya was the neatest we ever saw, because it was subsidized by Inti Raymi, the company who own and run, in conjunction with the University of Pittsburgh,

Bolivia's biggest gold mine a couple of kilometres downriver. As the boats drifted past groups of incredulous mine-workers, giant earth-moving vehicles rolled alongside them and occasional blasts of dynamite rent the air.

We were now quite near Oruro, a prosperous city in this mineral-rich region of the Altiplano. It has become a railway centre – though not visibly a very active one: the line runs down a main street and is frequently covered by market stalls. Nevertheless, it connects La Paz by rail to Chile and Argentina, and there is a branch line off to Cochabamba. Oruro was Bolivia's Swindon. In the Plaza de 10 Febrero, its thickly treed central square, is a fine gilded statue to Aniceto Arce, a former President and inspiration for Bolivia's railways; sadly, the network is now somewhat run down.

On the day we drove into the centre of Oruro, the square was ringed by police. Teachers were on strike. A demonstration was expected. They duly marched and afterwards, to drive their point home, others were arbitrarily blocking the city's main roads. John, Yoli and Richard, having completed their business, were heading out of town when banners were suddenly unfurled in front of the vehicle and the way barred by an angry crowd.

'Act ill,' John said to Richard, and leapt out of the Mitsubishi.

Richard extended himself over the back seat and pulled a suitably agonized face.

'Out of the way!' shouted John, 'I have a very sick man in the car. Move, please, move!'

Perhaps none of them was an English teacher. They seemed not to understand, and would not budge. Richard's gentle moans fell on deaf ears. With mounting road rage John ordered Antonio to turn and find alternative side routes. Circuitously and laboriously, we extracted ourselves from Oruro.

Later, on its way to help the boats down to Lake Poopó, the Support Group visited Oruro again. Once more the Plaza de 10 Febrero was cordoned off by police. This time it was a political rally by the MNR – the Movimiento Nacional Revolucionario, one of Bolivia's main political parties – in favour of its presidential candidate Juan Carlos Durán. Firecrackers sent the pigeons flying. A band led the party faithful, waving their pink flags. Once more we contrived to get through the mêlée and out of town to cross the Puente Español and head for Challacollo, our next base.

For torpor, this little town outdid anywhere else we had pitched up. Along the sides of the sleepy plaza nothing stirred. It was not lunch or siesta time. There was neither *Alcalde* nor *Corregidor* to be found. Eventually we were offered empty school buildings by Don Gregorio, who styled himself 'municipal agent'. The next day we saw him lurching unsteadily into shop doorways and picking fights. It turned out he was drunk most of the time and had nothing to do with the municipality; but we stayed in the school just the same.

On Good Friday night some of us attended the religious proceedings in Challacollo's rather grand adobe church – 'proceedings' rather than 'service': a throng of people constantly milling in and out. Central to all this activity was a fragile-looking glass-walled catafalque containing an effigy of Christ after his deposition from the cross. It stood on four spindly legs, one of which had become detached from the main framework. Every time a passing worshipper nudged into it, the wooden rod fell noisily to the ground and Christ in his glass tomb teetered slowly over, only to be repeatedly saved by the hands of anxious townsfolk rushing forward to catch him.

On the Saturday night the catafalque was carried round the unlit streets of the town to the accompaniment of a single dirge, sung over and over again. The catafalque was deposited for a moment in each group of houses as a corner was turned. The procession followed the gridiron street pattern round the plaza but one block back from it; and we followed the procession, ambling along in the darkness, Richard at one point stumbling calf-deep into a pothole full of green slime.

Earlier that day we had driven to the bridge over the Desaguadero where the boats from La Joya had arrived the previous evening. The crews had had to wade much of the way, and it was clear that we could not force a passage down much more of the river. Nevertheless, we rigged flags and the BBC filmed. *Pacha Kutec* cast off and drifted downstream towards the flat horizon which is Lake Poopó. The support vehicles bumped along the bank over reedy grazing land, nearer the river than they had ever been able to drive before. After 2 kilometres sandbanks broke up the river into a series of pools. We could go no further. The reed boat was hauled out and an impromptu farewell ceremony began. There was much mutual congratulation. Lieutenant Vladimir Terrazas fired ten rounds into the air. Then he made a speech. Then John made a speech. Rodolfo, the driver, had bought some squibs. A bottle or two of Bolivian wine, one of Chivas Regal and another of J & B materialized. We were making the best of a rather anticlimactic end to the voyage.

But if one thread of the expedition had run out, there was another waiting to be picked up: it was time to look for Jim Allen's canal. For twenty-four years Jim has been developing his beliefs that the 'lost continent' of Atlantis was somewhere in the Bolivian Altiplano. It has to be said that most other members of the expedition thought that this notion was fanciful, though John had written an encouraging foreword in Jim's book, *Atlantis: The Andes Solution*. However, when we set out from Challacollo we were all prepared to look at the ground with an open mind.

According to the great Greek philosopher Plato (427–347 BC), the island and city of Atlantis fell victim to one of the most cataclysmic natural disasters in world history. In 'a single day and night' in 9600 BC, he tells in his *Timaeus*, it was riven by earthquakes and overwhelmed by rain and flood. It had been a Utopian state, a peaceful, cultivated society of white-skinned, auburn-haired people, its ten regions ruled by ten kings, and with an overseas empire stretching over the Americas, parts of Europe and Africa. The capital city was built on an extinct volcano in the middle of a plain, and was ringed by three concentric canals guarded by walls lined with precious metals. There was hot and cold running water in the palace, and wild bulls roaring in its grounds; a racecourse and shipyards outside the palace walls. To one side lay a great irrigation system of canals laid out in a gridiron pattern, 3,000 stades long by 2,000 wide (a stade = 184 metres, so let's say 550 kilometres by 370). Plato's description of the city is so clear, so detailed, that artists like the nineteenth-century painter Thomas Cole have been able to reconstruct it on canvas. And it was all lost in an unimaginable catastrophe 11,600 years ago.

How did Plato know all this, living as he did in the fourth century BC? In *Timaeus* his grandfather, Critias, tells Socrates how when the great Greek law-giver Solon (*c.*640–569 BC) visited the Nile delta city of Saïs he was told the story by Egyptian priests, to whom it had been handed down over many generations. The tale was related originally by invaders from distant lands, 'the sea people', who attacked Egypt and Greece, to be driven off in their turn by a proto-Hellenic people who lived in an earlier Athens. These invaders came from a land 'larger than Libya and Asia combined' (geographical expressions which can mislead modern readers: Libya then meant most of North Africa excluding

Egypt, while Asia referred only to the Near East) which was located beyond the Pillars of Hercules, generally accepted as being the Straits of Gibraltar.

The exact location of the lost island or continent of Atlantis with its fabulous capital city has exercised Western thinkers since at least the time of Francis Bacon (1561–1626). In 1926 two Frenchmen reckoned that over 1,700 books had been published on the subject, and there have been a fair few since then. A good many, like one by US Congressman Ignatius Donnelly in 1882, place it in mid-Atlantic. The name of the ocean is itself suggestive, and there are islands there – Madeira, the Azores – which betoken the presence of a submarine mountain range that might have been dry land until flooded by some natural phenomenon in recent geological time. Old Portuguese charts show many more Atlantic islands, though most of these, like Hy Brasil, are mythical. Other writers – K. T. Frost in 1909, Galanopoulos and Bacon in 1969 – choose to ignore Plato's placing of Atlantis 'beyond the Pillars of Hercules' and 'at a distant point in the [Atlantic] Ocean' and identify it with the volcanic Aegean island of Thira (Santorini), which erupted about 1470 BC. The resultant tidal wave was said to have engulfed the Minoan civilization in Crete and the city of Knossos; if Thira was Atlantis, Plato must have seriously miscalculated the dating of the catastrophe by a factor of six or so. Eberhard Zangger, writing in the 1990s, claimed that Atlantis was Troy, destroyed by the Achaeans at a date even later than Knossos.

In more recent time Bimini island in the Bahamas has been touted as Atlantis, with reports of ancient roads and Greek columns on the sea-bed. John dived here in 1980 and found the roads to be a natural formation and the columns concrete cylinders from a modern shipwreck. In June 1998, twenty scientists from the Moscow-based Shirshov Institute of Oceanology searched for Atlantis on the Celtic shelf, 100 miles from the Scilly Isles. This was near the site supposed by Alfred, Lord Tennyson, to be the lost Arthurian land of Lyonesse off the Cornish coast.

Other putative locations presuppose some extraordinary world upheavals. Charles H. Hapgood, Professor of Anthropology and the History of Science at Keene State College, New Hampshire, came up with the Earth Crust Displacement theory (ECD). This postulates that on at least three occasions in geological time the axis on which the earth rotates has tilted, causing the relatively thin tectonic plates that make up the earth's crust to crack and slide across its surface. When this happens the North and South

Poles are shifted. Hapgood reckoned that the North Pole had at one time been in northern Norway, at another in northern Canada, before fetching up in its present position after the last ECD which, conveniently for Atlantologists, was about 9600 BC. Two Canadian librarians, Rand and Rose Flem-Ath, have used Hapgood's theory as the basis for their argument that Antarctica is Atlantis. Before 9600 BC, they suggest, the South Pole was not roughly in the middle of Antarctica but in the sea to one side of it. Then came the ECD and the southern continent, which had been somewhere near present-day Argentina and thus able to enjoy sunshine and wheat harvests as Atlantis did, slid inexorably to its present chilly location and was overlaid with ice, thus inhibiting archaeological investigation.

An attractive idea of Hapgood's – and Atlantean theorizing is nothing if not attractive, seductive even – is that before the 9600 BC ECD there lived in Atlantis a race of almost perfect human beings, possessed of many skills, one of which was the ability to navigate the world's oceans to acquire and then oversee their African and European dominions. To do this they made maps – maps that were lost in the inundation of 9600 BC or, if not then, in later sackings and burnings of the ancient library at Alexandria. Hapgood believed that antediluvian world maps existed because there are features on the old maps that we *do* have which could not have been known at the time they were drawn. For example, one shows an accurate rendering of the actual rock coastline of Antarctica, which for 12,000 years at least has been submerged under millions of tons of pack ice.

The most recent Atlantologist, Herbie Brennan, has an altogether more apocalyptic, cosmic view of what may have happened. About 12,000 years ago a supernova called Vela exploded in outer space. Bits of it entered our solar system, bouncing off the planets and scattering their satellites. Happily this debris did not hit the earth, but it came closer than our own moon and caused such gravitational mayhem that continents disappeared and sea-beds reared up to make new ones. Our moon works the tides: this monstrous intrusion caused whole oceans to well up and wash over mountains, carrying with them vast boulders (the 'erratics' that conventional geologists believe to be glacier-borne). In all this Atlantis was lost, along with all its people – except a very few who escaped with their maps and their knowledge to Mexico (the Aztecs?) or to Egypt, which had not suffered in the general global destruction. It makes a thrilling story. But Brennan is not too concerned with the exact siting of Atlantis, more in the manner of its going.

Jim Allen, for his part, is convinced that Atlantis was in the Altiplano of Bolivia. There is indeed a good deal of correlation between what Plato wrote and the high Andean plain that Allen has designated.

'Suppose it was not the island continent of Atlantis which sank into the sea in the space of a single day,' Jim writes in *Atlantis: The Andes Solution*, 'but only the island *city* which did. In that case, the continent would remain where it always was. Perhaps it is that continent that we now know by the European name of South America, so that the city sank not into an ocean sea but into a vast inland sea which exists in the centre of the continent.'

South America does lie beyond – to the west of – the Pillars of Hercules (less obviously so in Mercator's projection of the world map; more so in others) and may be considered an island continent if the Panama isthmus, so easily crossed by Balboa in 1513, is disregarded. Plato describes the city as being situated in a plain which was in the middle of the continent, next to the ocean, halfway along the continent's longest side, flat and rectilinear, high above the ocean, ringed on all sides by mountains. The Bolivian Altiplano meets all these criteria. It is one of the most level upland plains in the world, and if you trace round the 12,000 foot contour line west of Lake Poopó you will find a huge, flat, rectangular area, which furthermore has volcanoes, hot and cold springs, a tendency to be flooded (as it had been around 9000 BC) and a history of seismic activity. Bolivia, too, is a notable source of minerals: the Spanish conquistadors found a mountain near Potosí stuffed with silver. There are others containing gold, copper, tin and even the mysterious metal Plato speaks of – orichalcum, an alloy of gold and copper. Plenty of materials in the high Andes, then, with which the Atlanteans could adorn their city.

Andes, Atlantis – Atl-antis? Is there a linguistic link here? 'Antis' in the Quechua language means copper, and there is a tribe of Indians called the Antis who have given their name to the mountain chain. One of the four quarters of the Inca empire was Antisuyo, 'The Kingdom of the Antis'. A very common suffix in central and southern America is 'Atl': Quetzalcoatl, the plumed serpent of the Aztecs; tomatl; chocolatl; Nahuatl, the language in which 'atl' means water. Copper and water are both plentiful in the Altiplano. The Aztecs founded their chief city, Tenochtitlan (now buried under Mexico City), on an island in a lake. Some early disaster had driven them away from their first home, which had been on an island in a lake and was called Atzlan.

Jim Allen had told us all this and even to the sceptics among us it seemed very exciting; but we wondered, as we drove south of Challacollo, whether after 12,000 years there could possibly be any vestiges of his Bolivian Atlantis. Jim hoped to find traces of the deep canal which had run for 10,000 stades, or over 1,800 kilometres, round the sides of the rectangular plain. A former RAF air photo interpreter, he had studied satellite images of the land west of Lake Poopó and identified an interesting-looking gash running from north to south which he had visited in 1997. John and Jim thought we all ought to have a closer look.

After Toledo and Copacabana, tiny, forlorn settlements, we turned on to a rough road and headed south on to an area of the Altiplano that undulates slightly. Jim was clutching his GPS and when he reckoned we were near the canal Don René swung the Toyota on to the grass and headed off through the *tola*. After a bit it seemed pointless to keep driving over the bumpy ground, so we got out and walked on up the incline ahead – which also gave us more opportunity to study the place in detail.

'Did I tell you that my great-grandfather was an authority on Atlantis?' said Lee Smart suddenly. 'I've got with me the articles he wrote about it. He taught at the English College in Valparaiso in Chile from 1900 to 1904.'

Jim asked if Lee had been chosen for the expedition because of this connection, but it transpired that he had been nominated by Brigadier John Neeve, a senior Royal Signals officer who knew nothing of it. An odd coincidence.

Lee's great-grandfather was James Douglas Carmichael MA, of Bridge of Earn, Perthshire. During his time in Chile he came up to Bolivia and visited Tiahuanaco. He was much influenced by Plato's account and commented: 'There are in it no marvels, no myths, no tales of gods, hobgoblins or giants. It is a plain and reasonable history of a people who built temples, ships and canals, who lived by agriculture and commerce; and who in pursuit of trade reached out to all the countries around them.' Carmichael posited fifteen similarities between the New World and the Old and argued that there must have been some linkage, some 'ante-Columbian intercourse'. Atlantis, he thought, was the answer.

Lewis Spence echoed this view in 1925, in his *Atlantis in America*: 'I hold that the occurrence on either side of the Atlantic of a civilisation having certain cultural characteristics proves that

Europe and Africa on the one hand and America on the other must have received it from a common source – Atlantis.'

At the top of the gentle slope we found ourselves looking down into a shallow valley. It was a perfect rural scene: llamas, with red and pink tassels in their ears, grazing the green grass; flamingos and geese on a lake. Jim went on ahead to investigate in detail.

'It still has water in it,' he said as he came back up the side towards us, counting his paces. 'Seventy-four metres down, thirty-six across the flat, and seventy-four up the other side,' he announced triumphantly. 'That's a hundred and eighty-four metres, which exactly equals one stade. It *must* be the canal.'

It had been one of the great moments of Jim's life when he first stood on the rim of this low valley in 1997. But some of us harboured traitorous doubts. We had not expected to see plates of silver, gold or orichalcum sticking up out of the ground; 12,000 years is an unconscionably long time and 400 generations of herdsmen had wandered over the Altiplano with their sheep and llamas since the fall of Atlantis. But this shallow depression did not by itself seem wholly convincing. A motor recce proved that it ran south fairly straight for a mile or so, but some of us thought that it might just be a natural fault-line. However, scouting along the scrubby edges of the channel John and Oswaldo found remains of several small settlements of the Tiwanaku period and picked up a perfect stone hammer-head that was better than anything in the La Paz Museum. It was obvious that early people had lived here, but Oswaldo did not think there would have been a population sufficient to have dug such a huge canal.

'I think Jim will have to find some more evidence,' said Toby Marriner. And there is every indication that he intends to.

If Atlanteans and perhaps their successors did have trade links with Africa and Europe, how were these achieved? One obvious criticism of the Allen hypothesis is that the Bolivian Altiplano is a very remote place *vis-à-vis* the Old World. Even though Plato describes Atlantis as being at 'a distant point', a journey from the Altiplano to the Atlantic involves some 1,800 miles of inland waterways. However, the possibility that there may have been trade links from west to east was highlighted by revelations in the early 1990s arising from the work of a German toxicologist, Dr Svetla Balabanova of the Institute of Forensic Medicine, Ulm. She had found incontrovertible traces of cocaine and nicotine in the body of a mummified Egyptian priestess of the Twenty-First

Dynasty (1069–945 BC) in the Munich collection. Other mummies from the same collection were tested. These were authentically ancient mummies, from many centuries before the time of Columbus and not modern fakes. Balabanova scrupulously cleaned the equipment and ran the tests over and over again. The hair shaft test, which she used, precludes contamination. It was certain that these substances, at that time found only in South America, were present in corpses from the Nile valley. Coca and tobacco did not reach Europe and Africa until modern times, tobacco with Sir Walter Raleigh and cocaine in the nineteenth century; so how had they got to ancient Egypt? Balabanova explored many other possible avenues, but ended up believing them to have been imported.

While Jim carried on his search for indications of Atlantis in the Altiplano, it was perhaps time for John to examine the possibilities of trade routes from the Andes to Africa. The sixteenth-century Spanish conquerors of Peru and Upper Peru had developed a route for commerce from Lima through La Paz to Buenos Aires that was abandoned only in the early nineteenth century, so there could well have been traffic this way in antiquity. The Río Pilcomayo, which flows into the rivers Paraguay and Paraná and thence to the Río de la Plata and the Atlantic, rises only 60 kilometres from the southern end of Lake Poopó. It was here that we would begin our investigations.

PHASE II

PUERTO QUIJARRO—
BUENOS AIRES
1999

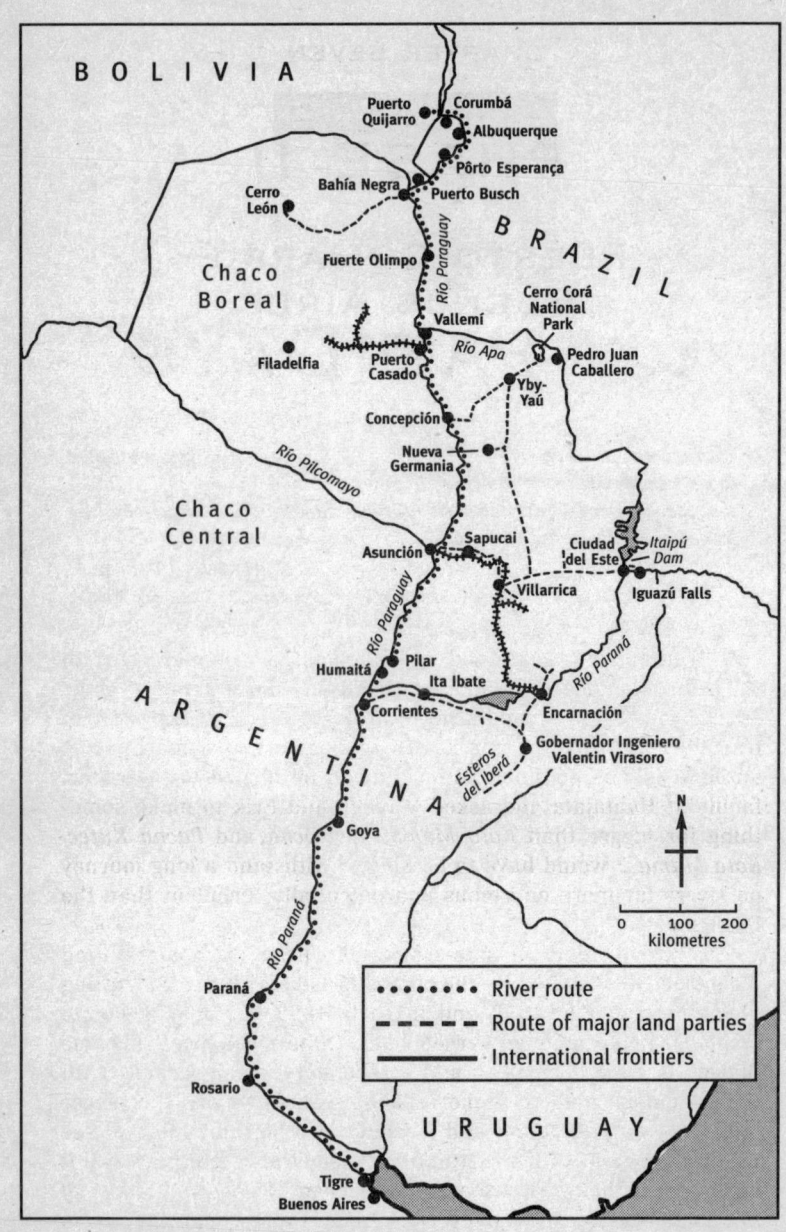

BOLIVIA

Puerto Quijarro
Corumbá
Albuquerque
Pôrto Esperança
Bahía Negra
Puerto Busch
Cerro León
BRAZIL
Fuerte Olimpo
Río Paraguay
Chaco Boreal
Vallemí
Cerro Corá National Park
Río Apa
Filadelfia
Puerto Casado
Pedro Juan Caballero
Yby-Yaú
Concepción
Río Pilcomayo
Nueva Germania
Chaco Central
Sapucai
Ciudad del Este
Itaipú Dam
Asunción
Villarrica
Iguazú Falls
Río Paraguay
Humaitá
Pilar
Ita Ibate
Río Paraná
ARGENTINA
Corrientes
Encarnación
Esteros del Iberá
Gobernador Ingeniero Valentín Virasoro
Goya

N

0   100   200
kilometres

Paraná
Río Paraná

Rosario

URUGUAY

Tigre
Buenos Aires

- - - - - - River route
– – – – – Route of major land parties
———— International frontiers

CHAPTER SEVEN

La Paz Days

We returned to the [San Pedro] prison gates via a catwalk from which there was an unimpaired view of Illimani, the mountain of 21,000 feet that towers over La Paz. It was silent, calm, majestic and [the prisoners] looked at it almost with reverence.

A. M. [ANTHONY] DANIELS,
'The Gringo Prisoners', *Spectator,* 21 December 1985

All that had happened so far was, it seemed, but an introduction to the main journey from Bolivia to the Atlantic. John decided that it would be best to assess the practicality of travelling this route to the sea in a boat designed and built as authentically as possible. So once again he turned to the Catari family at Huatajata and asked Máximo and Erik to make something far bigger than *Kota Mama, Viracocha* and *Pacha Kutec. Kota Mama 2* would have to be able to withstand a long journey on rivers far more enormous and potentially turbulent than the Desaguadero.

Size specifications, a time-scale and a price were agreed and a contract was signed. By the shores of Lake Titicaca the cutting of totora began in 1998 and in early 1999 ten men began to fashion a truly mammoth reed boat. Quite soon 'boat' became 'boats' as John decided to add a secondary, smaller reed craft: this would be able to make reconnaissances where the larger might not be able to go, and it would also be interesting to see if its single gaff sail made it more manoeuvrable and how well it stood up to heavy weather on the river. *Viracocha Spirit of Bahamas* was sponsored by Don Tomlinson, a supporter from Nassau, and was built along the same lines as the first *Viracocha.*

(We had another good friend from Nassau in Elodie Sandford, who raised money to send two Bahamians on the next leg of the voyage.)

The first challenge of the journey confronted us before ever we put boat to water. Early sailors would no doubt have built their boats close to a navigable point on the upper reaches of their chosen Atlantic-bound river. We had to build ours where the expertise and the raw materials were; so we would have the problem of transporting the boats to the river. At first the Río Pilcomayo looked the best bet. It rises high in the Andes between Lake Poopó and Potosí, and runs eastwards to join the vast Paraguay/Paraná river system which pours out into the Río de la Plata and the Atlantic. But research showed that previous expeditions had had a hard time getting down the Pilcomayo. In 1843 English carpenters from Chile built three boats which were carried in sections to Puerto Magariños on the Pilcomayo. Early in 1844 the flotilla covered some 30 miles in thirty-seven days – and then ran aground in 16 inches of water. While the crews were recceing the area, floods came and wrecked the ships. The survivors, harassed by Toba Indians, limped home. Colonel Andres Rivas took 200 men down the Pilcomayo in 1864 but was forced to return. Frenchman Jules Crévaux was driven back in 1882 by the hostile Toba, who accounted for twenty-two of his men. The following year the Paraguayan Admiral Daniel Campos, with a team of 195, managed to cover 1,185 kilometres of the river, but it took him sixty-two days. It was never going to be an easy route.

John's own investigations at the Royal Geographical Society turned up the map of an overland expedition of around 1900, which showed that near its end the river loses itself in impenetrable swamps before it enters the Río Paraguay. He then got in touch with James Wright, a well-informed Paraguayan farmer originally from Zimbabwe, who confirmed this. No further recce was necessary; it would clearly be foolhardy to attempt the Pilcomayo. Instead, John turned his mind to the Paraguay, an international waterway of known navigability. This meant that we could still begin our journey in Bolivia – just!

How Bolivia secured its right of access to the Río Paraguay is a complex story. For many years after the independence of Bolivia from Spain (1825) and Brazil from Portugal (1822) the frontier between the two states was left ill-defined. Although nine-tenths of today's Bolivia drains into the Atlantic and La Paz is in fact on the edge of the Amazon basin, Bolivians showed little urgency in establishing a frontier with Brazil, and the rivers to the east and north were for the most part explored upstream by Brazilians and Paraguayans, not downstream by Bolivians.

The Paraguay river might have seemed the obvious border, for between it and the foothills of the Andes lay only the Chaco, a flat, featureless desert covered in scrub and thorn. But, ignoring the old San Ildefonso line which runs roughly along the river and which was agreed between Spain and Portugal in 1777, the Brazilians had established settlements on the west bank of the Paraguay. Even Simón Bolívar, when he reluctantly accepted the setting up of Upper Peru (Bolivia) as a separate country in 1825, thought these Brazilian incursions were a threat. The Bolivians never seemed able to do much about them, however. Indeed, all three of their eastern neighbours, Brazil, Paraguay and Argentina, spent much of the 1860s and 1870s making frontier adjustments around the River Paraguay without reference to Bolivia, which was at this time at a low ebb and losing territory on other fronts.

In 1880 a Bolivian, Miguel Suárez Arana, got a permit from his government to build a road from Santa Cruz de la Sierra, the regional capital of lowland Bolivia, to Lake Cáceres, a shallow lagoon attached to Río Paraguay by a canal rather as the appendix is attached to the caecum. On the shores of this lake he built a port, Puerto Suárez. Sadly, Bolivia did not yet have the right to pass from this port down the Canal Tamengo to the main river, so in 1885 he founded Puerto Pacheco, further south on the Paraguay below Bahía Negra. This annoyed the Paraguayans so much that in 1887 they sent a gunboat, captured the port, declared the west bank a military zone and broke off diplomatic relations.

There followed various schemes to divide up the northern part of the Chaco (one to be adjudicated by the King of the Belgians), but while the Paraguayans were granting concessions to ranchers and loggers who in many cases began to push railway lines westwards into the Chaco, there was very little penetration of it by Bolivians. They stuck to the foothills south of Santa Cruz and concentrated on settling a border and developing trade with the Argentinians, who had built two railway lines up to the Bolivian frontier by 1922.

Not until 1903 and the Treaty of Petrópolis with Brazil did Bolivia gain access to the mainstream of the Paraguay river. The treaty gave Bolivia four separate 'windows' – Lake Cáceres and three others to the north; before this, Puerto Suárez was only viable in the high-water season. An Englishman, Henry Bolland, had in 1900 chosen a suitable site for year-round use, and the extended 'window' acquired in 1903 enabled Bolivia to inaugurate Puerto Quijarro, its easternmost town, which became a naval base and training establishment, and the passenger terminal on the railway line from Santa Cruz completed in the 1950s.

Bolivia's old claims to upper Paraguay were at least partially met by the award, also in 1903, of 330 square miles of land in a wedge shape north of Bahía Negra. This gave them a 31 mile stretch of swamp and tropical forest along the west bank of the Paraguay. In it today lies the optimistically named Puerto Busch, difficult of approach overland and guarded by a forlorn detachment of eight Bolivian *marineros* sitting on an engineless hulk in an almost permanent cloud of mosquitoes.

The next phase of our project was to be, as John put it, a 'reconnaissance in force' combined with the experimental voyage of the reed boats from Bolivia to Buenos Aires. The Hydrographic Department of the Bolivian Navy was to be involved and predicted northerly winds from August to October. This should enable us to sail for some of the time; but Jim Masters, a cautious man, insisted we fit a 25hp Suzuki outboard to the Avon that would allow us to push or pull the reed craft when the wind was contrary so that we could keep to a schedule. Experts including archaeologists, anthropologists, biologists and hydrographers would be in the team. In the time available detailed research would not be possible, but these specialists could identify tasks for future expeditions.

Governments were more interested in community aid projects than archaeology and there was much need for health work among the poor people along our route. Thus a medical and dental team would operate with us and Royal Engineers, serving and retired, would advise on construction tasks and give what help they could to the remote communities. As in 1998 there would be a link between schools in South America and Britain to foster friendship and understanding. By providing these services it was hoped to gain the cooperation of both the authorities and the people of the region, and to facilitate the gathering of scientific information. It was a well-tried and successful formula that the Scientific Exploration Society had often used.

Jim, Barry Moss and John, acting as an expedition committee, spent a year recruiting and seeking sponsors. In South America Yoli liaised with the governments, the navies and the boat-builders. We planned to get our craft on to the Paraguay river from Puerto Quijarro. But how were we to get them there from their spiritual home in the high Andes?

'What a hatter!' said Marie Peralta, one of our Spanish-speakers, as the Ministerio de Defensa low-loader breasted a rise in the Altiplano.

'Sorry?' said Shaun Linsley.

'What a hatter! That's it ahead of us.'

Some of us had been to Huatajata the year before; now Marie, a newly qualified barrister from Gibraltar, and Shaun Linsley, our anthropologist and husband of Julia, John's PA at Expedition Base in Motcombe, Dorset, were travelling to Lake Titicaca to fetch the boats as part of a team led by Jim Masters.

With the help of a pre-positioned crane lent to us by Crillon Tours, *Kota Mama 2*, over 8 tons of her, was lifted on to the low-loader.

'My God, it's vast,' said Jim to Andy Miller, our rusty-haired archaeologist.

'Do you think it will pass under some of those footbridges in El Alto?' asked Andy.

Jim had cause enough to worry. The road journey to El Alto would be straightforward enough; but thereafter problems loomed. Our patron, President Hugo Banzer Suárez, had said that he would be happy to commission our flagship on the afternoon of La Paz Day, 16 July, the anniversary of the city's independent foundation. But he had many duties in the morning and could only manage a *ceremonía de inauguración* in the afternoon – and it would have to be outside his seat of government in the Plaza Murillo and not up at El Alto as we had hoped. So *Kota Mama 2* would have to negotiate not only all the footbridges of El Alto but ever tighter right-angled turns as the low-loader drew closer to La Paz's ancient centre. And a myriad telephone lines and power cables all the way.

Out of interest Jim measured the big reed boat. It was 13.5 metres long: 1.5 metres longer than specified, and over a metre too high into the bargain.

'What happened, Máximo? Why is it so big?'

Máximo stood, eyes averted, his face an Aymará mask. A man of almost no words at the best of times, he shrugged just perceptibly. It transpired that he and Erik had lost the specifications we had drawn up with a road and rail journey in mind, and had just made it all up as they went along.

So the vast jaguar figurehead had to be taken from the prow, and the tail from the poop, and the mast lowered. Jim's team spent a wretched day, some guarding the boats at a dreary air force base in El Alto, while others worked out a route which might get them down to the Plaza Murillo. Jim himself survived the day on one slice of bread and jam.

Next morning he and his team left the Sucre Palace Hotel at 4.30 a.m. and contoured up the dual carriageway to El Alto. In darkness they manoeuvred the low-loader out on to the main road. Immediately a concrete footbridge loomed up.

'I think there was a side-road back there,' said Marie. 'Let's try and bypass it that way.'

Standing high in *Kota Mama 2*'s bows, Shaun Linsley soon encountered low-slung telephone wires which he pushed up with a wooden pole. Then there were two power cables separated by a spreader which he likewise looped over the high prow and passed over the cabin. As he pushed up another pair there was a blinding flash and a shower of sparks. There was no spreader and the wires had touched. Shaun fell back into the boat as the street lights of El Alto were extinguished.

Jim called John at 5.30 a.m. and again at 7.00, using the ENTEL mobile phone that had already proved such a boon in Bolivia. They agreed to abort the plan to take the flagship down. President Banzer would have to make do with *Viracocha Spirit of Bahamas*. It was a good job we had two reed boats – and that *Viracocha* was much smaller.

'I was put severely at risk of a fatal injury,' complained Shaun, as they looped down to La Paz in a taxi for breakfast.

'I could have booked a Saga holiday to Madeira,' said Jim.

The Sucre Palace Hotel was a hive of activity. Its charming owner, Lita Kushner, seemed never to mind the mountain of our boxes and kit-bags which continuously blocked its foyer. In 1948 Christopher Isherwood had dismissed it as 'big, pretentious, dreary' and chose instead the cheaper Italia. It still has a slightly spooky 1950s air, but is comfortable and friendly. Some of the bedrooms look out on to the streets of La Paz, a qualified blessing since in daylight hours there is almost always a demonstration of striking teachers or a parade of celebrating schoolchildren with attendant bands and firecrackers. Other rooms look into a dull interior courtyard. The lift doors often jam and there are discon- certing dints on their insides where trapped guests have beaten to attract attention. A first-floor restaurant serves, consistently slowly, good international food and we often enjoyed a snack of Palta la Reina (avocado, chicken and egg white). It is that rare hotel which still places ashtrays on its bedside tables; but, as in many Third World establishments with en-suite rooms, the best light is often in the loo. We had used it for five years and hoped to go on doing so.

John began here his regular habit – as regular as our daily taking of Paludrine anti-malarial tablets – of having an evening briefing, in this case in the coffee room. He would tell us what the situation was, what we had done, what we were going to do and who would do it. Others would report individually on their activities. It was an important point of contact for the whole group, as each day would see us scattering to different tasks – John and Yoli to visit presidential aides, admirals and ministers, the rest of us to deal with lesser fry, such as naval officers at the Hydrographic Department, the surgeon at the German Clinic, archaeologists at DINAAR.

On La Paz Day some of us went up to the Plaza Murillo to watch the ceremonial. It is a pleasant square, with trees and pigeons; the Legislative Palace flanks one side, the Presidential Palace and the cathedral another, and the fine-looking Gran Hotel Paris a third. The plaza is named after Don Pedro Domingo Murillo, a hero of national independence hanged there in 1810. There have been more recent excitements, too. A military coup led by Colonel Gualberto Villarroel in 1943 was particularly nasty. Villarroel brought Bolivia into the Second World War on the side of the Allies, but he also gave free rein to a chief of police who made political prisoners swallow lubricating oil. In 1946 students and soldiers became restive, and after much street rioting a light tank forced open the doors of the Presidential Palace. Villarroel and his aide-de-camp were shot, mutilated, thrown from the balcony and hanged from lamp posts. But they did put the President's statue up later in the centre of the plaza.

On the morning of 16 July 1999, however, it is all very peaceful. Bolivians, generally a tiny, stubby-limbed people, stroll about with their children and dogs. *Campesinas*, multi-skirted, shawled and jauntily bowler-hatted, sell chewing gum and matches. Policia Nacional Pumas in smart khaki are everywhere. They carry pistols, while the more sinister Policia Militar have rifles, some with tear-gas canisters fixed, plastic shields and belts hung with grenades. Bolivian presidents have learnt to be prepared for anything.

A band approaches, leading a smart contingent of the presidential guard, white-trousered, blue-uniformed and with helmets sporting white horsehair plumes *à la* Life Guards. Another band leads in a large company of naval personnel. As the morning wears on, some rather bored-looking members of the diplomatic corps emerge from the Presidential Palace. A group of army cadets march into it and come out bearing the flags of the nine provinces, which they rig to flagpoles. Finally, out come President Banzer and his consort. He mounts a platform on the edge of the square and raises, ever so slowly, the Bolivian flag with its bold bars of red, yellow and green, to all four verses of the National Anthem, which most of the watching public and soldiery sing. Then he lights an everlasting flame and walks off to the cathedral, next door, for Mass.

In the afternoon the plaza is still thronged with *Paceños*, and *Viracocha Spirit of Bahamas* is now there on the back of a small lorry, hung about with sponsors' flags and stickers and carrying, somewhat top-heavily, *Kota Mama 2*'s figurehead. It is the first of many big media occasions on the voyage. Peter Hutchison, our PR coordinator and another Spanish-speaker, gives an interview to a lady from Mexican television. Richard talks to a German reporter on the *Bolivian Times*, an English-language weekly which Peter once edited.

Platforms are placed on the pavement outside the Presidential Palace. Top naval brass arrives in droves, along with the new British Ambassador, HE Graham Minter, and his wife; and John in a dark suit which was not to see the light of day again for several weeks. And a priest. John speaks first; then comes Admiral Zabala, Chief of the Armed Forces. At the end of his piece, on cue, two naval officers unfurl a banner: *Hermanos Americanos, ayudemos a Bolivia a retornar al mar*. The British Ambassador looks uneasy. If this banner, adjuring Bolivia's American brothers to help it return to the sea, is displayed on our boats it could annoy the Chileans, who effectively closed Bolivia off from the sea by seizing its Pacific coastal province in 1884 and whose former President, Augusto Pinochet, was then under house arrest in Surrey. All very trying.

The mood is changed by the priest who says prayers, blesses the boat and censes it with holy water. But where is our Patron all this while? The VIP party retire into the palace and reappear on the balcony with President Banzer. In the course of the morning's ceremonial he has lost his voice, so he waves to us all

– from the balcony over which his predecessor was pitched in 1946.

'Why are the Bolivian and Paraguayan flags so much bigger than the Argentinian one?' the Mexican lady asks Richard disingenuously.

Oh dear; another diplomatic pitfall.

'They are just the flags they happened to give us,' he says. 'Nothing whatever to do with the Malvinas, in case you're thinking that.'

It was time now to start the move down to the river. The only practicable route for both boats and people was by road. There was quite a good one from the high Andes down through Cochabamba to Santa Cruz de la Sierra. However, a reconnaissance carried out the previous year by Toby Marriner and Chrysoulla Kyprianou showed that eastwards from Santa Cruz to the Paraguay river the road was an execrable one with poor bridges, deep rivers and primitive ferries unlikely to be able to cope with a huge low-loader. Fortunately, there was a railway from Santa Cruz due east to Brazil; it still operated and enquiries revealed that it could carry freight the size of *Kota Mama 2*. Less fortunately, its notorious nickname was the 'Railway of Death'.

A good many expedition members had flown from the UK direct to Santa Cruz, obviating the risk of altitude sickness, and so were already there. The rest of us began to move down from La Paz. John and Yoli, who wanted to go ahead and check the bridges and tunnels, went in a hired car – along with Andy Miller, who had eaten a pizza garnished with shellfish, an unwise move in a mountain city 400 kilometres from the nearest seaport, and was now packing his things in between bouts of vomiting. Tarquin Cooper, the *Daily Telegraph* reporter scheduled to write three 2,000 word pieces for the travel section of his paper, and Danilo Villamor, our anthropologist friend from 1998, and a colleague of his, all went by bus on the evening of La Paz Day.

The size of *Kota Mama 2* still presented a problem. The police had furnished us with details of obstacles on the road: 'Local bridges from Vinto which height is 4.80 metres and 5.00 metres until Sacaba.' Beyond Cochabamba, more worryingly: 'Two tunnels near Parajti. Tunnels height 5.20 metres in the centre part 4.95 and 4.90 on the side.'

At Jim's latest measurement *Kota Mama 2*'s height on its low-loader was 5.60 metres. A further 80 centimetres must go. There was only one painful solution: it had lost its head, now it must lose its neck. It was sad for Jim to watch, and tragic for Máximo and Erik to carry out the further truncation of prow and poop with a saw, and the dismantlement of the cabin – but it had to be done. Peter Hutchison and Richard went out one afternoon to measure the heights of the footbridges and cables they would meet on the way out of El Alto and to choose a route with the fewest of both. The whole expedition might be brought to an ignominious conclusion if we could not get the reed boats off the Andes.

It was a tense time. Shaun Linsley and Marie Peralta wanted to hire ten locals to come with us for the first few miles to lift the wires, manhandle the masts and generally ease the big boat under obstacles in the suburbs.

'On an expedition costing eighty thousand pounds it would be a drop in the ocean to hire ten men,' said Shaun, still shaken from his early-morning experiences.

John thought that we could handle the challenges ourselves. He had allocated Peter Hutchison, Marie, Richard and Máximo to go with Jim and the two vehicles.

'John is just buggering off in a taxi and I was nearly killed this morning,' said Shaun, red hackles rising. 'He doesn't appreciate the dangers.'

'No one listens to us,' said Marie.

The atmosphere in the foyer of the Sucre Palace positively crackled. It was a classic expedition flare-up.

'My job is to get these boats to Santa Cruz, and we're going to do it,' said Jim. The argument was concluded.

CHAPTER EIGHT

SLOWLY DOWN
THE ANDES

*Bolivia is the Switzerland of South America, a Republic without access
to the sea. In shape it resembles the hall of a great hotel, a huge green
carpet at the foot of a staircase that rises to a flat landing a good deal
nearer the stars. Nine-tenths of the population live either at the top or
half way down and the vast forest plain that merges into Brazil in the
centre of the continent is unknown.*

JULIAN DUGUID,
Green Hell, 1931

The boat escort left for El Alto early on the morning of 17
July. Also leaving the Sucre Palace that morning was a party
headed for the Altiplano to visit the Chipaya people, whose
problems had been noted in 1998 (see Chapter 5). This was a
unique, isolated community frequently threatened by the waters
of the Río Lauca. Toby Marriner and a fellow Royal Engineer officer,
Stuart McCallion, hoped to come up with some solutions to the
flood danger; Shaun wanted to make further studies of the Chipaya
people; and Mary Stewart (a retired nursing administrator) and
Graham McElhinney (a captain in the Royal Army Dental Corps)
went to give, respectively, medical and dental assistance.

The boat escort reached the Transportes Aerea Militar camp
in El Alto to find *Kota Mama 2* on its low-loader and *Viracocha
Spirit of Bahamas* on its smaller truck with the boats' two masts
lashed to its hull. DHL had brought an outboard motor and our
Suzuki generator. Led by two La Paz policemen on motorcycles,
the convoy turned into the main road and came up to the fateful

footbridge. *Kota Mama 2* now stood 4.73 metres and Peter and Richard had measured the underside of the bridge at 4.75. It was a nail-biter and we passed it with less than an inch to spare. The police obligingly held up the morning traffic and the convoy rolled imperiously through red lights.

El Alto's unsightly suburbs seemed to go on for ever – hardly surprising given that nearly half a million people now live here on the rim of the Altiplano. The small Nissan truck led (the police had said: 'If the load is special regarding width and height. Should be considered a vehicle with alarm and flashing lights. The same one should go in front') and the low-loader followed, slowing every now and then to allow Peter in the bows to push up a sagging telephone wire.

As the half-built or derelict brick structures began to thin out Rene Chambi Sosa, driver of the Nissan, said: 'I'm just stopping to get some alcohol,' which Richard didn't think boded too well. We pulled off the road by some shanties and soon Rene returned from a shop with a small plastic phial. But it seemed we had misjudged him. Minutes later, as we drove past some wooden shacks, he opened his window and spilt some drops out on the road. 'Barapuni. Holy place,' he said. This was a libation to Pacha Mama, Mother Earth. All the same, we noticed that he afterwards took a swig of it himself.

The first toll station posed a problem. *Kota Mama 2* passed easily *under* the canopy – but was too wide. One bulbous flank brushed the glass booth, forcing the cashier to keep his head tucked in, and the other threatened the columns supporting the whole station. A wooden mounting for an outboard engine had been tied into the reeds; projecting 6 inches from the starboard side, it now snagged against a row of concrete supports. It took Mark Terrazas Balboa, the driver of the Iveco low-loader, ten minutes of precision weaving back and forth to squeeze it through.

On to Calamarca; Patacamaya (soup and fried eggs); and Challacollo, where we left the main road running south down the Altiplano to Oruro, much traversed in 1998, and turned off eastwards for Cochabamba. Here the surprises began. First the terrain: we dropped down into steep-sided valleys dotted with adobe houses roofed with grasses and not mud bricks. Then snow-covered mountains appeared ahead and we snaked up into them. Over whitened cols we wound up and down through desolate, windswept, bitterly cold country.

'There's a lot more Andes than I thought,' said Richard. 'I wonder where we can pitch up tonight? Jim doesn't want us to drive after dark.'

'*No hay hoteles*,' said Rene helpfully when we put this problem to him.

Every so often we passed the remains of a grisly accident: a coach practically shorn in two by an artic. Lorries cross yellow lines to pass each other on curves, even when it says *No Adelantar*.

After the highest col at 4,496 metres (about 15,000 feet), where Rene spilt out a bit more alcohol, we began to coil down through the treeline. The road signs became legible, no longer masked with snow. We came into somewhere called Parotani – and Rene was right; there were no hotels. So we slept on or around the boats in the forecourt of a petrol station. It was a surprisingly comfortable night, despite barking dogs, busy night traffic and distant disco music. The only catch was that other lorry drivers had also chosen this forecourt, and so the small hours were punctuated by regular explosions of noise as juggernauts fired up and pulled out. At 3 a.m. the cockerels chimed in. Still, the heady mixture of Andean fresh air and diesel fumes ensured that we got our sleep.

Next morning we found ourselves in one of Bolivia's many patches of coca-growing country. Coca has been a money-spinner for the *campesinos* for centuries, and the industry has recently survived many national and international attempts to close it down. A couple of months later, in Argentina, we heard that the Bolivian Foreign Minister had promised to eradicate coca leaf production in three years and that General Barry McCaffrey, US drug policy chief, had praised Bolivia's efforts in this regard.

One thing for which it is difficult to give Bolivia praise is street hygiene. With our exceptional load we bypassed the centre of Cochabamba, the country's third city, passing under some footbridges that had alarmed John's recce group as we did so, and circled by Jorge Wilstermann airport and through the dismal, scruffy, impoverished suburbs: a wasteland of half-completed buildings, tatty little workshops, graffiti-stained houses and everywhere the accumulated detritus of plastic bags and empty Coke bottles. The Andean provinces of Bolivia have none of the domestic pride, a joy in tidy gardens or a lick of bright paint, that we were to see around more affluent Santa Cruz or in Paraguay and Argentina.

Minutes after an amazingly fat lady had served us a rough

lunch at the Restaurante Jasmin, we rounded a corner to see a warning sign – TUNEL 4.75m – and a gaping hole in the hillside. It was obvious that *Kota Mama 2* would block it completely, so Rene dashed through with *Viracocha* and parked at an angle, closing off the oncoming lane. Richard went forward and explained to drivers in Spanish why we had halted them. (They were remarkably understanding.) Suspense hung in the air. Then, like toothpaste from a tube, the low-loader oozed carefully out of the tunnel mouth. The entrances were of dressed stone, but inside the roof was jagged rock and the clearance had been tight.

The second tunnel, about a kilometre further on, was longer and required skilful timing – Rene had to be through and out the other side before Mark dared enter; the wait was a tedious as well as an anxious one, and it was with general relief that we saw two headlights emerging.

Even with these hazards behind us, there were 464 kilometres between us and Santa Cruz, and it seemed unlikely that we would, as had been hoped, reach the city that night. The Nissan could nip along at 110 kph, but would regularly have to stop for the low-loader to come rolling sedately up. On leaving Cochabamba we were still in respectably high folds of the Andes, but soon dropped into steep, thickly forested valleys. Down, down, down and again the surroundings changed: we were now among the wooden houses, banana trees and palms of a rain belt. The road became deeply pot-holed before we ran out into a flat landscape. It was 5.30 p.m. and Santa Cruz was still 240 kilometres away.

Our second night stop was a mouthful: Ivirgarzama. Also an earful: as we pulled into its main street we met an animated scene of shops, lights, people and noise.

'What do you think of the Alojamiento California?' asked Peter.

'Not a lot,' said Jim. 'It's right next to a night-club.'

So we settled for the Alojamiento Totoreño, which turned out to be next to a disco. The rooms were spare but clean, each with straw mattresses, a working light and a table. At 15 bolivianos (£1.50) per person, nobody could complain – even though the communal washroom consisted of one cold tap positioned over an oil-drum. Our kit was still stacked high up on *Kota Mama 2*, so Máximo and Peter slept on the boats.

The third and final day, the home stretch to Santa Cruz, saw the scenery metamorphose again – this time to a more developed countryside, with smart ranches, trim houses and painted fence-posts. In each little town – Entre Ríos, Yapacani, Villa St German,

Buena Vista – we were increasingly objects of interest. On one occasion an entire school was let out of classes to come and see the giant reed boat.

We were met at a toll station outside Santa Cruz by a party sent by John to guide us: Chris Brogan, a Royal Engineers captain and designated skipper of *Kota Mama 2*; Tomas Hughes, a Queen's Dragoon Guards trooper (whose mother is Spanish); and the expedition photographer, Charles Sturge, who videoed our arrival. Tomas took over the navigation, but the configuration of greater Santa Cruz, now a city of a million souls, is unusual: four concentric ring-roads, known as Cuarto Anillo, Tercer Anillo, and so on towards its old colonial gridiron centre, and Tomas got us seriously lost. Eventually we hired a taxi to lead us; and so it was that we delivered the boats, after three days and 882 kilometres, to the safety of the railway marshalling yards where John was waiting for us – in some anxiety, not having heard anything for two days.

The expedition had undertaken to carry out several tasks around Santa Cruz during the latter part of July. These were designed to occupy the whole team while the group at Chipaya did their work and the boats' crews took *Kota Mama 2* and *Viracocha* by rail to Puerto Quijarro and began the vital job of rebuilding them and fitting them out. On the very day the road convoy was bowling towards Santa Cruz another group, led by Captain Stuart Seymour of the Queen's Dragoon Guards, was starting an enquiry into some ruins near Samaipata, 120 kilometres south-west of the city. Oswaldo Rivera had wanted us all there the previous day, because a representative from UNESCO was to declare Samaipata a World Heritage Site; sadly, we were still in transit and so missed the occasion.

Samaipata itself is well known as a town in the foothills of the Cordillera Oriental, popular for excursions from Santa Cruz. Nine kilometres to the east of it is a hill-top site of mysterious origins called El Fuerte (The Fort), believed to be a pre-Inca ceremonial centre dating from 1500 BC. Despite its name it was probably never a fort; nor was it, as Erich von Däniken proposed, a launch pad for early spacecraft. When our group reached it the day after the UNESCO ceremony Oswaldo said to them: 'I have billed you as distinguished explorers, so please wear all your kit.' It was a hot day but they complied, and Gerry Masters, the tallest of the party, was duly garlanded with flowers by schoolchildren. With full pack and belt kit he then struggled up the 1,200 foot hill while the children, in shorts and flip-flops, raced on ahead waving Bolivian flags. At the top there was a park in which Oswaldo and other dignitaries had left their cars.

After the Samaipata group had left the Bolivian Navy barracks in Santa Cruz where most of us were lodged, a final team remained which was shortly to head south under Luke Cox's direction to investigate some archaeological sites. Meanwhile it was a quiet afternoon and John spent it happily trying on spectacles. An international organization which provides old, discarded glasses for the Third World and has no outlets in South America wanted us to collect and take out 5,000 pairs – many more than, in the event, we could carry. But we had scrounged seventy-one, and in various of these John looked like a Paraguayan general in sinister shades, a trendy punk, an old granny and a myopic schoolteacher. These all went very quickly in upper Paraguay and we could have off-loaded hundreds more.

But we had more to do in this vibrant, sophisticated city than experiment with eyewear. There were many things to be acquired while we had the chance. Sergeant Billy Huxter, the third member of the Queen's Dragoon Guards contingent, was our quartermaster and thus charged with the crucial duty of buying all the things we might need not only for the next two weeks but, in the case of hard-to-find items, for the whole journey. An entire morning, for example, was spent trying fruitlessly to locate gas regulator valves of the right size to link our Coleman stoves to the South American calor gas cylinders. In the end we found them only in Puerto Quijarro. Yoli, as usual, had her own, lengthy shopping list and a constant round of telephone calls to make, and sensibly she and Billy had the use of a hired station wagon.

Trips to downtown Santa Cruz were both necessary and popular. The city has an attractive colonial heart and most of us went there at one time or another to search out an Internet café, the post office or a bank. Founded in 1561 by Ñuflo de Chávez, a Spaniard from Paraguay, the original settlement was 220 kilometres to the east, but was driven by repeated Indian attacks to its present position in the 1590s. The central Plaza de 24 Septiembre has lofty trees in which sloths supposedly hang (the only ones we saw were in Santa Cruz's excellent zoo), and a statue to the not very Hispanic-sounding General Ignacio Warnes, Hero of Independence, 1816. Flanking the square are the imposing cathedral, the Prefectura, the Casa de Cultura, and a modern mall with a not particularly Irish Irish Pub.

It was here in the plaza that a last-minute thought in the UK, an International Driving Licence, came to Richard's rescue. Traffic approaching the square was unprecedentedly thick as he came in with four shoppers. Where to park? There was a demonstration in progress, this time by aggrieved *campesinos*, and police were funnelling vehicles straight through. On a sudden whim Richard turned the station wagon up one side of the plaza, but was immediately blocked by a log-jam of cars and a mass of demonstrators shouting *'¡No Pasa!'* It was just what he wanted – a chance to be stationary, a perfect parking spot. The shoppers nipped out. Soon a policeman approached. Richard played, convincingly, the dumb foreigner. Papers were demanded, so he helpfully handed over the international licence, open at the Spanish page. Soon the *campesinos* grew restless and began milling about the front of the car, batting the bonnet with their gnarled hands. As chance had it, a tape in the car was playing 'Rule Britannia' from the Last Night of the Proms. As a demonstrator moved one of the cars in the log-jam, Richard turned up the volume, raised his right arm in a clenched-fist salute, shouted *'¡Vivan los obreros!'* ('Long live the workers!') and drove straight through the narrow gap. It had been a bit of an ugly moment.

CHAPTER NINE

INCA OUTPOST

*Too much emphasis has been put on the demise of New World civilisa-
tions such as the Inca due to the Spanish conquest. One should be concentrating instead on what allowed their widespread success in such a
short time.*

ALEX CHEPSTOW-LUSTY,
Daily Telegraph, 30 May 1998

What is now the line of the railway from Santa Cruz south
to the Argentine border was once a cultural interface
between the highland Inca in their Andean fastnesses and the
lowland Guaraní of the Chaco. We had received information that
there were archaeological sites in the area and thought they
merited a few days' investigation. A man in Camiri, an oil town
260 kilometres south of Santa Cruz, knew about an ancient Inca
ruin in the Andean foothills. John wanted to pick his brains.

So the final group set out, marshalled by Luke Cox: John and
Yoli; our young IT wizard Owain Davies, fresh from his final year
at Clayesmore School in Dorset; Charles Sturge, the photographer;
Dr Noel Burrell, anthropologist Danilo Villamor, Richard, Peter
Hutchison, Sergeant Billy Huxter, Marie Peralta, archaeologist
Andy Miller and Patricia Weatherhead, whose job it was to keep
a record of everything the expedition did. This thirteen-strong
party packed itself into two vehicles, a Toyota Landcruiser and a
Nissan Patrol, with its gear stacked on the roof-racks.

Bolivian naval recruits begin their training in a hard school:
at 6 a.m. they were outside their barrack blocks breaking stones
with mallets like Victorian convicts. We left them at it and found

our way through Santa Cruz's rings to the road south – a fine, smooth highway for 125 kilometres. At Abapó the asphalt ended and we reached the banks of the Río Grande. This great river sweeps out of the Andes anticlockwise and runs up north to join the many Amazon tributaries – another possible route that early man might have taken to the Atlantic? It rises even nearer the Altiplano than the Pilcomayo does.

The girder bridge at Abapó carries road and railway together. An orange track inspection car tootled across; then several lorries came over from the other side, rumbling along the plank surface. Once across, we were on typically Bolivian mud and gravel all the way to Camiri. The mud takes its toll: in an effort to maintain the roads lorries dump earth at intervals for a grader to come and level out, and we came across one such lorry that had twisted over and spilled its load – in a single-track section. Queues had built up on either side, but Peter and Billy managed to jump them and drive the vehicles through. On another occasion Noel Burrell drove a bit too close to the edge and the Toyota slid off the road against a mud wall. We winched it out while massive petrol tankers festooned with lights trundled past. Hardening our hearts against a primitive restaurant at Tatarenda that offered sausages, cold rice and salad, we pressed on in darkness to Gutierrez.

We stayed here for three nights, as there was said to be some archaeological interest in the area: thirty years ago some large pottery funerary urns had been dug out of the ground, and there might be more. The priest would show us where.

If this had not detained us, nothing else in Gutierrez would have done. The school, Escuela Emilio Finot, its director and the children were most hospitable but their premises, like the rest of the town, were squalid and litter-strewn. The day after our nocturnal arrival was the Día de la Amistad – the Day of Friendship, a kind of St Valentine's Day – and they gave us a delicious tea of iced sponge cake, made by the girls, and plastic cups of lemonade; in return we gave them an illustrated talk on our expedition and showed them our technical armoury – our GPS instrument, personal CD player, BT Mobique satellite phone, and the JVC digital video camera, on which the children could see themselves. Then Charles entertained them on his didgeridoo. All this reminded us of how E. F. Knight, making his way up the Paraná in 1880 on board his yacht *Falcon*, had brought a concertina and a barrel-organ (and three bottles of gin) on shore to a ball he had laid on for the Guaraní Indians. (They seemed to like the entertainment; at least, Knight recorded that 'all went on well, and there was no grand finale of stabs and shots to mar the harmony of the evening.')

The priest on whom our hopes were pinned turned out – as was so often the case – to be away in the big city; undaunted, we spent two days digging for urns in the place he allegedly thought they might be. Sadly, nothing found.

Music was already blaring from a stall offering pirated tapes as Noel and Richard made a bonfire of all the school's litter. Then we packed and left for Camiri, 75 kilometres away on a rocky, potholed road described in the *South American Handbook* – with some justification – as 'terrifying', through scrub country with a simple *estancia* every now and then.

Camiri was an oasis of civilization – an airfield, paved streets, a superb plaza, a modern church, heroic statues everywhere, pavements, half a dozen *limpiabotas* touting for custom with their boxes of brushes and Kiwi polish, ice-cream sellers tooting horns as they hawked their wares. A town now of 30,000, in the years since the successful sinking of wells nearby in 1930, the production of liquefied petroleum gas and the opening in 1955 of pipelines to Argentina, it has become the oil capital of Bolivia.

It seemed appropriate to book in at the Gran Hotel Londres – not all that *gran*, but at least it had one hot shower. Afterwards we took a stroll in the nearby plaza, dominated by the statue of German (once again, 'Hair-Marn') Busch. It was the possibility of oil in the Chaco that sparked off the 1932–5 Chaco War between Bolivia and Paraguay, effectively won by Paraguay (which took most of the northern Chaco, leaving Bolivia only a fringe in the western part, in which Camiri lies). The Bolivian 'hero' of the war was General Busch, later the country's president, after whom the desolate little port on the Paraguay river is named.

Franz Michel, a tun-bellied French-speaking Bolivian sociologist, has a small museum of Guaraní artefacts which also shows Camiri's development since the discovery of oil. He told John of a possible Inca site found by archaeologist Erland Nordenskjöld in 1913, gave him a plan of the ruins and asked for an update of it. The site is called Inka-Ossi and is near the town of Lagunillas.

By midday on 26 July we were in one of the best examples of an old colonial town in Bolivia. Lagunillas has it all: arcaded streets, the traditional tree-filled plaza with bandstand, a church of mellow stone and brick, trim wrought iron seating – and a smartly trouser-suited mayor, Professor Mary Villarroel de Guzmán. It also has some interesting contemporary history. Ernesto 'Che' Guevara, familiar on T-shirts for his straggly locks and black beret, was a young Argentinian doctor who in 1959 helped Fidel Castro overthrow the Batista regime and set up socialism in Cuba. By 1965 this restless revolutionary aspired to 'liberate South America' and settled on Bolivia as the most suitable base for his small guerrilla band, which he established at Nancahuazu, a farm near Lagunillas.

'He came here early in 1967, ostensibly to buy land and set up a ranch,' Professor Villarroel told us. 'He was here for four months and in reality he was training his group. But two of them became disaffected and came to Lagunillas and tried to sell their rifles to my father, Sabino Villarroel. This alerted the townsfolk, who realised what Che Guevara was really up to. My father called in the army and the rest is history.'

The CIA, who thought Guevara had died in the Congo, sent American Special Forces to train up the Bolivian Army Rangers and they chased the now ailing Che, arthritic and asthma-ridden, first of all up north to Samaipata, where in July 1967 he hijacked a lorry, drove into town, overran the army post, seized weapons and took ten hostages, who were left naked in the road on the band's way out. After this success he went on to Alto Seco, where things began to fall apart. Far from starting 'another Vietnam in the Americas', he was now the disillusioned leader of a dwindling rabble. In a Lagunillas restaurant we watched a video of the Bolivian Army's recent re-enactment of how they ambushed him in the Quebrado de Yuro on 8 October 1967 and gunned him down, aged thirty-nine.

'Your father did very well,' said John, impeccably polite as ever.

John had been in touch with Ronald Larsen, an American who owns a ranch near Lagunillas and within striking distance of Inka-Ossi. Unfortunately, just as we had come to see him he had gone on business to Santa Cruz. 'Don't worry,' he reassured John over the radio. 'My people will show you where the Inca ruin is. You can stay in my church.'

Some way out of Lagunillas we turned off up the drive to the Hacienda Caraparicito and, sure enough, there was a small stone church in a wired-off compound looking for all the world like St Matthew's or St Mary's by some English village green. The church key, however, could not be found; so Ronald's manager was told to put us up in the main house. This gave us access to a kitchen in which Marie made a very substantial Spanish omelette for all thirteen of us.

Next morning the same question was on all our lips: Where was Inka-Ossi?

'You can see it from here,' said the manager and, taking us out on to the wide verandah, he pointed west to the top of a long ridge of mountains about five miles away. 'It is at the top of the pass near a shrine to the Virgin of Urkupiña.'

Accompanied by two ranch hands, we drove into deep tropical forest, heading for the foot of the mountains. In four-wheel drive and low ratio gears we ploughed up through the mud. Then, in a strange echo of our experience outside Abapó, round a corner appeared a stationary Volvo lorry completely blocking the way.

The driver is lying under his front axle, shovelling feebly. An old woman and two snotty-nosed kids stand watching. Peter starts helping the driver and Yoli tries to find out how it got stuck. Can we not all help by pushing? It seems that all the driver has to do is straighten his wheels and start the engine. But he does not budge, and soon does not even reply when we address him.

There might just be room to pass round him on the outside – a perilous few moments on a muddy precipice edge.

'Why won't he let us help him, Yoli?' asked John.

'I'm sure we could get past if we built up the road a bit,' said Luke.

'I think we ought to help him do what he wants to do—' said Peter.

'—Whatever that is,' said Billy. 'He's only pratting around under there.'

It was an impasse.

Suddenly John grabbed a shovel and began to clear a way round the outside. But in so doing he began heaping earth in front of the lorry's wheels and impeding its path forward even more. This concentrated the driver's mind and he crawled out from under his axle, got in his cab and started up. In moments, his rear wheels spitting back clods of earth, we pushed him clear.

It soon seemed to be impossible that any road could continue. Some of us, walking ahead of the vehicles, came to a near-vertical face, hung with trees. But there were noises of an engine halfway up and the ranch hands assured us there was a road over to the small town of Muyupampa (Villa Vaca Guzmán on some maps) in the next valley. We started on a series of tight hairpins which carried us slowly up, past two graders at work, to the col.

The shrine to the Virgin of Urkupiña looked modern and clearly attracted a steady flow of worshippers. Across the road was a lorry park, where a mother and child ran a small shop for the somewhat limited passing trade. Behind the lorry park, on a piece of rising ground, we found a place for a camp. But where were the ruins? Nordenskjöld's map, while full of detail of temples, walls and towers, gave no indication of where the ruins were in relation to the ground around them. The only building on our camp site was a recent but derelict wattle-and-daub hut – which we scrupulously avoided as being the typical haunt of the vinchuca, a South American insect carrying the parasite *Trypanosoma cruzi*, which causes the fatal inflammation and lesions of Chagas' disease.

There were two ways we could set about finding the ruins. We could search for them in the locality; or we could ask the natives. The second method proved useless: every *campesino* has a lost city up his sleeves with which to beguile the *gringos*. Our ranch hands knew nothing of their ancient history – but Apolinar Gonzalez, one of three other ranch hands who came up to help us, walked into our camp with stories of caves high on the hill opposite, which some Americans had recently robbed of their gold. There was, he said, an Inca palace some 20 kilometres along the ridge to the north. In our experience such confident directions led nowhere. So we looked – Peter, Luke and Andy on the tree-covered hill opposite our camp, John and the rest of us for 4 kilometres on what looked like a man-made road which cut along the top of the ridge to the north. Was this an Inca road? No. Richard noticed a tell-tale drill hole for dynamite high on a rock face; the road had been built in the 1960s by an American oil company that had set up a depot here and sunk some trial wells.

Gradually our efforts were rewarded. Marie found some pottery near the camp. Andy dug out a small stone-lined cistern on the top of a hill behind it; and Luke found that circling the site, and particularly down its western slopes, were many metres of unmortared cyclopean rocks forming the defensive walls of the ancient Inca settlement. After forty-eight hours it dawned on us that we were actually camped on what had been either a defensive outpost or a trading station, which had been destroyed almost completely since 1913 – partly by the oil company and partly by road builders who, even as we sat pondering these things, were gouging out the hillside to get material for their graders.

Intriguingly, a man in his fifties called Esteban came up from the ranch and told us he had been born in the next valley and, as a boy of eight in the 1950s, had seen buildings here, rectangular and circular, and doors with lintels, all of which had subsequently been razed to the ground.

Andy did a few digs, but Luke's walls, all 467 feet of which Noel and Richard surveyed, were the most important remaining feature. The site was a stupendous one, with commanding views to east and west. We saw how the Andean foothill ranges all ran north–south in parallel. There were three of them to the east before the uplands gave way to the hazy expanses of the Gran Chaco, just visible, which were to occupy us in days to come.

A third archaeological site had been reported at Saipuru, over to the east and near the Chaco proper. Getting to it involved a long U-shaped journey round the southern end of one of those ranges. John, Yoli, Owain, Charles and Danilo had been driven back to Santa Cruz by Billy to look at the work of Stuart Seymour's group, so it was just the Nissan Patrol, with a nasty clunking noise now audible in its driveshaft, in which Luke and the rest of the party drove south again to Camiri, along the road towards Argentina. We headed first for the small town of Boyuibe, held up rather bizarrely on the way there by a car rally, another of which we had also witnessed at Lagunillas. At Boyuibe we looked for a road east, but only the main roads benefit from Bolivia's green direction signs and we struck off rather blindly into scrub country, looking only for a *gasoducto* which cuts across the road north to south, carrying natural gas to Argentina; this we had to follow northwards. After a good while, passing the very occasional ranch but no people, we saw two surveyors by the road and stopped for Marie to ask: '*¿Dónde va este camino?*' ('Where does this road go?')

'Paraguay,' one of them said. 'Just over there.'

There probably would have been no border posts and we could easily have left Bolivia unwittingly and prematurely.

We retraced our tracks for some miles and realized we had missed the *gasoducto* because it was buried beneath the road at this point and the track running parallel to it was much overgrown. This track, built to support the laying of the pipeline, ran the whole length of it and was no respecter of gradients, taking us up hill and down dale on an often alarming roller-coaster.

At one point we turned off to cross the Río Parapiti, which roughly parallels the Río Grande and is the northernmost (almost the only) river in the Chaco. Here, as before, road and railway united to cross the bridge; but this time there was no superstructure or even a handrail. With his wheels outside the metre-gauge track it was a perilous drive for Peter Hutchison.

Despite a puncture and the continuing noise in the transmission we rolled that evening into another colonial gem: Charagua. It had a stunning plaza, which even sported waste bins marked PAPELES, LATAS, VIDRIOS. Not all beer-cans had found their way into the LATAS bins or bottles to the VIDRIOS, but it was a cut above other Bolivian towns in the civic pride league. On the plaza's sides were a fine church, with an astonishing blue and yellow glass dome over the crossing, and a very well-run establishment in which we stayed, the Alojamiento San Luis, which had spacious, clean rooms and hot showers for the standard out-of-town price of £1.50 per person per night. We tracked down a chicken supper and some bottles of Kohlberg red, the good wine from Tarija in southern Bolivia.

Next morning, 2 August, after having the tyre repaired we went off to look for Saipuru. This time asking the natives bore fruit, and after four or five enquiries we found ourselves negotiating a very rutted cart-track leading down to the Parapiti. We tried to ford the river and got seriously bogged down in soft sand. For an hour we struggled with rocks and baulks of wood and gunned the engine more than its delicate state deserved. Eventually we got clear. But it meant that the rock carvings we had come to see would have to be tracked down on foot.

This proved to be surprisingly easy. Luke, Peter, Andy, Marie and Patricia came upon a cliff overhang visible from the river only a kilometre and a half upstream, and it was Marie who first spotted some intriguing inscriptions – matchstick men, feet marks and the like – cut in sandstone. When Andy had drawn and photographed them we turned back to the main track, which ran north, parallel to the Santa Cruz–Argentina railway now, for 78 kilometres. After every gear change we still heard the ominous judder in the area of the clutch.

We crossed the road/rail bridge over the Río Grande and, in gathering darkness, Luke drove hard up the road, now *asfaltado*, to Santa Cruz. After 147 kilometres we were in the suburbs and on the cusp of a busy corner at traffic lights when an alarming clang told us that the clutch had finally gone. As far as the juggernaut and all the other vehicles behind us were concerned this could not have been a worse place for us to break down, but for us it was a merciful piece of good fortune. We were close to home; a short phone call would bring immediate relief. We could not help thinking what the outcome might have been if the failure had happened 225 kilometres to the south in uninhabited territory on the fringe of the Chaco. The train to Argentina runs only once weekly. We had no radio, little food, a finite water supply. Richard recalled a time in southern Ethiopia in 1966, on one of John's first expeditions, when, miles from anywhere in the Rift Valley, the universal joint of a Willys Overland Jeep had sheared and one end of the driveshaft fell on to the dusty road. The passengers walked. No doubt the same fate would have befallen us here: three or four days' delay, possible dehydration – and the certain prospect of missing the train to Puerto Quijarro.

CHAPTER TEN

BOLIVIA'S
GATEWAY TO
THE ATLANTIC

The second trail, that to the Paraguay [river] and Asunción, picked its
way eastwards through the sierras to the town of Santa Cruz, seat of
the seventeenth-century bishopric and the only important ranching and
regional centre of the plains. From Santa Cruz de la Sierra the trail
skirted the edge of the Chaco for about 400 miles through the Jesuit
province of Chiquitos. Linking San José or Roboré it ran out eventually
on to the Paraguay river at either Gaíba or Corumbá.

J. VALERIE FIFER,
Bolivia: Land, Location and Politics since 1825 (1972)

On 20 July, the day after the boats had arrived in Santa Cruz
by lorry, we were to load them on to ENFE's flat cars (the
Empresa Nacional de Ferrocarriles del Este runs the railway to
Puerto Quijarro). After listening, bizarrely, to the BBC Caribbean
News on John's Sony short-wave radio, we breakfasted on salami
and cheese and then set off for the Estación Guaracachi, Santa
Cruz's freight marshalling yards.

Cranes had been prearranged. *Viracocha Spirit of Bahamas*
was easy, but it took two to lift *Kota Mama 2*'s 8 tonnes with
padded ropes slung under her hull. When she was in suspended
animation the low-loader drove away and a flat car was rolled
underneath her in its place. Old tyres were scattered on the flat
car and the *balsa* was lowered with great precision on to them.

The two-day journey to Puerto Quijarro went smoothly and the only damage *Kota Mama 2* sustained was some scoring from thorn bushes on her rounded flanks when she went round some of the tighter curves. The boats' crew left by passenger train that same afternoon, but did not roll into Puerto Quijarro until thirty hours later. 'I can't wait to get to the river,' Jim had often said. Now he was there.

The rest of us buzzed repeatedly in and out of the city on various errands.

'I know we're near base when we get to McDonald's,' said Billy Huxter, negotiating traffic round one of Santa Cruz's ring round-abouts.

'We turn off by that enormous fat woman,' added Tarquin Cooper, on his way back from despatching a report to the *Daily Telegraph*. The fat woman was an allegorical statue of a Guaraní amazon. We were all in the last throes of preparing to move by rail to Bolivia's eastern outposts.

Most of us still in Santa Cruz were lodged in the Residencial Santa María which, conveniently, was just opposite the city's fine new station. All the metal plaques said it was built in 1992, but it was by no means finished and there were still workmen padding about the vast concourse. There is a train of one sort or another each day. However, the *South American Handbook* describes the timetable as 'flexible or pure fantasy', and even warns travellers coming from Brazil to Santa Cruz to arrive at Corumbá a week early to secure tickets and prepare for the 403 mile journey. After many years of local mismanagement the ENFE RED ORIENT (Eastern System) is now owned by FCOSA, a Chilean company, and things seem better. We had reserved places in the most comfortable class, and with a marathon journey of anything up to twenty-four hours ahead of us its reclining seats were a welcome prospect.

We spent the morning of 4 August moving our fifty-two pieces of luggage over to the station and into a secure area, and fell into conversation with a narcotics officer.

'Why is it called "The Railway of Death"?' some of us enquired nervously.

'*Descarrilamientos* are frequent,' she said. 'The previous owners put the money in their own pockets and didn't look after the railway.'

Apparently, the poorly maintained track – it seemed unlikely that there had been much investment at any time since its opening in 1956 – caused frequent derailments and the passengers on the roofs of the older carriages (only men were allowed to travel that way) were regularly pitched off. This also sometimes happened when the train, which bucks like a bronco, hit a sharp curve.

Seeing no sign of sniffer dogs, Noel asked, 'Is there much drug trafficking these days?'

'Oh, yes. I find about half a ton of cocaine a year. I can sniff it myself,' was her reply, straining our credulity somewhat.

'What happens to them when you catch them?'

'The traders get twenty years and all their possessions are seized. The carriers get seven years.'

Money can be made from the railway in more legitimate ways. As our 3 p.m. departure time drew near, the platform filled with hucksters. Up and down they went – '¡Hamburguesas, hamburguesas!' '¡Pollo, pollo, pollo!' '¡Soda, soda, soda!' – proffering their food and drink at every open window. For forty-five minutes they had a glorious sales opportunity and passengers had a chance to buy apples, torches, loo rolls, towels, mandarin oranges, *Time* and *Newsweek*, peanuts, sunglasses, cassette tapes.

Almost on time the *Empresa Ferroviaria Oriente* SA, the other *Orient Express*, drew slowly out. It was a not unpleasant beginning: the seats were quite comfortable, the carriages well sprung; the windows opened; the *baños* was tolerably clean – in fact, there was nothing to get dirty: everything had been stripped out and all the sides were lined with sheet metal, leaving just a hole in the floor.

'Miami Vice?' A man loomed over Richard with a pair of blue sunglasses. Another pushed past with a tray of yogurt. All the hucksters who had been on the platform were now on the train, and so an unending supply of *empanadas, café caliente* and the like, was on offer.

We rolled through fields of soya and rather ill-kempt ranches until the impressively long bridge over the Río Grande, flowing north to the Amazon system. Slowly, the height above sea level of the stations we passed diminished: El Pailon, 300 metres, Cañada Carga (Tres Cruces) 295 metres, Pozo de Tigres, 280 metres . . . What stories attached to that little halt, The Well of Jaguars? At a passing point we stopped to let another train through; for the most part this was a single-track line. On the straight bits the diesel locomotive touched perhaps 40 mph and the bogies beneath the carriages banged and clattered over the metre-gauge rails. Tall, earnest-looking Mennonites, blue-eyed and fair-haired, strode through in their blue dungarees. Darkness fell.

Sleep came with difficulty. Passengers need to equip themselves carefully for the night section of this trip (perhaps the week in Corumbá is not a bad idea). A blow-up neck ring is useful, and an eyeshade stolen from an airline to keep out the fluorescent light that is left on all night, its casing filled with the carcases of dead moths; and ear defenders to minimize the clanking of the wheels and the endless chatter of the youngsters in the seats behind.

It was black night now as the train rolled along a deserted platform.

'Hallo, unknown station,' Richard said, dimly remembering some army radio procedure.

At 10 p.m. we came to the principal destination en route and one where travellers prepared to take their chance on an onward connection often stop off for a few days. San José de Chiquitos has perhaps the best of the Bolivian Jesuit mission churches, built about 1750, and the frontier feel of a Wild West town. The original Santa Cruz was sited here and Father José de Arce founded the mission on its ruins in 1698. At night the citizens emerge to meet the train and sell their wares. It is possible in the brief time to disembark and eat a hot meal at covered track-side tables. Those who stay longer in San José de Chiquitos risk being caught, like the novelist Lisa St Aubin de Terán and her BBC film crew, by a rail strike and being able to continue their journey only by freight train.

In the small hours of the morning we passed close to an area about the size of two English counties with an exotic, somewhat sinister name – the Bañados del Izozog. At the northern end of the Chaco Boreal aridity gives way to swamp. Robin Hanbury-Tenison took eighteen days to drive 40 miles through it in 1957: it was the worst bit of his transcontinental journey. The name 'Bañados', suggestive of *baños*, the Bolivian word for loo, gives it a murky feel, and 'Izozog' is equally spooky. The only British equivalent is perhaps Grimpen Mire on Dartmoor.

The carriage lurched and swung onwards like a moving trampoline. John, his name surreally rendered by the rail clerks as SRELL BLANTORS, lay stretched out asleep as the train rumbled towards the dawn. At Yacuces it swung off the main tracks and then reversed back on to them down a spur line, so as to leave the locomotive at its head for the return journey. Here too an anti-narcotics squad came on board and began frisking passengers. At 9 a.m. we rolled slowly backwards into Puerto Quijarro. It had been a good journey: only eighteen hours of it, no derailments and, for Richard, who travelled as D. SWAILMAN, a rare chance to smoke a pipe on a train.

We found ourselves quartered in another naval base, this one much bigger, with a large campus which stretched down to Lake Cáceres. The expedition had the use of two dormitories full of double bunks, a draughty storeroom in which John slept and a canteen. Richard took over the lower bunk and unyielding straw pallet normally occupied by Marinero Paz Galarza Juan E.

There were opportunities for relaxation in these last few landlubbing days. Some went fishing; a trip on the Bolivian Navy's power boats was offered; others chose an early morning monkeywatch in the camp grounds. The younger among us tried the local night-clubs and made their first acquaintance with Brazilian girls. Saturday night in the crowded dormitory was confusing: at a very small morning hour the older generation was aware of shadowy figures with head-torches. Were they revellers returning from the 1054 Club in Corumbá and the Banana Club at the frontier, or were they keen zoophiles off early to watch monkeys?

The high-rise buildings of Corumbá were visible on the skyline, and their lights at night were an almost palpable lure. It was a bright nugget of civilization, perhaps the last we should see before reaching Asunción, the Paraguayan capital. By contrast, Puerto Quijarro was very run down. Named after the Bolivian minister in Buenos Aires in 1911, it had been at first just a frontier post, then a staging point for overland travel by horse to and from Bolivia's interior, then a railway town with a few shacks clustered by the almost always dilapidated station buildings. Now it was dignified a little by its smart naval barracks – but most visitors don't see these. Richard Gott, passing through the town in 1990, called it 'very poor and miserable compared with Corumbá'.

Our attention was now focused on the big ceremony to take place on Monday 9 August, just four days away, when our patron, President Banzer, would fly in with Admiral Zabala to preside over the official start of the river journey. John and Yoli negotiated constantly with Capitán Lido Ortiz, who helped us to secure the use of a support vessel. Captain Stuart Seymour, John's adjutant, began to form and drill a guard of honour. Jim and his crews, who had essentially finished their rebuilding work, rehearsed various manoeuvres with the two reed boats on the lake.

There was, however, time for a bit of dental work: the station had its own practitioner but there was still plenty of scope for our own naval dentist, Surgeon-Lieutenant Melissa Wingfield, and, after his return with the Chipaya party, Captain Graham McElhinney, RADC. It was disconcerting to see a poor *marinero*, too nut-brown to look pale after the extraction of half a mouthful, lying full length on the grass outside.

We felt a great sense of anticipation and excitement as we drove the 2 kilometres along the shoreline to the shipyard where the reed boats and our support ship lay. *Kota Mama 2* and *Viracocha Spirit of Bahamas*, masts stepped and fully rigged, looked splendid – particularly *Kota Mama 2*, which had its jaguar figurehead woven back on, its cabin rebuilt, two enormous steering rudders lashed on either side astern and a large lee-board on one flank. All was very shipshape and Bristol fashion on both vessels, as John found when he carried out an inspection. On *Kota Mama 2* a covered rear bunkhouse abaft the main cabin could accommodate three or four sleeping crew members; ample sail cupboards and a sturdy chart table had been installed. The roof of the main cabin had been replanked so that crew could keep watch from it and climb the mast more easily.

'Get John off,' said Jim after a while. 'He's started suggesting ladders here and there, and we've finished the refit.' Ever impatient with ceremonial, Jim wanted to get the boats sailing. But there is a necessary place for the formalities in big expeditions, and John spent a lot of time with Yoli and Commandante Ernesto Roca, the officer in charge of the naval base, and his staff, determining where the President would stand, where the naval band, where our honour guard. A programme of events was agreed and a timetable drawn up.

Those of us not crewing the reed boats were all keen to have a first look at the support vessel which was to be our home for the next ten weeks or so. This was a cargo boat, the *Puerto Quijarro*, which belonged to Dr Michel Chaim, a Brazilian citizen of Lebanese extraction who ran a shipping company from the nearby Brazilian city of Corumbá. His company, Cinco Bacia – Companhia Interamericana de Navegação e comércio – had been founded in 1989 and had a fleet of eighty cargo boats transporting minerals, grain and oil on the Paraguay/Paraná river system, as well as twelve ships of the type known in Portuguese as *empurradores*: powerful vessels of which we were to see a great many, designed to push blocks of barges up and down the waterways.

The *Puerto Quijarro* was by no means the flagship of this fleet. It had been built in 1973 in Corumbá and was, in essence, a 303-tonne barge with a large hold forward, a smaller one aft and a three-tier structure above the engine room astern containing crew accommodation, galley and bridge deck. She was currently on charter to the Bolivian Navy, from whom we hired her for $38,000 – the expedition's biggest single expense. This included fuel, mooring fees and food for the crew of ten (Shell Bolivia kindly gave us 2,000 litres of fuel, which cut the cost a little). *Puerto Quijarro*, or *PQ* for short, was marvellously capacious, perfectly suitable for a bunch of peripatetic expeditioners – beyond our most optimistic imaginings, in fact. There were steel stanchions supporting the roof of each hold, from which we could sling our hammocks. The steel hull, made at the Lanarkshire Steel Co. in Scotland, was clean inside, as was the thick plank flooring. For John and his immediate staff – Yoli, Stuart the adjutant, Owain the comms wizard – the boats' crews had built a wooden *sala de operaciones* on the deck, with desks and shelves inside and two bunk spaces below for John and Stuart.

'What am I going to do for light?' John asked.

Jim pointed to the wall of John's 'office', on which someone had drawn a spoof switch and a couple of portholes in white chalk. 'You'll have to imagine it,' he said. In the event, a line was rigged from one of the ship's spare batteries and bulbs hung from it at intervals, like Christmas decorations in a rather down-at-heel street.

Back at the naval base we sat on the grass, some of us smoking cheap Palermo cigarettes, listening to the merry chortle of the southern lapwings and watching the smooth-billed anis in the nearby bushes as the sun slowly set. There were no mosquitoes. The cautious among us had rigged nets, and Richard had been comprehensively attacked while waiting in the cab of a navy lorry at yesterday's crucial evening hour, but here, a little inland, we were spared.

This was our last weekend in Bolivia. What had we made of the country? Its founder, Simón Bolívar, *El Libertador*, described it in 1825 as a 'little marvel' – somewhat strangely, because at that time it was about the size of western Europe. But not everyone since then has been so generous. In fact, reactions to Bolivia have often been pretty negative. Queen Victoria was perhaps the most forthright: she allegedly had Bolivia expunged from her atlases after an astonishing diplomatic slight. The story goes that one of HE Graham Minter's predecessors, while being entertained by General Mariano Malgarejo, who was president from 1865 to 1870 and something of a tyrant, did not finish his *chicha*, a traditional Andean drink made from fermented corn. The affronted president then had the hapless minister plenipotentiary stripped naked, set backwards on a donkey and driven round the streets of La Paz. Victoria's first instinct was to send a gunboat but Malgarejo, holed up miles from the coast, could not be touched that way – so she just wrote the country off.

Malgarejo's six-year presidency was uncharacteristically long: since 1825 Bolivia has had 191 governments, most of them ended by *coups d'état*, and this has earned it a place in the *Guinness Book of Records*. Andrés Santa Cruz held power for ten years, the longest so far, but others have lasted only a fortnight. This instability has contributed to Bolivia's bad press over the years. 'The chances of gradual peaceful change are very slight,' wrote Christopher Isherwood in 1948. 'This unhappy country' he found to be potentially rich but hampered by poor infrastructure, under-developed, with still a severe Indian problem caused by racial hatred and the perpetuation of a kind of feudal system in the mines and on the big estates. Indeed, Bolivia has become a byword for remoteness and backwardness: 'What is the likelihood of finding a cash machine halfway up a mountain in Bolivia?' (*Daily Telegraph*, Family Finance, 28 June 1999); Mark Taplin, describing run-down Russia in the 1990s, called it 'a Bolivia with writers, a Bangladesh with rockets'.

In the last fifty years Bolivia, with a good deal of outside help, has made strides – but is still not much liked. Paul Theroux's views are characteristically bleak: on the Altiplano 'there were no cars in the villages, no roads, no trees; only mud huts and cows, and Indians wrapped up against the cold.' Theroux, like Isherwood, found that Bolivians hate and fear their neighbouring countries and were generally scathing about the rest of South America. Now, though, they have joined Mercosur, a trading partnership involving Argentina, Uruguay, Paraguay and Chile, and commercial ties, for example through Bolivia's export of oil and natural gas, have blunted some of the old animosities.

Theroux had been there when our Patron was first in power in the 1970s. 'The Bolivian election was held. There were shootings all over the country . . . and stuffed ballot boxes. It was generally agreed that the election had been rigged and then the head of state, General Banzer, "annulled" the election. A state of siege was declared and a new government was formed in what was officially termed "a bloodless coup". Within five months there was a counter-coup and another promise to hold elections.' We were certainly fortunate that President Banzer's second spell in office was a time of political stability.

Theroux did, albeit grudgingly, like La Paz, and described it as 'endearing' despite its being 'scabrous' and 'blighted' with 'urban gangrene'. We never heard a bad word spoken by any of our expedition members about Bolivia's extraordinary capital, and the country itself had by now won many supporters. Several of us proposed to come back with expeditions both archaeological and exploratory. We were sad to be leaving a land which, for all its persistent problems, had exerted its magnetic charm on us and shown us such generosity and friendship.

CHAPTER ELEVEN

ANCHORS AWEIGH!

5th Naval District at Calama *(HQ Puerto Quijarro). Three patrol craft and one BTL logistic vessel on the upper Paraguay river.*

Jane's Fighting Ships

Now that all the groups had come together in Puerto Quijarro, ready for the inauguration ceremony and the start of the 1,800 mile voyage, we had a few briefings on their various recent activities. Toby Marriner told how his Chipaya team had almost reached the Altiplano town near the Salar de Coipasa when they had themselves got bogged down in the troublesome Río Lauca.

'We were rescued,' he said, 'by two nuns on a motorbike, one from Chile and one from Birmingham.' These had been our old friends Sister Sylvia Sherwood and Sister Marcella Valenzuela.

This mishap behind them, Toby and Stuart McCallion had devised a system of dikes to be built in an inverted V-shape north of the town. Graham McElhinney had extracted 166 teeth and Mary Stewart had collected DNA samples and given sex education lessons. The British Ambassador's wife, Peter (*sic*) Minter, was also in this party.

Stuart Seymour's group had planned to start at Parabanocito, south-west of Santa Cruz, and trek with donkeys for twelve days; but Oswaldo Rivera had had to leave after the first day and no donkeys or guide were available, so they stayed on the spot and dug, expertly advised and assisted by Rolando, a Colombian archaeologist. A renowned authority on the Incas, Rolando had been driven from his Medellín home after a feud and trained at the Sorbonne.

Communication between groups was becoming a problem at this point, as John was largely reliant on his Bolivian ENTEL cellular phones, whose coverage was often limited to the immediate proximity of the larger cities. However, the BT Mobique satellite phones that had been loaned to the expedition were already proving their worth: with these, although John and Stuart did not speak to each other directly, messages were relayed via Julia Linsley back at base in Dorset using the e-mail facility. Thus it was that we learned of the expedition's first major discovery.

Using the Sight and Sound laptop and an army digital camera, Stuart had prepared a visual brief on his task. Sitting in the chromium-plated dining room of Residencial Santa María, we had to admire this innovative means of reporting.

In 1937 an archaeologist named Leo Pucher had discovered some interesting ruins east of Samaipata. Although he did not excavate the site, he did draw a plan and marked the location. Later, another archaeologist, Dr Albert Meyers, visited the ruins and found pottery belonging to a pre-Inca Amazon culture and some significant walls. Thus the place was believed to be an early fortress, possibly built by Amazon and Chaqueña people advancing from the eastern lowlands. Later, it might have become the most easterly outpost of the Inca. At Fortaleza del Parabanocito, as the site was known, there were fascinating architectural features unique in this region and clearly it was a place of considerable importance. DINAAR and Oswaldo wanted a detailed exploration carried out and Stuart's mission was to rediscover the ancient site and in particular to seek evidence of road systems. By finding a road, it was hoped to show that Samaipata and Parabanocito had once been linked.

The small town of Angostura straddles the highway from Santa Cruz to Samaipata. Beyond this Stuart had already experienced some bad landslides, which had temporarily blocked the road, so he was glad to find that to reach the site, to which Oswaldo directed him, he was to turn off into the jungle at this point. However, his experience here during an initial recce of the route gave rise for concern. On this visit a roadblock had been set up across the highway by some local villains demanding illegal toll fees. We all carried a letter from the President requiring us to be given safe passage and when Stuart produced this it had an electric effect. By now almost the entire village had turned out to see such an important document. It mattered little what was written but the words 'Presidente Hugo Banzer' were quickly noted and, after a short discussion and some ugly looks, they were allowed to pass. Nevertheless, arriving back at Angostura on the night of 21 July Stuart's party had some reservations, so he decided to ask the mayor for a camp site. As they were ushered into the dingy office, he realized to his horror that it was the same man who had demanded money two days before. 'You not *gringos*?' the mayor belched. 'No, no,' replied the cavalry captain, 'certainly not.' 'OK,' grunted the official. 'Two days ago some passed through here and did not pay me. I was looking forward to settling accounts.' Quick as a flash the British Army ID card came out. '*Británicos*, no *gringos*' the team echoed and were given a school playing field in which to erect their tents. At dawn they found themselves surrounded by children so Melissa Wingfield, our Royal Navy dentist, quickly went to work to repay local hospitality.

The day was hot and after a week of inaction the team sweated profusely as they marched in intense heat. The trek into the jungle with guides and three cargo mules took about four hours' hard walk along a steep path that led up the mountain to a stream where they established a base camp beneath the trees. That night they lay in their tents listening to the animal calls and wondering what evidence of long-gone civilizations they might discover. The next day was indeed very productive. Unexpectedly the muleteers and their beasts refused to go further, and simply set down the loads and departed. From here all movement was to be on foot, without load carriers. The group split into two, one team looking for the main site and the other going deep into the jungle to see if they could find an Inca road that might be an outlet. Stuart went with the road group along with Rolando and Doorman, two very interesting characters. Rolando, the Colombian archaeologist mid way through a doctorate at the Sorbonne, and Doorman, a Bolivian Indian, who is, through one of life's ironies, the most aptly named individual Stuart had ever met. Sultry and wide like an ox, if they were going to meet any of the mountain lions or indeed the even more aggressive mountain boar said to live here Stuart was glad to have this bear-like figure with him. They headed due south, Doorman crashing through the vegetation like a man possessed. A routine was quickly established and they all took it in turns to pathfind and mark the trail. After four solid hours of hacking Stuart decided to stop at a clearing for a rest. In truth, all were gasping for a cigarette. As Rolando threw his machete to the ground there was a 'clink'. Uncovering the topsoil revealed rows of cobbled stones that could only be one thing: an

Inca road. In archaeological terms the discovery of a road is crucial as it invariably leads to two places of relative importance. Having plotted its position with the GPS they returned to base camp where there had also been success and the outlines of some sort of fortification had been discovered.

The next day was to prove full of surprises. The main one being that Oswaldo had decided that he must go home on urgent business. This was a blow. Although they had two other very capable archaeologists he was the senior man. Two hours after he left, a chat with Doorman revealed that he had been promised that the expedition would pay him $20 a day for his services. Although this may not sound much, the fact that one of our taxi drivers made just $1.75 a day puts it into some perspective. When Stuart told Doorman that much as he liked him there were simply not the funds for this, he too left. So on day two the team were in the middle of the jungle having lost both the senior archaeologist and the guide. They still had thirteen days to go! However, Alvaro Fernholz of DINAAR seemed quite happy to carry on.

During the night a tarantula, the size of Doorman's palm, scuttled across one girl's foot as she sought the loo pit in the darkened forest. Millipedes were everywhere and the bugs began to bite. However, hearty meals of Beanfeast, McDougall's Sweet and Sour Chicken and masses of pasta sustained them. In spite of the claustrophobic atmosphere of the forest they were a happy band.

The next few days' discoveries really kept them going. Master builder and ex-sapper Gerry Masters (brother of Jim) was tasked to clear a path from one structure in the fortress to a wall. Noticing that some stones were still fairly well arranged in the shape of a room, Gerry, a very robust, no-nonsense West Country man, decided to dig and found a piece of pottery. They had their first significant find. An Amazonian pot dating to around AD 1000. There was much more to follow as the group discovered four different types of ceramics. There was, however, to be a real heart-breaker. In the room Gerry was excavating there were the remains of several large pots and a large stone around which he had been digging. Stuart called over one of the trainee archaeologists that Oswaldo had left behind, to ask him about this rock. 'It's just a simple sandstone rock,' he said. 'Get rid of it.' On his command and using a shovel as a lever, they heaved it out of the pit. It landed face up but split into three pieces. They could then see it was a finely carved mortar, pre-Inca, dated around AD 900 – and sadly broken. The team was deeply dismayed. It was, however, repairable and is now to be one of the exhibits at the museum in Samaipata. Panting his way to the summit of the nearby mountain, sixty-four-year-old Gerry had an unforgettable view of the Andes which made the whole exercise worthwhile. 'This is the life,' he said, later admitting that he had now caught the expedition bug.

The project had resulted in the exploration of fascinating twin fortresses built by Amazon Indians penetrating the Inca highlands around AD 900. Our team had excavated the jungle-covered defences, uncovered significant buildings and found a paved Inca road. 'The discovery of pottery enables us to date the period of occupation and, by finding the Inca road, we have located the link between the mountains and the plains. This road would have joined the forts and trading posts along the eastern edge of the Andes,' commented Alvaro. The question of Inca settlements in the Santa Cruz valley had been resolved and the cultural conflict between Incas and the eastern tribes revealed. This was an important step in the development of Bolivian archaeology. Stuart's group received a well-deserved round of applause as his impromptu audio-visual show ended. Those of us who had scrambled around the mountains seeking Inka-Ossi were filled with envy. Stuart's team had also seen evidence of treasure hunters at Parabanocito and it is to be hoped that the Bolivian authorities can protect this site before, like Inka-Ossi, it is destroyed forever.

The weekend of 7–8 August passed quickly in preparation for the great day that was to see the President's arrival and the launch of the next phase of the expedition. John and Yoli visited Gravetal, a soya-producing company whose splendidly named manager, Bismarck Rosales, had paid off some of our crane hire bills. The boats' crews rehearsed again, perfecting the gyrations out on the lake that they hoped would amuse our patron. Quartermaster Billy Huxter took Jenny Sambrook as his interpreter on a shopping expedition into Brazil: food was more plentiful and varied there and Corumbá had some good *supermercados*.

John had invited Rabia Siddique, a twenty-seven-year-old Australian barrister with an Indian father, to handle the expedition's sponsorship arrangements. In practical terms this now meant that she had to sort out all the flags and stickers that companies had sent us and allocate them to the boats. Where should we fly the bold white K on a navy blue field of J. P. Knight, the towage company based in Rochester, Kent, who had sponsored the flagship and helped us so much? Where hang the banner of American Airlines, who had given us sixteen free return flights from the UK to South America and whose two representatives, Liz Willson and Andrew Rae, joined us at this very point to take part in the first few days of sailing? It was a sunny morning and Rabia spread about thirty of these emblems on the grass. Then she was bitten by a dog and had to begin a course of anti-rabies injections. ('Rabia' may be Arabic for 'spring', but her parents may not have known that it is also, ironically, Spanish for 'rabies'.)

Marinero Valencia had four roots extracted by Melissa Wingfield. The Bolivian Navy band practised 'God Save the Queen', helped by Yoli's tape of the Last Night of the Proms that had helped to extricate Richard from the Santa Cruz demo. Tarquin Cooper, whose first front-page spread on the expedition appeared this Saturday in the *Daily Telegraph* travel section, worked on his next one.

On the Saturday afternoon John led a group 40 kilometres south of Puerto Quijarro to a site previously inspected by Toby Marriner. This was Mutún, where in the hardened igneous rock floor of a valley we found fossil imprints – of a two-toed creature and a giant trilobyte. There were also star-shaped man-made carvings near a site close by, showing evidence of recent open-air religious practices.

A more alarming discovery when we returned was that John had gone an extraordinarily bright yellow colour all over. It never enters the reckoning that the expedition leader might fall sick and John has, in fact, a very good health record (malaria three times, the odd vampire bat bite – nothing too grave). Now he began to look like a quarantine flag and Noel Burrell wasn't entirely sure what might be causing it. As a first measure, Noel took him off everything, including his anti-malarials – for his extensive travels John had been taking the more controversial Lariam rather than the Avloclor/Paludrine regime that the rest of us were on. Tests by a local lady doctor who ran a chemist's shop near the barrack gates showed that John was seriously lacking sugar, so a diet of fruit, brown bread, sweet jam and glucose was prescribed; eggs, fats, milk products, chocolate, red meat and alcohol were strictly forbidden. Feeling rather less well than he dared admit, he did not look forward to several weeks of such fare. Fortunately he was still allowed his favourite *mate de coca*.

This indisposition did not deter John from seeking, together with the energetic Yoli, a long list of items still required for the trip. Fortunately the manager of the local Zona Franca (free port) had become a good friend. Bill Brady, whose father Joaquin Aguirre is a prominent Bolivian historian, was a fund of information. He had himself once tried to build a fleet of reed boats at Puerto Quijarro, with imported totora, but was thwarted when they became infested by bugs. To avoid this happening to ours, Jim washed down *Kota Mama 2* and *Viracocha* with a powerful repellent called Baygon. However, this powerful chemical did not deter the local cows, who found the totora, of which our craft was made, to their liking. A cow guard was set up to prevent the fleet from being eaten before it had even sailed!

At this time, too, some good news came from our base in Dorset: Jaime Patiño, a famously rich Bolivian and a world-renowned figure in the tin mining business, to whom John had been introduced in London by our Bahamian supporter Elodie Sandford, had agreed to give us a donation.

On the Sunday morning eight of the expedition practised drill for Monday's parade. Captain Stuart Seymour took the squad through its paces. We were all dressed in what had become the expedition uniform: lightweight army longs; olive green polo shirts from J. P. Knight, with the Kota Mama badge and the company logo – a tugboat and the Knight funnel – on the sleeve; American Airlines baseball caps. (Alternative outfits were the smart navy-blue and red AA polo shirt and, for relaxation, an Aerosur T-shirt from our friends at the Bolivian airline.)

Then came a big let-down for us – and the Bolivian Navy – when we were told that President Banzer was not, after all, flying in for Monday's ceremony. Nor was Admiral Zabala. Some of us had half expected this: Bolivians are a volatile people and what is said is not always done. Yoli, a Colombian, put it well: 'I tell you about Bolivians: when you talk to them they are having their own thoughts.' This was no mere *lapsus memoriae*, however, as the President had had more pressing business in another part of Bolivia. The parade would, of course, go on, presided over by Capitán Ernesto Roca, the base Commander.

We all assembled in a forecourt by the lake where *Kota Mama 2* was moored. A master of ceremonies introduced John and Capitán Roca. Presently a distinguished figure in brown robes came forward. This was Padre Eugenio Cantor, a Franciscan *capilian* (chaplain) *militar*, who proceeded to bless the British and Bolivian flags. The naval band's rendering of 'God Save the Queen', despite careful practice, was eccentric; but they ground their way through it twice as Pat Troy, a retired Royal Marines

CREW OF THE SUPPORT SHIP
PUERTO QUIJARRO

Fuerza Naval Boliviana
Motonave [support vessel] *Puerto Quijarro*
Waterway Paraguay–Paraná

Personnel
Crew

TF.CGON.	Martin Vaca Vaca	Captain
TF.CGON.	Raúl Ferrufino Bascope	Pilot
ALF.CGON.	Milton Morantes C.	Pilot
SGT.2DO.	Florencio Pedro Cota	Chief Engineer
SGT.INC.	Jaime Valverde C.	Engineer
SEÑOR	Joselino Benites	Engineer
MARINERO	Pilco Quispe	Able Seaman
MARINERO	Casimiro Condori C.	Able Seaman

On Commission

TN.CGON.	Carlos Cespedes	Hydrographer
SGT.1RO.	Juan Delgado	Hydrographer

Harbour Pilot

SEÑOR	Gustavo Gallardo

TF.CGON. = Teniente de Fragata Cuerpo General Operaciones Navales
TN = Teniente de Nave
SGT.INC., 2DO, 1RO = Inicial, Segundo, Primero

major who was to navigate on *Kota Mama 2*, raised the Union Flag. Then he raised the red, yellow and green of Bolivia with exemplary deliberateness, never quite stopping, as they oompahed their way with obvious familiarity and relish through all four verses of the Bolivian anthem. Our honour guard, mostly civilian, drilled magnificently – though we somehow forgot to remove headgear and shout '¡Viva Bolivia!' as planned.

John then spoke at some length. After cataloguing ways in which a people can vandalize their own heritage, he said: 'Do not forget that we are not owners of the land but merely its guardians for our children and the future.' Capitán Roca then wished us well and stressed Bolivia's need to regain an outlet to the sea in the new millennium.

It was now time to break the traditional bottle of bubbly over *Kota Mama 2*'s bows. This might have been a problem on a hull made of reeds, so the metal jetty had been thoughtfully designated. Unfortunately, someone had forgotten the champagne; but the top brass in Bolivia are used to such moments, and small groups just chatted together in cocktail party fashion for a short while as one of us, remembering that Rabia Siddique had bought a bottle, sprinted to fetch it.

'What would you like, Colonel, for your expedition?' asked María, the daughter of Señora Blanca Soria de España, President of the Santa Cruz Chamber of Hotels. A difficult one, thought John, and simply said, 'Good weather.' A little later ten cases of Agua Mineral Natural Santa Ines arrived on board. She had misheard him, but the water proved a godsend.

The ceremony over, we were ready to go. 'Anchors aweigh!' shouted John. Jim reminded him that we had none. The only anchor we could find in the naval base was so vast it would have made our flagship seriously nose-heavy. *Kota Mama 2* and *Viracocha* cast off and moved away to the sound of clicking cameras, purring videos and the Navy band playing 'The Animals Went in Two by Two'.

The support team walked over to the *Puerto Quijarro*. We had moved our gear on board and slung our hammocks earlier that morning. Now the crew were standing ready. At 11.20 a.m. the captain, Teniente de Fragata Martin Vaca Vaca, gave orders to cast off. It was for us a historic moment. Amid beatific smiles all round, we continued to wave to our many Bolivian friends as the naval base slowly receded.

'All those months of work,' said Shaun Linsley, 'and now it's actually happening.'

CHAPTER TWELVE

THROUGH
THREE
COUNTRIES

You could stay a long time in Corumbá.

RICHARD GOTT,
Land without Evil, 1993

*Corumbá appeared to be a lazy, pleasant little town. The streets were
paved and wide and lined with trees. Merchants sat in the shade of
their forefronts . . . chatting with each other. Teenagers darted through
traffic on scooters. Barefoot children ate ice cream at sidewalk tables.*

JOHN GRISHAM,
The Testament, 1999

For most of us, there was a sense of unreality as
Kota Mama 2, propelled by its 15 hp Mariner outboard motor,
and *Viracocha Spirit of Bahamas*, bravely sailing, made their way
down the Canal de Tamengo. This serpentine watercourse is the
umbilical cord which links the Lago de Cáceres to the Río
Paraguay, and it has always been regarded as a very unsatisfac-
tory gateway. In 1911 the French explorer Paul Walle said:
'Sometimes the water flows from the bay to the river and sometimes from the river to the bay, according to the season.' Banks
of water hyacinth on our port hand, their rubbery dark green
stems and leaves bobbing in our wake, had changed little since
his time: '[The lake] is full of floating masses formed of algae and

Through three countries

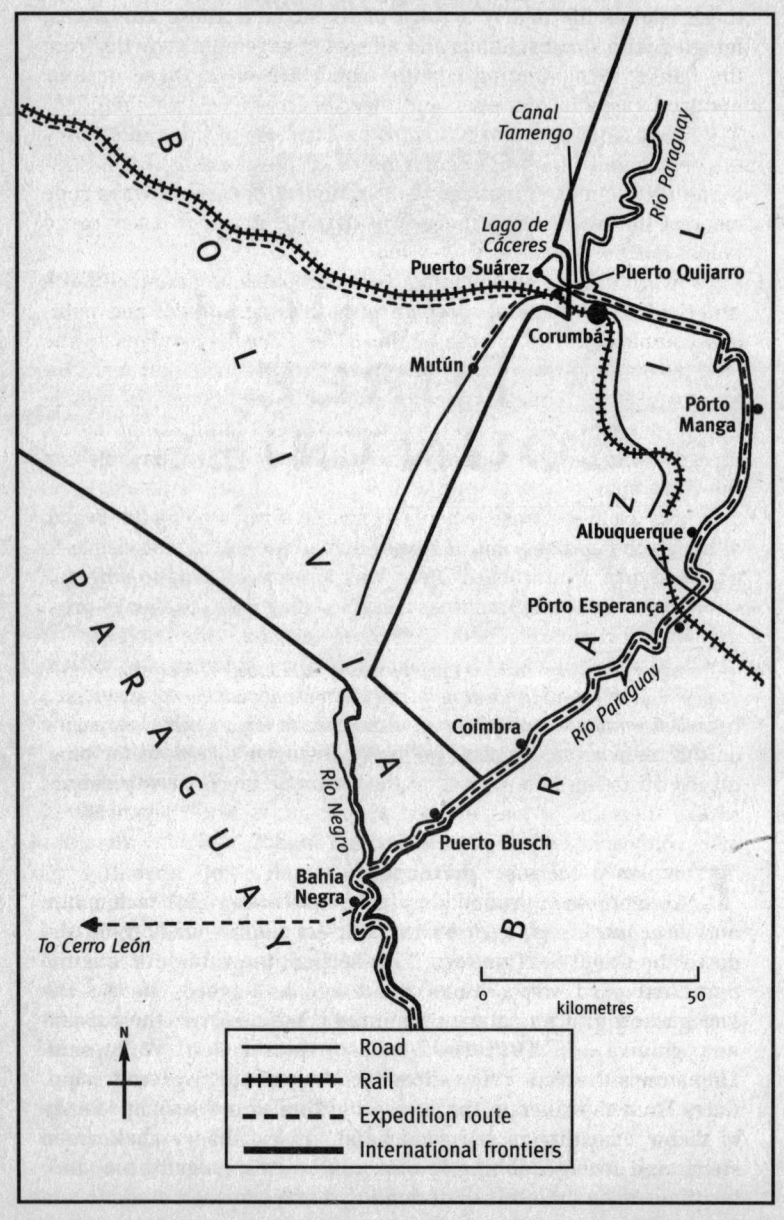

Canal Tamengo

Río Paraguay

Lago de Cáceres

Puerto Suárez

Puerto Quijarro

Corumbá

Mutún

Pôrto Manga

B O L I V I A

Albuquerque

Pôrto Esperança

P A R A G U A Y

B R A Z I L

Coimbra

Río Paraguay

Río Negro

Puerto Busch

Bahía Negra

To Cerro León

0   50
kilometres

N

—————— Road
++++++++ Rail
- - - - - Expedition route
━━━━━━ International frontiers

weeds known as *camelotes*. In the bay, which is covered with these islands for nearly a third of its surface, these *camelotes*, mingled with shrubs, lianas and all sort of vegetable growths from the banks, form floating islands which are often three or four hundred yards in diameter and more than twelve feet thick.'

Richard Gott said that Bolivians had the use of this outlet 'only for very small boats at certain times of the year', but the 303-tonne *PQ* seemed to manage well enough. Her bows always rode clear of the water since there was virtually nothing in her cargo holds, but her stern drew 3–4 feet.

We were moving slowly into a very odd portion of central South America's river system, a region of both geographical and political complexity. The course of the River Paraguay bulges to the east here and we were about to enter entirely Brazilian territory for about 210 kilometres, before reuniting with a part of Bolivia that projected like a wedge, on our starboard hand. Then, at the junction with the Río Negro, we would come to Paraguay, also on the right side only.

It was easy to sense when we passed from Bolivia to Brazil, although the actual point, if it was demarcated, was not visible to us. Suddenly, to starboard there was a stone esplanade with tall street lights and smart summer villas, exuding a definite air of prosperity and urban pride. Soon the strange arched bridge that carries Corumbá's water supply from a point in the middle of the stream came into view, and the broad Paraguay, with its burden of *camelotes* from the Pantanal in the north, swung in on the left. We were now on the main river. By noon *PQ* had passed under the water pipe, turned upstream and moored at the Corumbá quayside. We did not realize then that it was the last proper quayside for hundreds of miles: only smashed wooden jetties and muddy banks lay ahead as far south as Concepción in Paraguay.

KM2 approached and made a generously wide and rather late turn into the fastish current. Stuart McCallion, standing on the port-side projecting platform, gunned up the outboard engine. Ben Cartwright drove the Avon hard into the reed boat's stern and pushed. For an agonizing minute it seemed that the current was winning and *KM2* would have to moor lower downstream. Then, on maximum revs, she edged towards the mother ship. Gerry Masters waited in the bows with a coiled mooring line ready to throw. Able hands waited on *PQ*'s deck. The two helmsmen stood high aft on *KM2*'s bridge leaning on their steering oars like two figures on a Greek *krater*.

Gerry threw the line and dentist Graham McElhinney caught it. Navigator Pat Troy's head shot out of the cabin window. 'Take it forrard! Take it forrard!' he shouted. Graham cantered up the steel deck. 'Don't make it fast yet!' shouted Chris Brogan, the skipper. An aft line spiralled on to *PQ* and was caught. 'Tie it off now, Graham,' said Gerry Masters. 'Not yet, not yet!' said Pat Troy, beard a-bristle. 'Make fast the aft line,' came another voice. Jim Masters, Admiral of the Fleet, leaned phlegmatically against the cabin door. It seemed that everyone else was in charge.

Corumbá, founded in 1778 by the Portuguese as a defensive western bastion, was an impressive place, built on the top of high rock cliffs facing north – a natural site. In 1875 Marion Mulhall and her husband noticed the powerful fort, with guns pointing north, west and south. There were good shops even then and they found that great South American invention, the hammock, in this case made in Manchester. But not everyone liked it. Henry Grey, an Englishman sent to manage a Bolivian rubber plantation in 1911, reached Corumbá after covering 2,000 miles in the steamer *Cuyaba* in eleven and three-quarter days. 'The accommodation', he said, 'was comfortable but the food was execrable.' It was mid-August and the heat in the Hotel Galileo was oppressive: 'Lying on the bed under the mosquito net, I thought it would be a pleasant change to try the cool marble floor. Switching on the electric light with this idea in mind I was horrified to see the number and variety of insects that were crawling about the floor. Among them . . . the large tarantula.' Grey also noted the town's cosmopolitan character, with shipping offices run by Germans, French, Italians, Belgians, Spanish, Portuguese, British and Americans. Their ornate late nineteenth-century houses still lend Corumbá some distinction.

Theodore Roosevelt came in 1913 (expressing the same views of the same hotel), and Colonel Percy Fawcett in 1920. Julian Duguid, whose bestseller about this part of the world, *Green Hell*, was published in 1931, called Corumbá 'the most unpleasant place I ever saw'. The heat seems to have got to all of them, and whether or not it is just a case of everyone reading everyone else's travel books, they all tell the story of a local hotelier proving he could fry eggs on the pavement.

Teddy Roosevelt was met by town bands and civic dignitaries on river steamers and escorted into Corumbá. But then, he had been President of the United States just four years earlier. We rated a visit from the Vigilancia Sanitaria, three or four blue-overalled officials who inspected *PQ*'s loos and storerooms and didn't seem too pleased with them. Still, the Head of Tourism came too, and crowds of friendly townsfolk, fascinated by the reed boats, plied us with questions which Yoli, who does not speak Portuguese, managed to translate. A travel agent gave up his afternoon to drive John to the shops for stores and equipment and to the post office to send off the first batch of specially over-stamped postcards to sponsors, each one bearing the message 'Carried aboard the flagship *Kota Mama 2*'.

Like Roosevelt, we admired Corumbá's tree-lined streets, scrupulously swept; we saw its fine plaza, with a statue of General Coelho, Brazilian victor of an 1867 battle in the War of the Triple Alliance against Paraguay, and a brightly painted steamroller built by Marshall and Sons & Co. of Gainsborough and London. Then it was evening, and we had to tear ourselves away from Corumbá and its multi-hued inhabitants. Stuart Seymour organized a night guard, an hour at a time, because the port area was ungated and much desirable kit lay on deck. The last man on watch glanced down at the raft of *camelotes* that had become wedged overnight between *PQ* and *KM2*. A metre-long silvery snake arched up from among them and tried to slither on board.

Dawn was as magical as sunset had been. Olivaceous cormorants rested between bouts of fishing; southern screamers and yellow-billed terns zoomed about. And up the Paraguay, towards the Pantanal, roared a steady stream of *pescadores*: for Corumbá is a tourist destination for sport fishermen as well as a well-run, characterful town attracting visitors in its own right. The hunters come to the Pantanal for *dorado* (Portuguese: *dourado*), a superb fish which goes golden when dead and is a sort of South American salmon, spawning in the Atlantic and swimming all the way up to the Mato Grosso. From here until well into Paraguay we were kept company by noisy speedboats driven by baseball-capped, life-jacketed fishing enthusiasts, most of them Japanese, whose lodges are springing up fast along the Paraguay's banks.

On Tuesday 10 August *KM2* left Corumbá at 7 a.m. and *PQ* half an hour later. There was plenty to see on our way out of the town: its industrial suburbs, its white-walled Fort Limoeiro, its shipyards and, later, its opencast iron mines. It is for the iron ore, among other things, that the trains of barges come, pushed upstream by the powerful *empujadores* or 'pushers' owned by a variety of companies, Paraguayan, Argentinian and Brazilian – like Cinco Bacia, proprietors of our own *PQ*.

The actual route we took down the broad River Paraguay was determined either by *PQ*'s Bolivian officers or by *KM2*'s navigator, Pat Troy, or by all of them in consultation. Pat is a man steeped in Royal Marines lore, full of sagas from service life; a very competent seafarer, he lives in Jersey, where he keeps a yacht in St Helier. The charts he was now using on *KM2* were twenty-five years old, and the arrangement was that he and Captain Martin would update them every evening in the light of the day's experience. Pat pointed out that they were stamped 'Empurrador Tracey E. Jones'. Interestingly, we almost immediately passed the *Tracey E. Jones* in a dry dock.

It was a gorgeous, sunny morning, our first on the river proper, tinged with golden promise of a unique journey to come. White-rumped swallows dipped about, sometimes cheekily settling on *PQ*'s foredeck. The trees on the banks, often over 100 metres away from the river's centre line, sported a profusion of pink flowers. One of us, settling down with Graham Greene's *Travels with my Aunt* (which is set at its end in Paraguay) read: 'One long avenue was lined with oranges and trees bearing rose-coloured flowers, which I learnt later to be *lapachos*.' There were also occasional strands of trees in bright yellow flower: tajy amarillo, we were told, or *Tabebuia chysantha*.

Quite a few of us – Jim Masters in his cabin on *KM2*, Ben Cartwright in the Avon inflatable, John and Richard on *PQ* – had a distinct sense of *déjà vu*. The Río Paraguay looked uncannily like the Zaire (Congo) river, which these four, and two still to join us, had navigated in giant inflatables in 1974–5: clumps of water hyacinth floating by, distant banks hung with primeval tropical vegetation, limitless swampy flatlands beyond.

Soon to become a familiar sight leaning over the rail of *PQ*'s upper deck in his white ducks was thirty-five-year-old Teniente Carlos Cespedes, a Bolivian Navy hydrographer. His task was to gather intelligence about the river: its depth, width, rate of flow, bankside installations and the like. Similarly employed, but for a foreign government, and a century and a half before, was Captain Thomas Page, United States Navy. In 1853 he sailed up the Paraguay in a paddle steamer called *Water Witch*, with instructions to survey the tributaries above the Río de la Plata and carry out scientific and agricultural studies. Edward Hopkins, a young American diplomat assigned to Paraguay in the 1840s, had returned to New York and lectured on the commercial potential of the upper part of the river. It was this that encouraged the US Navy to send Page. He met Hopkins in Asunción but got on rather better with President Carlos Antonio López, who gave permission for the onward journey but forbade him to leave Paraguayan waters. Page was fascinated by the native tribes of the Chaco and formed a very rose-tinted view of the possibilities of the area for development by European immigrants. So attracted was he that he steamed on into Brazil and to Corumbá, which surprisingly he found in 1853 as yet a very forlorn settlement. His breach of López's instructions soured Paraguayan–US relations for some time; but no doubt he delivered a full rivers survey to his naval superiors. Teniente Cespedes was certainly able to give a thorough technical report to his in La Paz after the Kota Mama expedition.

The battle of loos (not the 1915 one) was quickly won by the ladies. There were two aft on *PQ*'s lower deck (none, of course, on the reed boats) and it was agreed that our eight females should luxuriate in the sole use of one of them, with its shower, while the men – thirty-six of them including the Bolivian crew – queued impatiently for the other. This old-fashioned gallantry soon broke down when confronted with the practicalities of daily life: men about to take off for a long stint on the reed boats, or returning from one filthy and exhausted, needed a cold douche urgently; so later on both loos became unisex.

Our second day afloat was a good one: 90 kilometres run, mostly on engines. *PQ* tied up to a few trees and *KM2* and *Viracocha* tagged on outside her. As the mooring lines were being secured, a movement in the river caught John's eye. Through binoculars he saw an extraordinary sight: a small horse appeared to be swimming towards them from the far bank. He questioned Captain Martin, who corrected him. 'No, Coronel, it is *capyvara*.' And indeed it was. Quite unconcerned by all the activity, a capybara, the world's largest rodent, paddled past, pulled its body, the size of a sheep, up the bank, shook water from its fur and gave these visitors to its swampy domain an inquisitive stare before ambling off into the undergrowth. Mosquitoes came in with a vengeance at 5.30 p.m., but by 6.30 they had fled to the darkness. Frogs croaked to order, like sound effects on a BBC2 wildlife feature. Three caimans (caimen?) took up station in the lee of *PQ*'s bows and we periodically wandered up to stare at the orange glow of their eyes. John, an enthusiastic animal lover, returned to his

wooden-walled *sala de operaciones* to read up about this creature, the crocodile of South America, and its reptilian colleagues.

The Admiral of the Fleet must have temporarily forgotten the
disposition of his ships, for when Jim got up in the middle of the
night and stood on the starboard planking looking out over the
river, plaintive voices came up from Luke Cox and Melissa
Wingfield on *Viracocha* below him: 'You're not going to pee on
us, are you?'

Day three and the sun was a livid red orb, rising from a tropical forest fringe.

'Just like in Scotland,' said Billy Huxter, with a leap of his
imagination.

During the morning, in an effort to be heard above the constant
thrum of the ship's generator, John borrowed *PQ*'s loudhailer but,
mercifully, it didn't work.

'Owain,' he shouted, 'can you fix this thing for me?'

Apparently, he had dug out two loudhailers from the stores at
Motcombe, but as a result of some subterfuge neither was packed.
Stuart Seymour and Billy had been sent off to price and buy one
in Corumbá but to everyone's relief none could be found. Owain
even managed to fail to make the ship's one work. It was not
until Concepción that John could acquire one of his favourite
means of waking everybody up in the morning. This he did with
military ditties recalled from his days as a private soldier. Later
he would quote Kipling, sing snatches of rousing hymns or read
snippets from the New Testament that he has always carried since
the Zaire River expedition.

However, on this day, Wednesday 11 August, with a good sailing
wind freshening from the north-east, the crews needed little
persuasion to be off. At 7.30 a.m. the reed boats swung out into
the current and hoisted sail. They were a magnificent sight and
Ben Cartwright was soon carrying our photographers around the
fleet in the Avon. The barometer was rising and the temperature
quickly reached 95°F. Those not engaged in sailing, or helping
Billy Huxter to sort out the stores in the aft hold, spread themselves on the deck until it was too hot to bear.

At Pôrto Manga a car ferry brought vehicles over to the
Corumbá road. Anything man-made in this stretch was remarked
upon, but it was the prolific wildlife which mainly held our attention on these first days: a caiman basking on the bank, big brown
capybaras munching grasses above it. Pale-necked heron
abounded, and ringed woodpeckers, but the prince of birds was

the jabirú: a stork, black, white and vast, apt to stand on the tops of trees like a television aerial. This was the place for exotic avifauna – the zone-tailed buzzard, the crested caracara, the anhinga or snakebird with its S-shaped neck and long yellow beak.

Photographer Charles Sturge, Graham McElhinney and Shaun Linsley began fishing from the stern end of *PQ*. Their catch could never be big enough to feed the whole expedition, but it could provide a *bonne-bouche* for a few. They pulled in piranha (very bony eating), small *surubí* weighing up to 13 kg or 28 lb (these catfish can grow to an enormous size), *pintado* (not the Cape pigeon, but a fish), *dorado* and *paraputanga* (delicious).

Large islands began to divide the stream, reminding us again of the Congo, and sometimes *PQ* would go one way and *KM*2 the other. We stopped for petrol at the small town and fishing station of Albuquerque and shortly afterwards some construction workers, sinking a caisson for a new road bridge, tooted their ship's siren in salute. The first big landmark enabling us all to pinpoint our exact position – Pat Troy had his own GPS and could do this at any time – was the existing rail bridge at Pôrto Esperança. This had been completed in the 1950s when Brazil finally honoured earlier promises to continue the line into Bolivia. Before then, travellers detrained at the rail terminus, Pôrto Esperança, struggled with their baggage to a shallop in which they were rowed out to a waiting steamer for the slow run upriver to Corumbá.

Albuquerque, a little way to the north where the Río Miranda joins the Paraguay, and Pôrto Esperança have always been natural crossing points for travellers journeying east–west from Brazil over the northern Chaco via Chiquitos to the foothills of the Bolivian Andes. There is every likelihood that this was also the way early west–east traders came, perhaps to launch off down-river to the sea.

It was here that the first European ever to enter these parts had crossed the river. Aleixo García, a Portuguese, made an astonishing journey from the Atlantic coast of Brazil to the fringes of the Inca empire in 1524. He was probably a crew member with Juan Diaz de Solís, the first European discoverer in 1516 of the Río de la Plata, which he called El Mar Dulce, 'the freshwater sea'. The expedition was attacked in Uruguay and returned to Spain but some ships, including presumably García's, were ship-wrecked off Santa Catarina in Brazil. Courageously, Aleixo García and some fellow sailors went inland, learnt Guaraní, the principal

A PARAGUAYAN CHRONOLOGY

1524	Aleixo García is the first European to cross Paraguay
1526	Sebastian Cabot sails up Paraná and Paraguay to Asunción
1537	Asunción founded by Domingo de Irala
1544	Alvar Nuñez Cabeza de Vaca overthrown by coup
1609	Jesuit missionaries first in Paraguay
1620	Asunción ceases to be principal Spanish city in central South America
1631	Mission at Trinidad del Paraná founded
1685	Mission at Jesus de Tavarangúe founded
1767	King Charles III of Spain orders expulsion of Jesuits
1775	Franciscan church at Yaguarón built
1811	INDEPENDENCE
1811	Fulgencio Yegros and Dr José Gaspar Rodríguez de Francia in charge
1816–40	Dr Rodríguez is 'El Supremo', dictator for life; Paraguay sealed off from rest of world
1840–4	Confusion
1844–62	President Carlos Antonio López; Paraguay opens up to world
late 1850s	Building of Central Paraguay Railway begun
1862–70	President Francisco Solano López; Paraguay on war footing
1864–70	War of the Triple Alliance (Paraguay vs Brazil, Uruguay, Argentina)
1870–1932	Thirty-two presidents (two assassinated), six coups, two revolutions, eight attempted revolutions
1886–93	Elisabeth Nietzsche at Nueva Germania
1890s	Argentinian Carlos Casado acquires land in Chaco
1880s–1961	British build and run railways
1927	First Mennonites arrive in Chaco from Canada
1932–5	Chaco War (Paraguay vs Bolivia)

1954–89	President Alfredo Stroessner heads a dictatorship
1961	Railways nationalized
1966–91	Itaipú dam built
1967	Chaco ceases to be a military zone
1989–93	General Andres Rodríguez (President 1991–3)
1991	Paraguay joins Mercosur, the South American common market
1993–8	President Juan Carlos Wasmosy
1998–9	President Raul Cubas
1999–	President Luis Gonzalez Macchi

Indian language of Paraguay, heard of the distant existence of gold and silver, came down the Río Miranda and crossed the Paraguay at a place called San Fernando, which was most probably today's Albuquerque.

He then marched with a scratch army of 2,000 Guaraní Indians through the swamps of the northern Chaco to a point near the Inca city of Chuquisaca (now Sucre, the Bolivian legislative capital). He loaded up with silver, copper, jewellery and cloth and returned to the Paraguay, where he sent two Portuguese colleagues ahead to the Atlantic coast with the good news. It is through them that we know his story; for Aleixo García, waiting by the river, was butchered by Indians. He was the first transcontinental traveller and it had been a stupendous achievement.

'About noon we passed the highest point which the old Spanish conquistadores and explorers, Irala and Ayolas, had reached in the course of their marvellous journeys.' So wrote Theodore Roosevelt of the time in 1914 when he steamed up past Pôrto Esperança. Juan de Ayolas arrived here on Candlemas Day, 2 February 1537, and so he called it Puerto de la Candelaria. He had been second-in-command to Pedro de Mendoza, the first founder, in 1535, of Buenos Aires, and had taken over when Mendoza, riddled with syphilis, sailed home to Spain. Juan de Ayolas, with his colleague Domingo de Irala, immediately had eight shallow-draught ships built and sailed up the Paraná and the Paraguay. He founded Asunción in 1537 and took three ships and 175 men on up to La Candelaria in the territory of the friendly

Payaguas Indians, the first Spanish conquistador to reach these parts. Following in the steps of Aleixo García, after a few days he set off for Peru.

News had reached Spain of Francisco Pizarro's defeat of Atahualpa, his conquest of the Incas three years previously and subsequent acquisition of unimaginable wealth in gold and silver. It had been Mendoza's plan, and was now Ayolas's, to reach the source of all this wealth from the east, via the river that Sebastian Cabot in 1529 had renamed, somewhat optimistically, Río de la Plata – 'river of silver'.

Domingo de Irala stayed behind to guard the base at La Candelaria while Juan de Ayolas, guided by an Indian who claimed to have been García's slave thirteen years before and with an army of 300 Payaguas porters, marched over the northern Chaco, crossed the Río Grande and reached the foothills of the eastern cordillera of the Andes. He built a fort but had to fight several battles with Indians on his way back with his gold and silver to La Candelaria. To his consternation, Domingo de Irala was not there.

A shortage of food had driven Irala to retreat to Asunción. An old Spanish friend of his, a shipmate in the original Mendoza armada, had come upriver to visit him. The firing of a cannonade of welcome had scared off the Payaguas, Irala's main food suppliers, and they had not come back. He returned to La Candelaria twice more and was both times driven back to Asunción. He made a final effort in 1539 only to discover that Juan de Ayolas, like Aleixo García before him, had in the meantime been murdered.

As we slid below the box girder railway bridge and took our pictures of the neat little Brazilian town of Pôrto Esperança, we paused to remember these frantic comings and goings and to reflect that it was from this place that the first great westward marches from the Paraguay river to the Andes had been made.

Although the current at this point was only 2.6 kph, we had to admire the skill and tenacity of these early navigators who tacked or perhaps man-hauled their clumsy wooden caravels into the interior of the continent. *Viracocha* was having difficulty maintaining direction in the fluctuating wind and kept drifting to the bank. 'Why don't you use your dagger boards?' asked John over the walkie-talkie, but skipper Luke Cox was determined to prove that he could sail without. However, it did make us wonder how the ancient reed boat sailors might have managed.

'Perhaps they simply used reed craft to go downstream,' suggested Richard, 'and made dugout canoes to come back. There would be plenty of timber for them to use, and the reeds would certainly have begun to rot in the time they would have taken waiting for favourable northerly winds to carry them down.'

'We have 2,600 kilometres to go to find out,' said Graham who, resting from his dental duties, was helping to navigate *PQ*.

Domingo de Irala survived, and in 1542 sailed with three ships and ninety-three men further upriver past the site of Corumbá to find a new route to the west. He reached Lake Gaíba, another of the curious lacustrine appendices, like Lake Cáceres, the western parts of which belong rather uselessly to Bolivia. Irala thrashed through the swamps for three days but had to retire in the face of rising waters.

Five years later Irala himself got to Peru from San Fernando. He left behind a well-provisioned, stockaded base camp guarded by forty Spaniards, and with 250 others fought his way across swamp and desert and over the Río Grande. An unexpected shock awaited him: Spanish-speaking Indians led him to a Spanish official in Cochabamba. The Inca were defeated. Upper Peru with its mines had fallen to other Spaniards from Lima in the north. In 1549 he returned, empty-handed save for a couple of thousand slaves, to Albuquerque.

The town grew and prospered, serviced by its friendly Indians. It narrowly missed having something permanent to show for it: in 1766 Albuquerque was set to have had a Jesuit mission, but the Jesuits were expelled from South America in the following year by the Spanish king, Charles III.

On 11 August 1999, resplendent in the topee specially made for him by Lock's, John had gone ashore at Albuquerque with Yoli to meet Brazilian officials. The following day, with ever stronger winds blowing perversely from the wrong quarter, thus inhibiting sailing, we motored on. The geography of the next few miles began to confuse.

'Is it still Brazil both sides?'

'Yes, until after Fort Coimbra, then Bolivia comes in on the right.'

'We should see Puerto Busch and some Bolivian naval presence. I've seen on a map that there's a railway, or maybe a canal, projected to run to it. It could become as big as Puerto Quijarro.'

'Wow! Stand by, world!'

The surrounding country was becoming hillier. Suddenly, round

a bend, there appeared a large white fort dominating a spur
running down to the starboard bank: Fort Coimbra, Brazil's
defence against dastardly Paraguayans coming upriver. They had
not done so since late 1864, when President Francisco Solano
López launched his first campaign of the Triple Alliance War.
Transports carrying 3,000 men and two field batteries, and towing
two flat-bottomed gunboats each sporting an 8-incher, set off
northwards from Asunción under Coronel Vicente Barrios, the
President's brother-in-law. Another force, cavalry and infantry,
was marching in parallel up the eastern bank from Concepción.
Coimbra, though its 14 foot high stone scarps seemed barely preg-
nable, soon fell to Barrios. The fort's elderly commander, Coronel
Hermenegildo Portocarrero, survived one day's assault, but stole
away with all his men in the ensuing night. Unspiked guns,
powder, ammunition all fell to the Paraguayans. It was their first,
most glorious, but almost only victory in this bloody six-year war.
Barrios pressed on to capture forts at Albuquerque and Corumbá,
but his successes in the Mato Grosso campaign brought President
López no strategic gains, though the captured war *matériel* proved
valuable.

Today at Coimbra there are cannon, ancient and modern, and
a large football pitch for budding Rivaldos, but very little movement in these more peaceful times. Four hundred Brazilians had
defended the fort in 1864. A century later, the place had played
a big part in the epic solo journey in an Avon Redcat inflatable
boat made in 1964 by Robin Hanbury-Tenison from the River
Orinoco in Venezuela to Buenos Aires. He had no Brazilian visa
and so passed Corumbá on a Saturday night to avoid alerting
customs and immigration. But later on he had to get out of Brazil,
with equal stealth, past Fort Coimbra. He hid behind an island
opposite this last Brazilian outpost and waited until nightfall
before cooking his supper, but an armed patrol boat saw him and
picked him up. Hanbury-Tenison, then flaxen-haired and an Old
Etonian of considerable charm, so impressed the sergeant
arresting him that he was invited to dinner by the Commandant
and the following day breakfasted and lunched in the officers'
wardroom. The Brazilians, characteristically laid back, let him go
and wished him well. We identified the island where he hid, and
after the evening briefing Richard gave a short resumé of Robin's
journeys.

As we waited for Bolivia to come up on the right-hand bank,
the noon sun drove people on *PQ* underneath a large metal canopy

over part of the deck. There was some competition for shade on one or other of the wooden benches that Noel Burrell had made, or on one of the white plastic chairs that some of us had bought in Corumbá. On his last expedition in 1547 the sixty-year-old Domingo de Irala had been offered the three daughters of a Guaycurus chief. Richard and Noel, recalling Corumbá and the half-hour they had spent in a street café watching some of its more attractive girls pass by, lamented the passing of this pleasant custom.

Eighty kilometres downstream of Fort Coimbra we reached that putrid, insect-ridden wedge of swamp that stretches from the Bolivian Chaco to touch the Paraguay river. As usual, John woke before dawn. Jim Masters was already up, trying to light the Coleman stove. 'Bloody wind,' he growled as the gas flame died for the third time. In the pitch black they felt the biting chill, and the wild flapping of the SES flag against its pole told them the wind had gone round to the south and was rising fast. White-topped waves were breaking against *KM2*'s hull, bringing groans from those still struggling to sleep. The barometer was plummeting and the temperature had dropped dramatically.

'It's the scirocco and that means a punch from the south,' said Yoli, who also rose early and had already talked to *PQ*'s crew.

'No sailing today,' moaned Jim, peering into the grey dawn.

This was our introduction to the foul weather for which the Paraguay is notorious. Most of us had come expecting a semi-tropical climate, and few had the heavy duty clothing that today's conditions demanded. Former members of the 1998 phase pulled out their Henri-Lloyd yachting gear, and the boats' crews borrowed warm garments from those travelling on *PQ*. Pushed by the faithful Avon, *Kota Mama 2* took *Viracocha* in tow and then, using her own steering motor as well, managed to make some headway into the gale.

We re-entered Bolivia almost without realizing it, alerted by a single pyramidal concrete pillar on the starboard bank, one of a series erected on the border with Brazil by a Boundary Commission between 1957 and 1962; and we passed Puerto Busch only distantly, just glimpsing the remains of a huge dry dock given by the Argentinians in 1970.

President Banzer had told John how, as a young officer, he had escorted three German geologists from Puerto Quijarro to Puerto Busch.

'We had to wade up to our waists in water for a week,' he said.

'The geologists thought they would die, the mosquitoes were unbelievably bad and there were snakes everywhere. When we reached the outpost they refused to march back with me. We waited a long time before getting a lift home up the river.'

John had wanted to visit this godforsaken station and Captain Martin had supplies for the small Bolivian Navy guard, but by now the river was being whipped into a fury of small white-crested waves. This was no place to stop. Through binoculars we watched the shivering *marinero* dip his flag in response to our salute as we sailed by. It was perhaps fitting that the outpost had been named after a president who shot himself after an all-night party.

We looked next for the Río Negro, a stream coming in on the right which forms the border between Bolivia and Paraguay. John wanted to do a recce up it to assess its navigability. Somehow in the wind and spray we could not find it. Pat Troy must have been having an off day.

It was, in fact, Friday 13 August and the superstitious among us had so far been having the kind of time they expected: Noel had fumbled the casting off of *KM2* in the morning, causing the reed boat to drive straight into a bed of water hyacinth; the strong south wind continued, buffeting our boats' noses; we had not yet become used to high winds and this one carried away a few items left on deck, including a recently purchased plastic food storage box. It was rough. *KM2* and *Viracocha* pitched and lurched, and on *PQ* most hands stayed below. We only managed to run 45 kilometres all day.

In mid-afternoon each day, instead of following the reed boats in stately procession, *PQ* would forge ahead of them and look for a mooring. About 4.30 p.m. Captain Martin, consulting his charts for depth and heading towards the deeper shore, would select a clump of stout trees and run *PQ* into the bank so that his men could leap on to land with machetes and tie up to two or three of them. The reed boats then followed in alongside. Today when we moored, although the wind had now eased a little, the temperature was only 62°F after the previous day's 100°F, so a wood party got a fire going on shore. Everyone washed and changed into long trousers and long-sleeved shirts for the nightly strafing by mosquitoes; supper was cooked and scoffed. John's evening briefing prepared us for our entry into Paraguay the next day. We had heard the magical name of Bahía Negra, Paraguay's northernmost town, and we waited for tomorrow with keen curiosity. What would we find in this isolated settlement?

Monocled old Nazis drinking schnapps at café tables to the strains of Horst Wessel on a cracked 78?

It turned out that we had passed the Río Negro and at this moment were already on Paraguayan soil. We had said a final goodbye to Bolivia after just 40 kilometres of it. Richard thought it appropriate, after the briefing, to tell the story of a remarkable Bolivian, Ramiro Carrasco Quiroga, a former university lecturer in La Paz and Oruro. In 1992, tired of working for the World Bank and growing sceptical about the usefulness of government in general, he took off from Puerto Suárez in a reed boat the size of our *Viracocha* but without the mast. He paddled it alone down the Río Paraguay for 1,380 kilometres, all the way to Asunción. Without charts he frequently became lost in the maze of creeks and lagoons. One stretch that we ran in three days took him twenty-six. Twice his totora boat became waterlogged and broke up under him. He once spent sixty-two hours without remission paddling past banks of water hyacinth looking for something solid to tie up to. A visionary, perhaps also an eccentric, he tried to continue the journey in 1994 from Asunción, but his final boat collapsed somewhere near Formosa in Argentina. Why did he do this at the age of sixty-six? He left a note pinned to a tree at each campsite explaining his purpose: to draw attention to Bolivia's need for an outlet to the sea by flying the red, yellow and green all the way down to the Atlantic. This the Bolivian Navy saw as our purpose, too.

CHAPTER THIRTEEN

TROUBLED WATERS

An island surrounded by land.

AUGUSTO ROA BASTOS
Novelist, on Paraguay

Liquid spinal cord of my country.

HELIO VERA
Essayist, on the Paraguay river

As the days went by we all became very friendly with one another. Tarquin became Tarks, Rabia became Rabs and Melissa Mel. We began to borrow freely among ourselves: money, film, books, cutlery (spoons are always the first things to go communal on an expedition). This was natural, with many of us sleeping and eating in, on or around the mother support ship. Exactly where we slept often depended on the weather. Most of us had fixed abodes and the *KM2* crew tended to sleep aboard their own boat, but some people moved their billets on an almost nightly basis like paranoid dictators.

Equally naturally there was some pairing off, noticed fairly early on by most of us but not commented on at first. This sometimes has a disturbing and divisive effect on other members of a team. John never likes it and on a large expedition can easily despatch one partner on an important mission far away from the other, or send them both packing. Fortunately, there are always a number of small reconnaissances which need carrying out. In any case, the expedition was not much disrupted by its inevitable quota of romance; the rest of us passed rapidly from amused interest to acceptance, and on we all went.

There was some rivalry between the reed boats' crews and the rest. They were, after all, sailing the damn things (or, most often, motoring them) on a day-by-day basis. And they looked like boats' crews, striding about in the hot weather in a state of semi-undress, exuding machismo. Gerry Masters, John Teague, Chris Brogan, Stuart McCallion and Luke Cox began to take on the air of Viking seafarers – especially after they bought some plastic Norse helmets in Asunción, horned and silvered and good for a joke photograph. Working dress was very casual, sometimes bizarre: Tomas Hughes would disappear for long periods, then emerge walking jauntily along in a flimsy pair of black shorts and sleeveless black T-shirt, with a wristwatch round his left ankle – more the pirate than the Viking. Luke sported the battered leather hat he had worn on the 1998 expedition, Billy Huxter regularly appeared in his royal-blue Rangers football strip, and there was a fair sprinkling of ARMY – BE THE BEST T-shirts.

We all dressed very smartly and fairly uniformly, however, for our arrival in Bahía Negra. There was still, on the morning of 14 August, a viciously high wind. The recce to the Río Negro was cancelled and the fleet sailed at 8.30 a.m., *Viracocha*, with Luke Cox, Erik Catari and Jenny Sambrook as crew, relishing the crosswind. *KM2* always needed a following wind, but *Viracocha*, with its gaff rig, could nip along with the wind on the beam. And nip along we did. It was the coldest, most blustery day so far: the temperature in Brazil had been up to 100°F in the shade, but at dawn on this day the cold air from Patagonia had brought the thermometer down to 54°F; even at 9.30 a.m., as we butted along through the waves to the low, white buildings on Bahía Negra's riverfront, it was only 62°F.

The townsfolk were lined up, an impressive number of them. The pretty red, white and blue Paraguayan flags snapped in the breeze. Stuart Seymour had ordered out the whole complement of *PQ*, and we fell in rather too close to the rail-less edge of the deck – hoping *not* to fall in. As the ship swung round we leaned forward perilously into the gale like circus clowns with elongated boots. Banners of welcome on shore threatened to take off as naval ratings shot up a succession of firecrackers. A forward mooring rope, urgently thrown, almost scythed down a part of our lined-up guard. It was all a bit chaotic, but in the teeth of the scirocco we had to admire the crews' skill in mooring at all.

The Paraguayan naval station pulled out the necessary stops. Their patrol boat, *P08*, dressed overall, escorted in the reed boats. On shore waited Stuart, Yoli and Melissa, who had gone ahead the previous day in *PQ*'s tender, the 'tin boat', to liaise with the local authorities. Also with them was Lieutenant Tomas Galeano, the jolly Paraguayan naval liaison officer who was to accompany us throughout the voyage in his country. Capitán Angel Chamorro, the officer commanding the naval base, made a speech replied to by John and Mrs Peter Minter, the wife of the British Ambassador to Bolivia, and the Navy laid on a very welcome meat and rice lunch in an upper room of their HQ. We were in another country.

The crowds that met us were made up mainly of Chamacoco Indians, interspersed with a few hospital staff, naval personnel and American missionaries from the controversial New Tribes Mission, expelled from many countries but still active here. It was a touching welcome. Whereas in earlier days explorers would bring beads for the natives, now the natives gave them to us: Jenny Sambrook and some of the other ladies received seed neck-laces, wicker baskets and straw hats.

Admiral Ocampos, Commander of the Paraguayan Navy and also a Vice-President of the expedition, had charged Capitán Chamorro with our welfare, and he took his duties seriously. Thus he insisted that Peter Minter and John should stay at his house. Although the hour was late when they made their way up the waterfront, the thought of a warm, comfortable bed was not unattractive. Loud South American music blared from a *cantina* where many of our younger members were relaxing, aided and abetted by some attractive Latin ladies. However, the Capitán was anxious and had several of his armed sailors at the disco. 'You must warn your people,' he told Yoli, 'all is not as it seems; these women with whom your men dance are the girlfriends and partners of the *vaqueros* at the bar. This is not England. A Paraguayan only kills for two reasons, a cow and a woman.' As the cowboys drinking in the darker recesses of the dance hall were well armed and getting rapidly sloshed, this was sound advice. Keeping such situations under control was to be a constant headache for John as we made our way downriver.

We had brought with us some wooden planking to use as ramps to get four-wheel-drive vehicles on to *PQ*'s deck. Two such vehicles had been driven all the way from Asunción to Bahía Negra for this purpose. The plan was that we should have our own wheels instantly available for project work ashore. But it was the first of many plans that had to be modified. We found at Bahía Negra no convenient wharfside, just a bank too degraded to get vehicles down and ramps that would have been too steep to drive them up. So the planking went to make a more windproof galley, and later on we borrowed or hired vehicles as and when we needed them.

For now, though, we needed the two 4 × 4s for John's planned trip from Bahía Negra into the heart of the Chaco. Each came with a driver: James Wright, who had a vast ranch in the eastern parts of Paraguay, and Pablo Kirchhofer, of German–Swiss parentage. Both were big men – James, knowledgeable and smiley (a smile somewhat disconcerting as it lacked the upper front teeth); Pablo, more the sort of man you would not wish to be on the wrong side of in a bar-room brawl.

We had two main projects while based at Bahía Negra. John and a group of thirteen were to drive 300 kilometres inland in the two vehicles, to Cerro León in the heart of the Gran Chaco, to carry out zoological tasks. The First Lady of Paraguay, the President's wife, Susana Galli de Gonzalez Macchi, who was to become our Paraguay Patron, was to meet them there and inaugurate a new guard post on the nature reserve. Another group of eleven, under Stuart McCallion, was to be conveyed downriver by the patrol boat *P08* to a Chamacoco Indian settlement now called Puerto 14 de Mayo and left there for four days to advise on flood relief, make some anthropological studies and examine the mysterious shell mounds that might offer evidence of an early civilization. Back in Bahía Negra, meanwhile, more dental work would go on at the hospital.

All this was revealed to us at the evening briefing of Saturday 14 August – as was the fact that John was very unwell: subdued, almost inaudible, and still a distressing shade of yellow. Noel was becoming increasingly concerned about his condition. Clearly he needed thorough tests to enable a proper diagnosis to be made. Somehow he must be got to a fully equipped hospital. A distinct question mark hung over the whole expedition.

Gracie Elsam, the wife of a British businessman who was assisting us in Asunción, had e-mailed to say that there was a hospital at the Mennonite community of Filadelfia in the middle of the Chaco, which John and Yoli had visited on their earlier reconnaissance. It was not known if this remote medical facility would be able to make the examination, but the alternative was another long day's drive to Asunción or an air ambulance. And this at least could be amalgamated with the Chaco trip already planned. 'You may not feel too bad,' Noel told him, 'but you are very sick and you must do whatever the hospital doctors advise – even if it means returning to England,' adding, 'you may need surgery.'

Not feeling very happy, John packed his gear, handed over maps, copious files and planning documents to his adjutant and told Jim and Stuart that they would be in charge until further notice. Neither looked pleased. John would not hear of calling for an aircraft while he could still walk and decided to take the two vehicles beloging to ANDE, the Paraguayan government electricity company, which the First Lady's office had sent up to help us. They had arrived that day, bringing in reinforcements: Captain Nathan Arnison, who would take over from Toby Marriner as leader of the Royal Engineers' team, and an enthusiastic young outdoor specialist, Edmund Ledsam.

At dawn on Sunday 15 August the thermometer in the *sala de operaciones* read 10°C. John had not slept well, trying to remember all that he should tell Stuart and Jim in case he did not return. Fortunately, Yoli had been party to all the planning and, having been on the recces, knew everyone involved from La Paz to Buenos Aires. Nevertheless, with almost 2,500 kilometres and two months to go, it would be a great blow if John did not come back.

At 11 a.m. the Chaco convoy formed up: James's and Pablo's vehicles, the ANDE cars, and Capitán Chamorro's lorry – filled with well-armed sailors. Even the civilian drivers carried pistols under their seats as the area was noted for banditry, drug production and smuggling. James assured us that he had spoken to the local narcotics baron who had agreed to leave us alone, but no one was taking any chances. John's two vehicles would travel with them as far as Fortín Madrejon, when the convoy would stop the night at a National Park guard post. At this point he would be driven on the 200 kilometres south to Filadelfia.

John and Yoli knew the Gran Chaco from the recce they had done with the Paraguayan Army in 1997 and were well aware that this wilderness, once a Pleistocene sea, had little human habitation and was virtually impenetrable. The road left Bahía Negra as a narrow causeway running due west through swamps crawling with caiman. A herd of giant peccary, a species of pig and one of the world's most recently discovered large mammals, appeared at a waterhole and the column stopped to photograph this comparative rarity. After a band of waving yellow pampas grass, there came thickets of cane and then the forest of low, bushy trees with thorns up to four inches long. Like a solid mass of barbed wire, it is a complete obstacle to man, yet animals can move relatively freely beneath. Here and there is a tree called *quebracho* – 'the axebreaker' – said to be one of the hardest woods on earth. Fifteen-foot cacti stood like sentinels along the road. 'You can get water from one of those,' said James. 'Which one?' asked John. 'Haven't seen that one yet,' he grinned. 'But if you break down in this place in the dry season, you die of thirst very quickly.' Apart from a few birds and a couple of fluffy titi monkeys, they saw little wildlife. Those in the following vehicles were enveloped in a cloud of dust and saw even less.

James was a mine of information on the bush. He had seen two jaguar on the way up and now he talked of electric eels that deliver a 600-volt shock in the swamps, stingrays, snakes and insects. The cold weather was keeping these pests at bay and even the tiny *jejen*, a small black midge, did not appear.

They continued on the only road through this otherwise trackless forest. There were no paths, nor any landmarks, but occasionally a gate with a warning to keep out appeared. 'Aeroplane farm,' grunted James. 'They simply grow aeroplanes.' It was said that cocaine paste is processed here and shipped out of Paraguay with little inconvenience to the government. 'There are many shoot-outs,' hissed Pablo, waving his automatic pistol as they stopped for a pee.

It was bitterly cold when they reached the army post at Agua Dulce: two white buildings, an airstrip and a volleyball pitch. The lieutenant seemed pleased to have visitors at his lonely camp. These were the first buildings and people that the convoy had seen for 180 kilometres.

At Fortín Madrejon the Chaco National Park begins, and here John left Jim with the team that would go on to Cerro León next day. It was dark when the electricity company vehicles pulled out. Again the road was straight and dusty. Fernando, the driver, was nervous and protested loudly if asked to stop, but with John drinking several gallons of water a day, pauses were inevitable. At every comfort halt Fernando feared bandits and pulled out his pistol while watching anxiously as John relieved himself at the roadside. However, apart from the deer and foxes that appeared in the headlights, the route was deserted. Nearing Filadelfia, they stopped at a shack that served as a transport café to buy more bottled water. Seeing John's jaundiced appearance, the shopkeeper's wife made a brew of herbs, 'for the liver', she said – and John, willing to try anything, downed the awful concoction.

Reaching the hospital at midnight, they found it closed. Yoli did her best to persuade a nurse to take John in, but to no avail. 'Come back *mañana*,' was the reply. Most hotels in the little township were also closed. Mennonites are not night birds and it took two more hours to find a bed, by which time Fernando was almost asleep at the wheel.

Dr Erwin Hauf had been warned of John's visit by the Elsams and, with typical Teutonic thoroughness, had everything ready. Yes, he had all the necessary equipment. Indeed, he was as well equipped as a Harley Street specialist. There was even an ultrasonic scanner with which to inspect the colonel's internal organs, he explained! In two hours the tests were complete. Several doctors gathered to give the verdict. 'You have drug-induced hepatitis – probably a reaction to the Lariam you have been taking against malaria,' they announced. A strict low-protein diet was prescribed, with masses of sugar and water, and John happily paid $100 for one of the most thorough medicals he had ever experienced, in the shortest possible time, in one of the more remote areas of South America. 'Oh,' called Erwin Hauf, 'and give up Lariam – there is hardly any malaria here anyway.' A chatty English-speaking nurse from Winnipeg sold them a load of glucose and they waved farewell to this incredibly modern hospital. As it was possible to make an international call from the town, John felt he should tell his wife, Judith, what had happened.

However, the call produced fresh worries, for back at home Tarquin Cooper's revelatory and rather lighthearted reports on the *Electronic Telegraph*, which he was sending through every month or so, were upsetting supporters of the project. Expedition Base had received one or two complaints, chiefly along the lines that no sponsors were ever mentioned, there was too much reference to the extra-mural activities of one or two members of the team, and very little was said about the work the expedition was doing or the fascinating area through which it was travelling. Yoli, who had devoted much of the last four years to Kota Mama, was furious. 'Is he deliberately trying to make a joke of all we are doing?' she demanded, as they drove north through the gathering dusk. John later spoke to Tarquin about the tone of his reports, but an element of tension remained.

On the way back to Cerro León John dozed most of the time. A graceful jaguarundi bounded across the road and a young armadillo was captured by Fernando, photographed and released. The cars reached the camp at 9.40 p.m. to find the team settled in, Jim very relieved to see the leader back and Noel delighted that his diagnosis had been proved correct. A roaring fire was going, and they toasted some of the fresh bread Yoli had bought in Filadelfia, consuming a whole pot of strawberry jam with it. However, Pablo, the driver, had got the fire going by burning some of the park's carefully cut log stools and this, coupled with firing his pistol when lost, had not endeared him to Jim, still very much the professional soldier.

The next little problem came after all had retired. Stretched out in the front of Fernando's car, John awoke to see another driver attempting to push the car in which Yoli was sleeping towards the tent containing Jim and Gerry. John was about to sort him out when he realized that the fellow was very drunk and simply trying to stand up. However, as the man had a gun and a dagger in his belt, he felt that discretion was better than valour; thankfully, Fernando arrived to drag his inebriated colleague away.

To assist the Chaco Foundation we had agreed to design a biological conservation centre for the park and seek funding for it. So, while we awaited the arrival of the First Lady, Jim and Gerry set to work, while Shaun Linsley, Jennifer Sambrook and others went off with James Wright on a zoological observation trip.

It was late morning when the President's wife arrived. 'She's a stunner!' said photographer Charles Sturge as Señora de Gonzales Macchi appeared in a beautifully tailored trouser-suit and high heels. Tossing her blonde hair, she came straight over to our team and talked to them all in English. By now a large crowd of Paraguayan and Bolivian government officials, members of the American Nature Conservancy and other conservationists had gathered. Speeches and the unveiling of a plaque were followed by a walk up a steep hill-side to a viewpoint over the vast park. Impressively, the First Lady managed the 600-foot climb in her high heels with no effort at all, followed by a retinue of puffing and panting officials. At the barbecue lunch afterwards we briefed her on our programme and plans, and were delighted when she asked if she could come aboard *Kota Mama 2* in Asunción.

Leaving Jim and his team to follow on, John took Bahamian

Geoff Tomlinson (son of Don, who was sponsoring *Viracocha Spirit of Bahamas*) and headed back to Bahía Negra. They made good time until a forest fire flanked the track. The flames were dying down but a hardwood had fallen right across the road and as Fernando's chainsaw would not start, it took half an hour of hacking with machete and John's razor-sharp kukri to clear a way through.

Stuart was delighted to see John back, even if he was still bright yellow, but another problem was looming. It had been a very long day and John decided to get some sleep before tackling it.

Back in the chill, windy darkness of 5 a.m. on 15 August the Puerto 14 de Mayo party had crept along the mud banks to go on board patrol boat *P08*. Clutching the necessary stores, organized by Stuart McCallion, eleven of us piled into the patrol boat's tiny cabin and fell asleep. After a fast downriver run of an hour and a half, *P08* swung under a sheer mud cliff which seemed to be made up of large snail shells compacted together. This was one of the many points of interest in the briefing that Yoli had had in 1997 from the *cacique* of this village, Bruno Barras. Had there been an ancient community of snail eaters there? Did the shells have any ritual significance? The Chamacoco name for Puerto de 14 Mayo was Kalchabalut or Karchabalhut, the Place of Big Shells. Andy Miller was with us to investigate this possibility.

Bruno Barras had also told Yoli that the village needed help in dealing with devastation caused by the occasional flooding of the Paraguay. This problem had a long history. James Minchin, addressing the Royal Geographical Society in March 1881, had said: 'The annual variation of water-level of the Paraguay does not exceed ten feet, yet this is sufficient to inundate the lowlands along its courses.' Over 300 years earlier, a Spanish expedition exploring the upper part of the river in 1543 had noted that 'When the waters are low, the people from the interior come and live on the banks of the river . . . and pass their time in fishing. They lead pleasant lives, dancing and singing night and day . . . but when the water begins to rise, which is in January, they retire inland, because at that season the floods begin, and the waters rise two fathoms above the banks of the river.' So wrote the secretary of the new *Adelantado*, or Governor, of South America, Alvar Nuñez Cabeza de Vaca, appointed by Charles V of Spain to replace poor Pedro de Mendoza, now dead of syphilis. Cabeza de Vaca, a conquistador whose odd name means literally Head of Cow, had sailed up to explore the Pantanal and, like Domingo de

Irala, had reached Lake Gaíba in his search for a new way through to Peru. Despite his distinction as the explorer over a period of eight years of what are now the southern states of the USA from Florida to northern Mexico, Cabeza de Vaca was now forced back to Asunción by his mutinous men, where, always unpopular, he was in 1544 the first ruler in the history of Paraguay to be toppled by a *coup d'état*.

Now here we were in an upper Paraguayan village whose people had in the past been driven westwards 17 kilometres by the same flooding Cabeza de Vaca had noted. What to do about it? Our newly joined Royal Engineers officer, Captain Nathan Arnison, and his fellow sapper, Stuart McCallion, had come to address the problem between them.

As we stood on the high grassy bank, waving a farewell to patrol boat *P08*, we noticed building work in progress on a stilt house. All the other houses in the village, single-storey and made of split palm trunks, were on ground level. We were offered one of them as a base – at 5,000 guaraníes per person per night. This would have cost the eleven of us 220,000 guaraníes, which was only $71 and thus not a bank-breaker; but we had come equipped to camp and this we preferred to do rather than occupy a bug-infested hut.

We crossed a five-a-side football pitch to get decently out of the village and put up our tents and hammocks. Here Andrés, the young deputy *cacique*, visited us.

'Are you a military organization?' he asked.

We wondered whether he might better have asked if we were a religious organization. From 1956 these Chamacoco were kept at Bahía Negra by the New Tribes Mission, who sought to win their souls for Christ and erode their tribal customs, and only escaped to set up their village in its present site in 1990.

As he led us back to show us the village, we explained our aim: to help the villagers – 105 Chamacoco in thirty families – in whatever ways we could in the next four days. Temporarily tied to the bank was a mobile river shop with sacks of potatoes, flour, cheese, biscuits and beer. As we looked it over and made some small purchases, we heard distant sounds of chanting coming from a line of houses a little way inland. We were led over to them, whereupon there occurred an event which the villagers could not in the brief time available have arranged just for our benefit. From some thick bush behind Andrés came six men, shuffling and calling out, carrying red flags and shaking maracas. Their naturally brown bodies had been blackened and white splodges applied. Their heads were completely covered in rhea feathers, and tin anklets rattled as they stamped. They danced and sang round and round a large clump of thorn and grass in a well-worn circuit.

'They do this daily,' said Andrés, 'for three months at a time.'

'What for?' asked Peter Hutchison.

'It is to propitiate the gods and to revive our culture. If they don't do it they will be punished by the gods. There will be no rain, poor crops. There is a secret, sacred area behind in the bush called Towich which outsiders cannot visit. Masculine rituals take place there. They dance from there down a track called Behet to this public dance area, Harra.'

Sadly, none of us had a camera handy; presently the dancers retired down the secret track where the ululations went on for a while.

Back by the river bank there was another surprise.

'Do you want to see the museum?' Andrés asked.

Sure enough, there is a Chamacoco museum with artefacts on the walls and in glass cases, boldly labelled in Spanish, English and Chamacoco. It was built in the 1990s by Earthwatch Earthforce, an American ecological group which undertakes projects abroad, and is well kept up. On the wall was a telling dictum: 'We know the kind of future we want because we do not forget our past. Our ancestors fulfilled all their needs in the forest working united and harmoniously. Let us follow their example.' One in the eye for the New Tribes Mission.

'You might be interested in this,' said Andrés, taking a thick, printed tome from a desk drawer and handing it to Richard. It was in Spanish, and translated its title read *A View of the Chamacoco-Ybytoso settlement – Ecoculture of the Chaco Woodlands of Upper Paraguay. A Thesis* by Carolina Cattebeke Figueredo, Faculty of Architecture. A graduate of the National University of Paraguay in Asunción, trained in Cuba, the author had spent a year producing a full ecological survey of the Chamacoco in 1998. So it seemed that since Bruno Barras' briefing of Yoli in 1997 his people had been thoroughly anthropologized, and our attentions in this field were now rather superfluous.

Nevertheless, there was plenty to do over the four days: Richard produced a map of the village; Peter Hutchison, Mary Stewart and Andy Miller asked a host of questions; and our expedition artist, Andrew Stevenson-Hamilton, sketched away happily. It was felt that we should also help the village in a way that had not been tried before and one for which there was an obvious need: dental treatment. So Nathan Arnison and Peter Minter returned to Bahía Negra to fetch Melissa Wingfield and her dental gear, and by 18 August her surgery was established in the museum. Thirty-eight rotten teeth were extracted from fifteen people on her first busy day.

It had been immediately clear to us on our arrival that we were not the only Western agency at work in the village. A Bolivian-based ecological group called Hombre y Naturaleza (Man and Nature) had people in the field, hoping to develop tourism and operating a boat with an outboard motor. It was this group, part of Doña Ana, a Spanish charity in Seville, that was building the stilt house, their new operational HQ, with paid local labour. On top of this, an Argentinian, Mario Blaser, had been working in the village for several months on his doctorate for McMasters University in Canada. And a German organization had begun to build a new school (but had left it half completed). So we resigned ourselves to the probability that we would for ever be viewed by the locals with a tinge of doubt, as a four-day wonder, typical of that kind of international do-gooder outfit which descends on a Third World village, asks a lot of questions, draws up plans and then shoves off, never to be heard from again.

Mary Stewart tried, with limited success, to interest the small existing school in some extra-curricular guidance, but teacher and pupils were apathetic. Perhaps too much foreign interest had come their way. Villagers sat out the long afternoons sprawled in wooden armchairs in their front yards, children chased hens, cats lay prone in the dust. We began to find the same sleepiness overcoming us – Chacolepsy, someone called it.

For, although only on the edge, we were now in the Gran Chaco. As we ranged wider for firewood we found the notorious Chaco thorn bushes everywhere. Satanically designed, the thorn itself, horn-like in texture and harder than the stem it sprang from, could be seven or eight inches long. Almost all bushes seemed to have thorns on stems or leaves somewhere or other, sometimes invisibly small but wickedly barbed.

It was not a pleasant place to be. The sun, still rising as a red orb, seemed never to penetrate a curtain of haze. We could look it directly in the eye, yet the days were still cruelly hot and humid. An element of frustration beset all our work. Although the Indians reported finding the bones of some exceptionally large people,

Andy Miller concluded after some trial digs that the dense layers of shells below the surface were a natural phenomenon. Nathan and Stuart decided it would be prohibitively expensive to attempt to build flood defences round the village and the only answer was to raise the levels of houses – the Spanish Stilt Solution. We were glad to be packing up and making ready to be collected by the fleet coming downriver.

By the time the boats reached us the expedition had been through its trickiest 'diplomatic incident' so far – of which John learnt only on his return from Cerro León. Before leaving for his hospital examination, he had suggested to Stuart that we should organize a dinner for our Paraguayan hosts and some of the local Indians. Capitán Chamorro kindly offered the use of his mess dining room. However, it was unlikely that the guests would appreciate dehydrated rations and no meat was available in the village. Fish was considered too commonplace. 'They love caiman,' said the local doctor; and although caiman is listed as an endangered species, the Navy confirmed that it was quite permissible for the Indians to hunt them for food. Indeed, riverside villages were often littered with caiman skins. A local hunting party was organized and Stuart invited to go along. Upriver in a swamp they found their quarry. Several shots were fired with little effect, so the rifle was passed to Stuart who finished it off. His companions were delighted and a special caiman dish was prepared for the feast.

However, there were those in the expedition who felt very unhappy that, even though the hunt had the approval of the local authority and caiman were plentiful, we should be seen as encouraging their hunting. Shaun Linsley, although a keen sport fisherman, was especially upset. James Wright was fairly neutral, but Pablo, the other driver, who had no affection for the Paraguayan Navy and may possibly have been peeved after John's having reprimanded him for brandishing his pistol, was incandescent.

John, himself a keen conservationist, was in a tricky position. While he did not wish to condone the incident, neither did he wish to criticize our hosts. Stuart, mortified that he should inadvertently have caused such distress, had apologized immediately, to critical expedition colleagues and Paraguayans alike. Capitán Chamorro assured them that no harm had been done and the matter was closed. 'The problem is with your own people, not ours,' he said. Nevertheless, to avoid further repercussions the caiman was taken off the menu and an apology sent to our patron, the First Lady.

Ironically, as our team debated the issue at Bahía Negra the locals carried another dead caiman along the foreshore . . . .

While this mini-crisis was simmering away Ben Cartwright went out to the Bahía Negra airstrip, where a C47 of the Aerea Militar de Paraguay had crashed in 1994. It had been comprehensively stripped but, ever resourceful, Ben took from it some D-shackles to make strongpoints for towing in the Avon inflatable.

In another significant development at Bahía Negra, Luke Cox had bought a piglet for $6. He had seen it being carried uncomfortably in a plastic bag and thought it might well be fattened up on scraps for future consumption. So when the Puerto 14 de Mayo party were picked up in the late afternoon of 19 August, one of the first things they noticed was a long-haired auburn addition to the population, tucking into eight stale rolls.

The 'dinner crisis' was not over yet. Back aboard *PQ* after a plateful of tasteless reconstituted powdered chicken curry, John met a highly disturbed Captain Martin. Why had he and his crew not been invited to the dinner? Were they second-class citizens? In fact, Stuart had invited them, but in spite of his faultless Spanish, the message had not got through. John poured oil and said we would try harder to ensure that the *PQ* crew always understood that they were part of the team. He was about to go to bed when he heard that *P08*, the Paraguayan Navy's only patrol boat at Bahía Negra, had been sent downstream with our dental team against the orders of the Commandant. On the way back it had broken down and was now stranded halfway between its base and Puerto 14 de Mayo. Capitán Chamorro was clearly not a happy man, and the officer responsible was probably in chains. More oil: John said how much he appreciated the Navy's help and offered to use *PQ* to recover the stricken vessel next day.

While all this was going on, the wake of a passing tug had hurled *Kota Mama 2* against the side of *PQ*, damaging the steering oar transom, which had then to be replaced.

In his log that night, John wrote: 'Running this expedition is like walking a tightrope over a pool of piranha. Now I know what it must be like to be a UN Commander in Kosovo.'

At least the thermometer was rising again.

CHAPTER FOURTEEN

WORKING OUR
WAY
DOWNRIVER

*The routine of travel was invariable. It was odd how grateful one was
for that element of routine. It gave form and substance to those date-
less days . . . Routine is the most portable form of domesticity and uncon-
sciously but gladly we took refuge in it. We were nomads by numbers.*

PETER FLEMING,
Brazilian Adventure, 1933

We now embarked on a long haul south, with the occasional
rather forlorn settlements and cattle stations of
Paraguay's Gran Chaco on our right hand and Brazil, swampy
and virtually uninhabited until Pôrto Murtinho, on our left. We
were only ever to stop on the Paraguayan side, at places whose
local names always seemed to be at variance with any on our
selection of maps. Which was Puerto Voluntad? Where was Puerto
Mihanovich? Were Puerto Leda and Puerto Lidia one and the
same? (No.)

As we went, Stuart McCallion measured the current. In 1881
J. B. Minchin, FRGS, had reckoned it at 2,700 yards per hour.
Not surprisingly there had been no significant change: Stuart
recorded it at 2.934 kph. This was a good speed: 'We're moving
faster than estimated,' John told the team at the evening briefing
on 19 August.

This was just as well, for at 1 p.m. on 20 August the steady thump of *PQ*'s German-built diesel engine stopped. She had split an oil pressure pipe. Captain Martin took her into the bank for emergency repairs by Pedro the engineer. The breeze had died and we were hit by a wall of heat coming from the forest margin. John, working at his chart table, noted the temperature: 101°F. Fortunately, a repair was effected within the hour.

It was the first of many mechanical problems to afflict *PQ*; she was, after all, a 26-year-old tub in need of constant maintenance. Apart from this, she suited us fine. Capacious holds housed our personal kit and our expedition stores. There were serviceable loos and cold showers aft. John and Stuart had their custom-built wooden *sala de operaciones* amidships, which was soon roofed and doored against the ravages of sun and wind. In front of it a wooden galley was erected, too exposed at first until we turned it round to shield the two gas cookers from the gales. Refinements were made to galley and operations room throughout the expedition: there was continual hammering as another map went up, another coat-hook was fixed.

It was a noisy ship, her main disadvantage the need to keep the generator going round the clock. All day, all night (until it, too, broke) the ship's metalwork reverberated to its incessant drumming. It gave the impression of movement when we were still tied up, a sensation heightened by the swish and gurgle of the river against the moored hull. John and Stuart Seymour, those on *KM2* and light sleepers everywhere else also had to contend with deafening music from the crew's galley, whence the sound-track from *Titanic* resounded at all hours.

'The cook must be stone deaf,' complained Jim after a disturbed night.

It was no surprise, then, when at the end of August John's patience gave out. A polite request to Captain Martin produced no improvement and he exploded in wrath. The captain kept to his bit of the ship for a few days but the decibels were reduced.

'What are you whingeing about?' one of our saltier old members asked. 'This is a river expedition, not a Swan Hellenic jolly.'

Lying in the steel hold, wishing he'd brought some ear defenders, Richard felt like an Irish emigrant on his way to the United States in steerage, or a lascar in the chain locker of a British India cargo boat. At dusk we were reminded of Oscar Wilde in Reading gaol: our little tent of blue was the rectangular hatch through which, as we lay on our sleeping bags, we could see the ghostly tracery of Paraguayan trees.

Another problem was *PQ*'s almost unbroken flat deck, across which fierce gusts of wind blew, often catching us with possessions scattered about. On the afternoon of the pipe repair the wind got up again. It was a northerly and the reed boats hoisted full sail. It became Force 6, gusting 7, and *KM2* tore her gaff. She carried on at a cracking rate with her square sail acting like a spinnaker, while the crew got out the repair kit and began stitching.

Spray was blowing over *PQ*'s side when a potentially dangerous event occurred. In the middle of the deck between the aft hold hatches stood a hemispherical plastic reservoir, 6 feet in diameter, which held our chlorinated drinking and cooking water. It was kept covered by a circular plastic lid. A flurry of wind suddenly caught this lid and flipped it overboard into the river. Owain Davies, our young IT wizard, was already notable for his attachment to his hammock and the general sluggishness of his movements, but with great presence of mind he now dived from the deck and swam for the lid. Almost immediately he was left behind by the boat's onward progress.

This was an area notable for its piranha population. Only a day or two before, Peter Hutchison, out fishing in the tin boat, had teasingly poked a corner of his book in the river. There was a ripple and a snap and he withdrew it to find that a quadrant had been neatly bitten off. Captain Martin, seeing Owain drifting abaft the ship, grabbed a lifebelt and a line and plunged overboard himself. Owain swam to him and slowly both of them, with the lid, were hauled aboard. It had been a brave effort, and our media team justly made a meal of it. It was on the website that night and Owain, lately of Clayesmore School, was soon to be lionized by all the sixth-form girls.

Towards evening we reached María Elena, known locally as Pitiantuta after a big Chaco War battle from the site of which the villagers had earlier emigrated. It was desperately run down. There were traces of an airstrip, and a large wooden building on stilts with steps leading up which looked like the cricket pavilion of some seriously negligent club, but turned out once to have been an eight-roomed hotel. Tomorrow we would investigate it all.

In pre-dawn darkness early stirrers moved up and down to the two washrooms: Jim and Gerry Masters, Yoli, Patricia Weatherhead and whoever was on breakfast duty.

'Wakey-wakey, rise and shine, You've had your sleep, I've had mine. Hands on socks . . .' but John forbore to complete the jingle because of the sensitive female souls in the hold below.

Until we grew a bit more resourceful and the Delia Smiths among us emerged, breakfast was often instant coffee and two hard-boiled eggs with whatever buns or bread Billy had been able to procure in the preceding days. Restaurant furniture was limited, and Noel sometimes came over all mock irritable: 'You go and buy a chair of your own, young Graham!' Some of us had bought white, moulded garden armchairs, and one had NBO on it: Noel's Bottom Only. We chatted in groups as we shelled the eggs or, on special days, spooned up our porridge, and the morning mosquitoes circled the juicily exposed ankles which were their breakfast. 'When I was in Belize it was much worse,' Mary Stewart would tell Patricia, while Peter Minter would discuss how she might get flights back to her husband Graham at the Embassy in La Paz.

As the red disc of the hazy sun appeared over the Brazilian palm trees, everyone began to go about his or her morning business. John had skilfully divided us into groups so that we all had a job to do. The anthropological team, Shaun Linsley, Peter Hutchison and their patient interpreter Luis, a Paraguayan sailor who had joined us, went inside the cricket pavilion for a conference with the local chiefs. Interpreters were necessary because, although Peter speaks good Spanish, some of the Paraguayans in these remote stations understand only Guaraní or other local languages. Almost all hispanophone Paraguayans also speak Guaraní, the Indian *lingua franca* of central South America; indeed, Paraguay is the only truly bilingual Latin American state.

Another valuable addition to our complement for the Paraguayan stretch of the voyage was Teniente Tomas Galeano, the naval liaison officer who had joined us at Bahía Negra. Apart from being a keen soccer player who turned out for most of the games between us and the local teams, this jovial, roly-poly figure also had a good knowledge of the river. While he gave the impression of not having a care in the world, he was an unflappable ally whom John came greatly to appreciate, always smoothing our path and ensuring the cooperation of government officials along the river line – and often inland too. Yoli discovered that he had his own direct radio link to the Paraguayan Navy chief, Admiral Ocampos, who always knew our location and was well informed of any problems, not least *PQ*'s breakdowns. The admiral in turn kept the First Lady's office briefed, which was to guarantee us a good welcome everywhere.

The communication kings in the ops room on *PQ* were always

busy. News had come through from Asunción that the First Lady, who had made such a striking impression on some of us at Cerro León, was going to join the fleet some kilometres north of the capital and sail the home stretch with us. *KM2*'s crew relished the idea of this former Miss Paraguay as a temporary shipmate. She had also agreed to take part in one of the regular satellite telephone exchanges which the expedition had arranged with British and German schools. Mindful of this, she asked Richard to prepare a list of possible questions that we could plant among the young audience. One of them was 'What are the qualifications for being First Lady of Paraguay?' Her reply: 'Marry the leader of the opposition party and wait.'

Today Melissa and Graham were pulling teeth again, this time in the former hotel lobby. They did not need interpreters and were now getting on very well with '*¡Abre la boca, por favor!*' at the commencement of treatment and '*¡Escupa aquí!*' as they indicated the spit bucket at the end. Bizarrely, they sometimes worked against the distant background noise not only of the generator but of the didgeridoo. Charles Sturge had brought one from Australia and had become quite a convincing performer, sometimes accompanying Gerry Masters' mouth organ, much to the joy of local children.

The people here were still Chamacoco Indians, but belonged to a sub-group called the Tamaráho and were not of the same stock as their fellows we had met further north. We heard of a small inland village in need of some help and so moved downriver a little way next day to Puerto Boquerón, which offered an easier approach to it. Here was a shop, a police station and a road leading spear-straight into the interior. Fences made from wooden sleepers gave us the clue: the road had once been a railway line and Puerto Boquerón a terminus for one of the many light railways that ran into the interior of the Gran Chaco – in this case to carry cattle for transport downriver. Moored up next to us was a deliciously clapped-out cattle boat, the *Doña Clarissa G.*, built in Argentina in the 1950s and waiting to convey its cargo of 250 cows to Pôrto Murtinho on the Brazilian side. Charles Sturge was later able to film the vast herd being driven down the road by heavily armed *vaqueros*.

It was a hot slog down the straight road and then through groves of palms northwards to the village of Cuareí. After 8 kilometres we stumbled into a primitive hamlet of just thirteen souls. Melissa and John Teague set up a dental clinic, but there were few takers (she and Graham had extracted ninety teeth the previous day, so the respite was welcome). Noel examined a very sick old lady, said to be a hundred but more likely about eighty.

The chief wanted help with the completion of a house. Every building here was made from 10-foot sections of palm tree trunk, but the only available ready-cut wood was already employed in the form of a perfectly good animal corral. 'Take it down,' said the owner, so we dismantled a (for some reason) not so OK corral and carried the wood to Stuart McCallion and Nathan Arnison, who very quickly built most of the man's new house.

An interesting reversal of roles then occurred: instead of the visiting white man learning survival techniques from the cunning natives, as John and Richard remembered happening to them with the Shankilla in Ethiopia in 1968, Gerry Masters and Luke Cox found themselves teaching the local men how to make fire-hardened pegs and how to employ the ancient bow drill to create holes to insert the pegs in the hard palm wood. Two village elders responded by painting their bodies, donning rhea feather head-dresses and putting on a half-hour dance show for us – joined by the octogenarian woman who was not so sick after all. The only really sick person was John, who lay propped against a tree stump most of the time, faint and shaky from the long walk in the heat. The hepatitis was still with him, though he was now more gold than canary yellow. Some slugs of glucose and water helped to get him back to the river.

Towards lunchtime on the next day, 23 August, we saw two bumps on the southern skyline ('reminiscent,' said Stuart Seymour, 'of a young girl sunbathing on a flat beach'; we had been away some time). This was the site of our first fairly large Paraguayan town, Fuerte Olimpo, capital of Alto Paraguay. There was plenty of work for us here – historical, zoological, medical, dental, constructional. A police officer took our passports and, as we waited for official clearance into the country, we scanned the two hills. One of them, to the north, was crowned by both cathedral and fort and looked an interesting area. The town, protected from floods and hidden from our sight by a high levee, lay sprawled between this hill and the next.

We made first for the northernmost hill, where Sister María, from Treviso in Italy, let us into the locked cathedral church of Sta María Auxiliadora, a fine white Italianate structure with a spire at its west end and two towers at the east. Built in 1927, it was the mother church of the Vicariate of the Chaco. The fort was older, built by Captain Antonio Zavala y Delgadillo in 1792, in the days of Spanish colonial rule, to keep the Portuguese out. Known originally as Fort Bourbon, after the Spanish royal family, it was one of a chain of fortifications safeguarding Spain's use of the Paraguay river. It is roughly square in shape with a squat circular bastion at each corner and one watchtower looking upriver. Inside was a commander's house with kitchen, guard-room, chapel, storeroom and barrack blocks. Double bunks in one of these hinted at fairly recent occupancy. Richard, Luke Cox and Pat Troy surveyed it all.

The fort was obviously quite widely known and, though generally kept locked, open to the occasional visitor. What was not known was the location of some walls that had been built between 1824 and 1827, in the early days of Paraguayan independence, on the orders of President Francia, to encircle the town and its landing stage and so protect them from the depre-dations of Chamacoco Indians. Though largely destroyed, they had originally been about 3 kilometres long; traces of them were said still to exist, but had become something of a local mystery. There was also said to be a tunnel running into one of these hills. But where and to what purpose? Richard and Luke made it their business to solve these mysteries.

First, though, John set about one of the most intriguing tasks offered to us by our archaeological and anthropological mentor in Paraguay, Licenciada Adelina Pusineri, Head of the Museo Etnográfico 'Andrés Barbero'. This was to search for the fossil remains of mastodon thought to be somewhere in the hinterland. Paraguay was short of trained experts, and information was sketchy, consisting largely of reports that a Polish priest, Father Zislao, had found huge bones 25 kilometres west of Fuerte Olimpo. Yoli phoned him to confirm this and learnt that some of the bones were in the cathedral museum. John, Yoli and Andy Miller went straight there and met Father Aguero, priest-in-charge. He knew about the mastodon find and was ready to help us. Andy's eyes lit up as he spotted a well-preserved tusk in a glass case. It was, without doubt, mastodon – but where was the rest of the creature? 'On an *estancia* near Santa Fé,' said Father Aguero.

A four-wheel-drive vehicle was hired in which John set off with Andy, Yoli, Tomas Galeano, Jennifer Sambrook and an off-duty armed police officer. An hour out of Fuerte Olimpo they met a sight straight out of Hollywood: 300 head of cattle being driven to the river. As the team pulled off the track, cameras at the

The Catari family building the boats for Phase II

John explains the expedition to Bolivian President Hugo Banzer Suárez, at the Presidential Palace in La Paz. British Ambassador Graham Minter is on the left; Admiral Zabala on the right

Kota Mama 2 emerging from the tunnel near Cochabamba. In the centre of the tunnel the boat cleared exposed rocks with only centimetres to spare! (*Richard Snailham*)

The Bolivian Navy band plays 'God Save the Queen' as the fleet prepares to set sail from Puerto Quijarro

The pre-Inca carved mortar discovered by the team at Fortaleza del Parabanocito (*Stuart Seymour*)

Anchors aweigh! *KM2*, red ensign flying, sails into Brazil

Viracocha Spirit of Bahamas in the Pantanal

Stormy weather: Trooper Tomas Hughes adjusting *KM2*'s rigging (*Charles Sturge*)

One of the major hazards along the way: the giant barges in operation on the Río Paraguay

Ayoreo Indians performing a dance to bring rain and food

Gerry Masters demonstrating how to use a bow drill

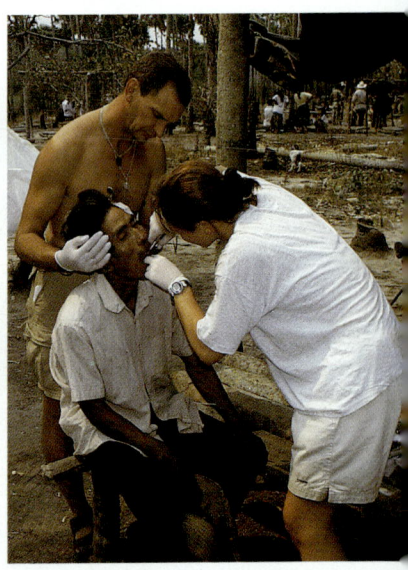

Melissa Wingfield and nurse John Teague extracting teeth

Sergeant Billy Huxter and a Bolivian sailor proudly display their catch, a fine *surubí*

Don Carlos, the engine built in Leeds in 1916 and discovered in a workshop in Puerto Casado, Paraguay

Forest fire at Cerro Corá

'Runic' script discovered near Villarrica in south-east Paraguay

Admiral Luis Ocampos with Erik Catari, who built our reed boats

KM2 entering Asunción (*Charles Sturge*)

The BT satellite phone was used to link up with Clayesmore School in Dorset: the English schoolchildren had the chance to chat to the First Lady of Paraguay, with Richard looking on, and to pupils of the Vuelta Del Ombó School in Argentina, with Yoli helping out

John is a wildlife enthusiast and was rather taken with the capybara, the giant aquatic rodents abundant in South America

A rare sight: the endangered marsh deer photographed by John from a microlight near Lago De La Luna, north-east Argentina

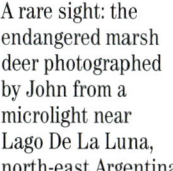

The reed boats battling through a *pampero* on the Río Paraná, and the resulting damage to *KM2*'s bows

Tired but triumphant: the team at the end of the journey near Buenos Aires (*Charles Sturge*)

ready, the bovine torrent swept by, lowing and kicking up clouds of dust. Gunshot whipcracks and yells from the attendant *vaqueros* kept the herd moving. With battered sombreros shielding their narrowed eyes, the men gave toothy grins. In their belts were six-shooters and daggers, and several carried carbines in long leather holsters. Most of them wore worn leather chaps. A man from a Marlborough advert greeted Yoli.

'*¡Buenos días!*'

'You seem well armed,' commented John.

'*Sí, Señor,*' he said. 'My cows are worth two hundred dollars each and there are many thieves in the Chaco, so we shoot them.'

Fierce bush fires sent up black columns of smoke along the way. There was much wildlife to see: raccoons, rhea, caiman. The policeman pointed out a green swamp. It was a heaving mass of caiman, squirming over each other in the black mud. Yoli drew everyone's attention to an anaconda moving deliberately along among them. It was an awful sight, and called to John's mind stories of Chaco War prisoners being lowered feet first into such places by way of interrogation.

When the team finally reached the gate of the Santa Fé settlement they found it chained, padlocked and adorned by a notice declaring visitors not welcome. The policeman climbed over and returned shortly with the Brazilian manager and a heavily built, heavily armed Paraguayan police officer. The owner had left strict instructions that nobody was to be allowed in, and only Tomas Galeano's quiet insistence gained them access. Seeing a newly built hangar, John wondered if this was another aeroplane farm. Once inside, however, the manager relaxed, and his wife kindly offered *yerba mate* (*Ilex paraguayensis*, a strong, bitter green tea drunk through a straw from a gourd).

Several kilometres into the estate they came upon the mastodon site. Here delight was followed by frustration. After the initial excavation, in which the creature's head and hindquarters had been recovered, the pit had become a reservoir and was now, to Andy's profound disappointment, filled with a few metres of slimy green water. However, John could report to Adelina Pusineri that the story was true and that excavation might be possible later, in a dry period.

Meanwhile, Noel had had one of his busiest days, seeing forty-seven patients in the morning, and Richard's team had measured up the fort, produced a plan of it and made numerous enquiries in the town about walls and tunnel, drawing a blank each time.

Eventually, as is often the way, a couple of eleven-year-old boys solved one problem: Carlos and his friend knew of the missing tunnel and led the way to it. *La gruta* or *la vieja mina* was an old mica mine driven horizontally into the hillside about a kilometre out of town in the mid-1940s.

The walls were more difficult. On 24 August Luke got up early to avoid the heat of the day and climbed the second hill. He scoured painstakingly over rocks and through thorn but found nothing – except that the second hill had obscured two others from view as we had looked downriver from the north. The three grouped together were clear to those coming upriver and were known as *las tres hermanas* (the three sisters). The next day, our last in Fuerte Olimpo, Richard and Luke set off to circumambulate the other two hills. Thrashing through bushes high on the middle one they came upon what they sought: a superb stretch of wall, neatly dressed, smooth on both sides and running for about 100 metres down towards the col between the middle hill and the end one. It stood an impressive 1.8 metres high and was still in good order. A report on all this was written and given to the town authorities.

As we prepared to leave Fuerte Olimpo, two members of the expedition had to leave us: Eduardo Esteban, a thirty-three-year-old Argentinian park ranger who had been with us since Puerto Quijarro, took a riverboat to Asunción, and with him went Peter Minter who, after much soul-searching and telephoning, had decided after all to rejoin her husband in La Paz to help entertain Clare Short, Britain's International Development Secretary, who was due to arrive shortly in Bolivia on an official visit. The rest of us, with some sadness, left the pleasant township on 26 August. Characteristically, the youngsters from the local school, in their trim blue uniforms, turned out in force to see us off. Their touching letter (see opposite) arrived later.

It was a cold, cheerless morning with a strong south wind: no sailing for the reed boats until it changed direction. We were headed for the next place where work awaited us, Colonia Peralta, and so passed straight through Puerto Guaraní, a place which looked to have much of interest: a big church in Saxon style, a barracks, evidence of an inland railway, archaeological possibilities. This led to one of those conversations at cross-purposes that John and Richard occasionally have where neither seems to hear the other:

3 January 2000   Fuerte Olimpo, Alto Paraguay.

TO THE MEMBERS OF KOTA MAMA II EXPEDITION

It was Monday 23 August and in Fuerte Olimpo arrived 'Puerto Quijarro' Vessel followed by two very rare boats. It was our first time to see these type of distinct boats, then a deep curiosity came to our insides.

With great amuzement and gladness we received a visit of two persons, who we reckoned were foreigners because of the different way they dressed and walked. They were Cor. John and Señorita Yolima. Outside of our classrooms in the yard all of us were formed by organised groups according to our grades. We listened them. Señorita Yolima spoke in Spanish (our language), meanwhile the Cor. JBS spoke in English which gave us a great joy, because it was the first occasion we heard someone speaking in English, so our natural response was with infantile laughs.

We were thrilled by their invitation to see the expedition boats very closely.

With our hearts full of joy we went home and told our parents about our new experience.

You all have a definite aim, perhaps you don't know or you don't imagine the impact and range of your activities in everyone of us, because not only is the remembrance but also of the aid to the most need people and this is a high value. You left a good seed with the example of your actions that we fight for fear ideals without rest, they can be achieved.

God and Virgen accompany and bless you for everything you do all over the world.

Special gratitude to Cor. JBS

Teacher: Gricelda Abreu de Benitez and students of 6th Grade of Escuela (school) Mayor Ramón Bejarano No. 117, Fuerte Olimpo, Alto Paraguay (High Paraguay).

RICHARD: John, look. Those are surely two old locomotives on the waterfront there . . .

JOHN *(scanning the bank with his binoculars)*: Adelina Pusineri told us there was some pottery in the bank sides somewhere here.

RICHARD: They could be locomotives, because there were a lot of lines running into the Chaco to the big cattle *estancias*.

JOHN: Keep your eyes skinned for pottery shards.

RICHARD: That one has a firebox but the funnel is missing.

JOHN: An interesting stratum of clay runs along just below the surface. Do you see it? Might be pots there.

Such is obsession.

Later Richard enjoyed that privilege treasured by many a blue-rinsed widow on board the larger cruise ships: luncheon with the captain. For some time now Captain Martin had invited small groups in turn to his tiny dining room where a cooked meal rather than our usual scratch snack had been prepared by his two orderlies. Fish, expertly caught by the Bolivian crew, always featured.

The flat, unchanging landscape of palm tree and swamp on either side was relieved in the afternoon by the appearance of some substantial hills, one a *mesa* of 1,788 metres and several smaller. The river narrowed between them, at one time to as little as 230 metres, in almost a gorge, and the stream manifested, if not rapids, at least swirls. (There was not, in fact, a single rapid in the whole length of our Paraguay/Paraná route, which was where it differed most of all from the Congo/Zaire.)

Jim, sensibly, did not like the support ship to motor on any later than about 4.30 p.m. By the time the reed boats had arrived and tied up alongside, and their crews had cleaned themselves up, there was only an hour or so left to light a fire ashore and prepare and eat supper before darkness fell. Barely able to keep awake, we would then have a Briefing, and so to bed.

This night it was more of a Griefing: there was a great fear of fire aboard. Drums of petrol were stacked on *PQ* astern (and later in her bows also). *KM2* carried fuel for the steering motor, and both reed boats were highly inflammable. Smokers were reminded that they must confine their habit to the galley area of *PQ* or the hold. Jim had asked permission to keelhaul one of our few slaves to nicotine who had flicked his butt-end over the side towards *KM2*'s cache of fuel. Nor was this all. The hold was a mess. Kit strewn all over the place. What did our Paraguayan visitors at Fuerte Olimpo make of the spread of detritus round everyone's bed space? There might have to be army-style inspections. Finally, a water-bottle and two unwashed mess tins had been found lying about. Standards must not be allowed to slip. The Lost and Found box was full. Would people please have a look through it and reclaim their kit?

As we breakfasted next morning, the sun's rays were noticed warming a heap of bedding on *KM2*'s cabin top. In it was Chris Brogan, oblivious of the heavy dew and equally of the lovely tree with yellow candles to which we had moored up the previous night. After the Griefing he had seen, some 4 or 5 kilometres downriver, the lights of a town twinkling seductively: a distant string of pearls on the Brazilian side lining the foreshore of Pôrto Murtinho. It was too much. The prospect of bars and night-clubs and lissom Brazilian girls, with what Noel had so graphically described at Corumbá as 'their tight little bottoms', had induced him to join the ship's crew in their tin boat for a trip to town. They had not come back until 4 a.m.

As it happened it did not matter. We were not going anywhere for a little while. It was strangely quiet. No generator. *PQ* had a problem with its batteries. There was to be an enforced hiatus.

After breakfast some of us liked to spend a bit of quality time with Rocket. The little auburn piglet had already wormed his way into several affections. Luke Cox, who had bought him, was Chief Carer, but many of us took the trouble to carry scraps of food up to his den in the forecastle. He responded now to our approach and would obligingly roll over for the anticipated stomach tickle. He spent the nights on the shore, tethered by a long line and snuffling about among the water hyacinths. One morning we found him with a hind trotter inextricably bound up with frayed twine; Peter Hutchison carefully cut it free, to much squealing. There had been a lot of this squealing in his first days on board, particularly when he once walked off the edge of the deck. Fortunately he was securely tied to his girth strap and merely had to be hauled up. We began to work out a Pig Overboard drill, but he never caused it to be put into action. He visibly grew fat: dry bread rolls, banana skins and the remains of the spag bol (kept in a bucket marked ROCKET FUEL) soon transformed him. Was this what we wanted? 'I see him as food,' said John Teague, and Luke had regarded the $6 expended as an investment. There was talk of bacon butties; but others wondered if in Paraguay somewhere there was a home for overweight, semi-domesticated porkers.

Colonia Peralta lay opposite Pôrto Murtinho up a creek – well, not strictly a creek but a channel. The Paraguay meandered here and it looked as if the river had cut through the neck of the meander to form a new channel and an ox-bow lake, but that for some reason it had not worked out: the main channel carried on round the meander and the new cut had silted up.

Soon the tin boat was marshalled and our various work teams, correctly lifejacketed, were ferried downriver. Patricia Weatherhead, Charles Sturge and Stuart Seymour went on horseback to carry out a wildlife survey in the Chaco. They saw and photographed wild otter and anaconda, as well as caiman. Noel and Mary Stewart worked in the health centre at Colonia Peralta. Graham pulled about seventy more teeth.

The bulk of us were scheduled to walk to a nearby village of Ayoreo Indians, a visit arranged by the local priest. A guide, Mario, himself Ayoreo, led us through palms for several kilometres to a group of huts on rising ground – Isla Alta, a 'high island' in time of flood. Here were Indians inhabiting that grey margin between the natural life of the rain forest and the civilization of the river line. The village seemed to be exclusively populated by big, fat girls in T-shirts, skirts and flip-flops with their grubby-faced children. All looked distinctly Amazonian – pudding-basin haircuts, protrusive lips and pendulous breasts. When they smiled, it became apparent that none had any upper front teeth: all four had gone, leaving an expanse of gum between two fierce-looking canines. This did not necessarily make Melissa's job any easier, because all the rest of their teeth were rotten. The gap was attributed by some to the ready availability of *caramelos* and fizzy drinks, others to a perception that it enhanced their attractiveness.

Melissa and Richard set up a surgery in the wooden church. The Stations of the Cross lined the walls; giggling girls peered through the unglazed windows.

'I bet it's the first time you've worked in a church,' said Peter Hutchison, who was making an anthropological survey with Shaun.

'Last time it was an old hotel lobby, before that a museum . . .' Melissa said. 'All I need is a chair, a bucket and good light.'

Her spirit stove soon had the water boiling and the instruments sterilized. There must have been a lot of dental pain about because the queue of patients never dried up. Docilely they sat down and received their injections. Was it fortitude or fatalism? They never demurred.

'I've never seen such terrible teeth before,' Melissa confessed. 'They all need ten or twelve extractions.'

It was not long before she broke an expedition record by removing ten teeth from one patient, and immediately beat it by pulling twelve from another. Only one side of a mouth can be desensitized at any one time, so the maximum possible was sixteen. The bucket was steadily filling with spittle and gore. Richard proffered extractors, elevators and swabs, and held the head for obstinate removals: one of the trickiest was from Mario, our guide. Hens picked about the dusty floor and cockerels crew outside as Melissa toiled away until her wrists and forearms ached.

Back at Colonia Peralta we found the reed boats – but no support ship. The battery problem had persisted and Captain Martin had gone off in his tin boat for a replacement. Our only recourse now was the Avon inflatable, and so in gathering gloom Ben Cartwright made a series of runs, four passengers at a time, upstream to *PQ*. Each round trip took an hour. Scanning with the headlamp, we got up on the plane and expertly scudded over the millpond river, narrowly avoiding clumps of *camelote* and occasionally hazarded by completely unlit fishing boats roaring past, outboards at full throttle.

'You'd better have a break, Ben,' said John as he brought in his penultimate load.

'No chance. I'm enjoying this. Best day yet!'

CHAPTER FIFTEEN

RAILWAY MANIA

*The line itself was so fantastic that I could only stare at it in mute,
horror-stricken silence. It was approximately two and a half feet wide,
each rail worn down and glossy with use, so buckled that they looked
like a couple of silver snakes wriggling away through the grass.*

GERALD DURRELL,
The Drunken Forest, 1956

On our last night in Pôrto Murtinho, 28 August, after Patricia
had masterminded an excellent supper, Richard continued
his series of lecturettes – on Aleixo García, Sebastian Cabot, Robin
Hanbury-Tenison and Ramiro Carrasco – with a post-briefing talk
on Gerald Durrell. How did the famous animal collector and
founder of the Jersey Zoo and Wildlife Trust come into the picture?
In 1954 Durrell went with his first wife to collect fauna in
Argentina. There were problems with their transport to Patagonia,
so they switched their sights to Paraguay instead and flew via
Asunción to Puerto Casado on the Paraguay river. This was our
next important objective.

After Puerto Sastre, another derelict port strangely reminiscent of river stations on the old Congo (broken-down warehouses,
water towers, collapsed jetties), the first geographical feature of
interest was the influx of the Río Apa on our port side. This river
marked the formerly much contested frontier between Brazil and
Paraguay, and once we had passed the junction we would have
Paraguay on both banks. In Spanish colonial days Fort San Carlos
had guarded the Apa against Portuguese incursions from the Mato
Grosso, but in 1867 Colonel Carlos de Morais Camisão crossed it

and led a Brazilian force of 1,600 towards Concepción in the war of the Triple Alliance.

As is often the way with significant landmarks, we missed the Apa altogether and came soon to Vallemí. This town reminded some of us of Middlesbrough: a big cement factory belched white smoke into an overcast grey sky, and lime kilns lined the pock-marked bank. We had a rendezvous here with some Argentine colleagues, and a caving assignment to do; also, *PQ* had now developed a problem in her water-cooling system and was running at half speed, so some more time for repairs was needed. This was another headache for John. Would the support ship actually reach Buenos Aires? Yoli fired off more messages to the owners.

Eduardo Esteban rejoined us, and with him Adrian Giménez Hutton and caving expert Enrique Lipps, members of the Argentine Chapter of the Explorers' Club who were to spend a week with us. Adrian had been helpful in paving the way for us in Argentina and John, feeling grateful for this, did his best to lay on an interesting programme. However, Adrian did not seem very well and, after a quick look at *PQ*'s very simple accommo-dation, decided to stay in a local hotel. Attempts by Yoli to bring the pair into the fold came to naught, and after one sortie to see some caves the visitors announced they were going home. Adrian assured John that nothing had annoyed him and they parted on good terms. Nevertheless, John was mystified by this sudden departure and questioned cavers and others in the hope of finding a reason for it. He found none; but he had good cause to be concerned, as we were to discover later.

Unaware of all this, *KM2* had set off southwards to Puerto Casado, shown on some maps as Puerto La Victoria. A pencil-slim mast, visible from a distance, turned out to be a tall factory chimney; nearby was a collapsed jetty that provided us with a mooring. Puerto Casado had been founded in 1893 by Carlos Casado, who owned 5 million hectares of northern Paraguay west of the river and made his fortune from the extraction of *quebracho* wood from the Chaco and the production from it of tannin. Tannic acid ($C_{14}H_{10}O_9$) is used in the manufacture of leather from hides, and at one time 1,500 workers were reducing 160 tons of wood to 30 tons of it each day in the factory which still dominates the river bank and the town.

Quebracho is one of the hardest woods known; extremely heavy, with a specific gravity of 1.38 it does not float in water. 'You cannot hit a nail in it with a hammer,' Miguel Angel Burgos told

Richard at the factory; 'you have to drill it.' The trees take 100 years to reach maturity, so replanting is impractical and loggers in the early days had to range further and further into the Chaco to find them. Consequently, in the late 1890s Casado found it necessary to build a light railway into the interior. This eventually penetrated as far as 180 kilometres westwards and had several branches.

Around the factory a large company town grew up with an imposing castellated hotel, wide boulevards and tree-lined avenues stretching, it seemed, to the horizon. People from Asunción came on honeymoon to Puerto Casado, which had electricity before the capital. There were still plazas everywhere; but squatters, donkeys and hens occupied the Casado Hotel and the whole place now had a dusty Wild West look: goats in the streets, few shops, a distinct torpor in the suffocating heat. The railway had ceased operation in 1983 and the last tannin, from *quebracho* brought in by boat all the way from Bahía Negra, was produced in 1995. There were 250 workers then, but now only sixty remained, engaged on repairing tractors, drying rice and maintaining the irrigation of the paddy fields 4 kilometres away. The word was that the Casado family, now based in Argentina, wanted to run the place down. We wanted to see if it was desirable and feasible to build it up, perhaps to attract visitors. There is a burgeoning interest worldwide in ecotourism, and an extant railway system, which still possesses nine steam locomotives, four of which might easily be brought back into service, was of inestimable value. The track was in a dismal state and Puerto Casado is now hard to get to, but we felt it was worth looking at. So Stuart McCallion and Nathan Arnison, with Tarquin, Owain, John Teague, Shaun and Tomas, took a small pickup and went off into the Chaco to look at the state of the permanent way and the wildlife there. The two dentists, assisted by Mary Stewart, set up a clinic in a local office (there was a hospital and a doctor in Puerto Casado to tend its 3,000 people, but no dentist). Richard headed for the station and engine sheds.

Here is an Aladdin's cave for railway buffs. The nine steam locomotives stand quietly rusting away, all but one of them under cover. There is even an employee, Don José Feliz Riveros, appointed to look after them. The oldest, made in Berlin in 1901, is proudly billed as the First Locomotive of the Paraguayan Chaco. Eight were built in Germany, just one in Britain: the 0-8-0T *Don Carlos*, made by Manning, Wardle in Leeds in 1916. The last

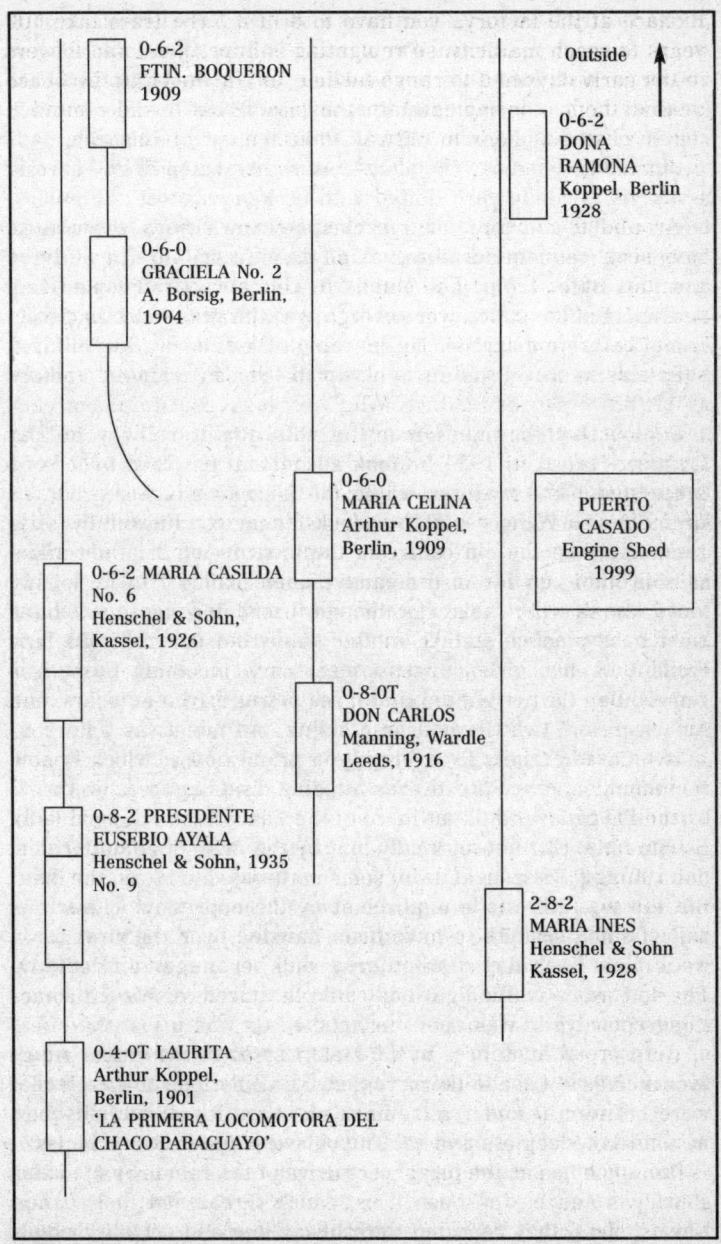

0-6-2
FTIN. BOQUERON
1909

Outside

0-6-2
DONA
RAMONA
Koppel, Berlin
1928

0-6-0
GRACIELA No. 2
A. Borsig, Berlin,
1904

0-6-0
MARIA CELINA
Arthur Koppel,
Berlin, 1909

PUERTO
CASADO
Engine Shed
1999

0-6-2 MARIA CASILDA
No. 6
Henschel & Sohn,
Kassel, 1926

0-8-0T
DON CARLOS
Manning, Wardle
Leeds, 1916

0-8-2 PRESIDENTE
EUSEBIO AYALA
Henschel & Sohn, 1935
No. 9

2-8-2
MARIA INES
Henschel & Sohn
Kassel, 1928

0-4-0T LAURITA
Arthur Koppel,
Berlin, 1901
'LA PRIMERA LOCOMOTORA DEL
CHACO PARAGUAYO'

arrived in 1935, when the railway was kept busy ferrying troops to the front in the Chaco War against Bolivia. Don José has few resources and does little but sit about in his workshop (another treasure-house for engineering enthusiasts); but he did remove a couple of name-plates to burnish them for our photograph.

Immediately outside the sheds nature has taken over. There is a vast marshalling yard dotted with broken wagons, old boilers, bogie wheels and three or four classic steam cranes (there must have been frequent derailments), all made in Britain – by Stothert and Pitt, Bath; Taylor and Hubbard, Leicester; Grafton and Co., Bedford. But the tracks were overgrown with grass and the points unmovable. We marvelled at the rapid rate of decay, for Yoli had been able to travel some way down the line by train as recently as 1997.

Gerald Durrell makes much of this quaint railway in *The Drunken Forest*. In 1954 he took an *autovía* powered by a Ford 8 hp engine and travelled along the 2½-foot gauge line for 25 kilometres to Waho (Guajho) to look for jaguar. He and his wife Jackie lived in the old centre of the town in what he describes as a brothel run by an eccentric madam called Paula. Nobody today knows where this was, though it may, incongruously, have been by the police station on the waterfront (Durrell tells how Paula took her girls down to meet each incoming passenger vessel). Ben Cartwright did find three petrol-driven autocars, one American and two German, in a siding, but none was a Ford 8.

The Casado family lived in quite a grand house, which is now a nunnery; another prestigious building, La Chaquera, was used by the Paraguayan military hero of the Chaco War, Mariscal Felix Estigarríbia. Our house, kindly lent by the municipal authorities, had running water, light, even some mattresses to lay on the floor. But life was still made unpleasant by the oppressive climate. A pall of smog seemed to have been hanging over the river for a week now. Each day dawned grey, dull yet muggy and stifling. The sun was a traffic light and could be stared at. We felt something apocalyptic was about to happen. Or was it just the effect of widespread bush fires in the Mato Grosso to the north? At all events, Puerto Casado never cooled. The only tolerable moments were between 6 and 7 a.m. Each night we lay under mosquito nets naked, sleepless and in a muck sweat until after midnight.

Our track inspection party were driven back into town by water shortages and by the bush fires, which threatened their camp. Nevertheless, they reported the railway line and certain bridges over culverts to be in a reasonable condition, and capable of being put into good shape. So we left Puerto Casado in a mood of qualified optimism. 'The only tannin factory in the world still working' (though not producing tannin) had an energetic Argentinian manager, but he realistically pointed out that the amount his plant currently earned would not pay for the extensive modernization required. Richard noticed that *María Celina* had greased working parts, suggestive of recent use. And 'your British locomotive, *Don Carlos*, only needs a grille in the firebox and one water tank and it would go,' said Don José, more perhaps in hope than expectation.

Puerto Casado had had its mosquitoes, and also a biting fly which the locals called a *viuda negra* (black widow): a creature like a miniature Stealth bomber that was very difficult to swat. But for Richard the night after we left Puerto Casado on Friday 3 September was The Night of the Mosquitoes *par excellence*.

Everybody has his story of some dire tropical occasion when the *Anopheles* genus got the upper hand. Certainly everyone on this expedition will have his or her memory of a time when they were worse than usual. The low-lying, swampy flatlands of central South America are as deeply mosquito-ridden as anywhere in the world. Bernhard Förster, who set up the anti-semitic colony of Nueva Germania with his wife, Elisabeth Nietzsche, wrote: 'No one who has become acquainted with the Paraguayan mosquito in all its industriousness and suffered its attentions on a hot, still summer night on the Río Paraguay will ever forget the experience.'

It had been another smoggy day with no wind. The heat was beginning to addle the brain. Pat Troy said: 'I've got a story for your book, Richard, but I've forgotten what it is.' We tied up on the Isla Caá-Pucú-Guazú. Guaraní names are like that. Gerry Masters cleared an area of bank and lit a fire. Following some unspoken natural agenda, the entire crew of the reed boats was busy – some collected wood, some washed, others erected tents. While Richard set about preparing the essential first hot drink, Pat kindly put up a tent for him – to which he did not immediately go, leaving the tent door unzipped.

After supper a myriad insects of all types were wheeling and diving within. Richard crawled in and zipped up: a clear case of the stable door and the bolted horse. Thrashing about with his Aerosur T-shirt he seemed to enrage rather than annihilate them. A more piecemeal slaughter cleared the tent top fore and aft and he fell into a troubled sleep while for four hours a legion of mosquitoes injected their anti-coagulants and sucked. At 1 a.m. it was clear the battle was not won, so for the next four hours Richard fought it. Like fighter-bombers taking off in waves from some East Anglian airfield in the Second World War they attacked first at one end of the tent then the other. But where from? How were they finding their way in? Where the vertical and horizontal zips at the door almost met there was a small triangle, into which Richard stuffed his underpants. 'That should fix them,' he thought, 'I've had those on for five days.'

The warning whine went on. Mosquitoes land imperceptibly and can only be zapped when seen. If over the next several aeons they could genetically breed out the whine, they would become a very formidable foe indeed. Most were now gorged and when Richard, with a practised snatch of the left hand, caught one in mid-air there was a satisfying gout of blood on his fingers. So englutted were they that they seemed to be flying like heavily laden Hercules C-130s; they even looked bigger than before and were more easily taken. Soon Richard's hands were squishy with his own blood and the tent walls similarly spattered.

But every time he believed the battle won, switched off the head-torch and settled back on the Thermorest there was another whine around the head. This was a different class of enemy. The Very Advanced Mosquito did not obligingly alight on the tent's sides but hid in the interstices of Richard's kit until it was dark again. Then the VAM, a leaner and more wicked-looking beast, would emerge and, like the Red Baron diving out of the Flanders sun, deliver its blow. Richard shot down his last mosquito at 5.45 a.m., dressed and emerged to find many hundreds more circling in the still morning air.

He was soon absorbed, however, in a more general drama. The previous afternoon the support vessel and the reed boats had become separated, and Stuart Seymour and Mark Barth, a fifteen-year-old American boy living with his parents at Vallemí and the genius who had mended the fault in *KM2*'s outboard motor which had eluded Ben for so long, had set off downriver in the Barths' tin boat to check up on *KM2* and *Viracocha*. They had not begun their return journey until dusk at 6 p.m., and at nightfall they had still not arrived back at *PQ*. Where were they?

PQ had itself set off on 3 September but was only a few kilometres south of Vallemí when it broke down again. This time it had been the main gasket, and two Yorkshiremen who had just joined us – Les Winterburn, an old Zaire River expedition hand and an experienced engineer with long service in the REME, and Roger Godfrey, with a diploma in mechanical engineering – climbed down into the oven-like heat of *PQ*'s engine-room to see what could be done. *KM2* and *PQ* had now lost radio contact.

'Why can't they listen out?' complained Jim. 'There'll be no more Mr Nice Guy when I see them.'

In fact, *KM2* was now so far ahead it was out of radio range – which was why it was decided to send Stuart downriver with young Mark. Stuart left at 2.30 p.m. and ran the 54 kilometres to *KM*'s position alongside the Isla Caá-Pucú-Guazú, where he delivered some rations and set off back at 6 p.m. When darkness came and they had not returned, it was clear that they must have broken down – but where?

The river is a dangerous place at night. Sandbanks become invisible; vast blocks of barges are pushed along around the clock by powerful boats that take up most of the deep channel; very few beacons light the course, and caiman abound.

By 10.30 p.m. John had ordered a search, but Captain Martin's tin boat had gone up to Vallemí. At that moment the Barths arrived in their old motor cruiser, the *Robin Hood*, which had once belonged to Eva Perón.

'Oh, I expect he's broken down and is being eaten alive by mosquitoes,' said Jane Barth, showing remarkable sangfroid at the news that her son was missing. Her husband, John, planned to mount a search at first light.

PQ was now once more repaired and ready to motor, but early risers learnt that Captain Martin had come in from Vallemí and had shot off immediately in his tin boat to hunt for Stuart and Mark Barth on his own. Without success. So a systematic search was laid on. At dawn *PQ* set off in midstream while *Robin Hood*, with Charles Sturge on board, combed the reed beds and creeks on the port bank, and the tin boat, with Marie Peralta translating radioed orders to the Bolivian crew, searched the starboard side. Local boats coming upstream were asked if they had seen any moored or abandoned craft. John's misgivings increased when one after another they reported seeing nothing. Islands divided the stream. John could not be sure every corner had been looked into. To make matters worse, he had spotted with his powerful binoculars some water containers caught in the reeds. They were like the ones Stuart had carried.

Then Marie's excited voice came up over the radio: 'There's a boat coming up. I think it's them.'

Stuart's outboard had broken down twice, and each time Mark had stripped and repaired it with screwdriver and fingernails. He had managed to undo a size 11 nut with a size 14 spanner. Going ashore to seek help from a small farm, Stuart had been taken for a thief and chased away by the señora with a broom. They had had one hour's sleep and had been comprehensively devoured by mosquitoes and the like.

Pamela Coleridge, once a nurse and John's PA in Zaire, put away her medical kit with obvious relief and later joined in a happy reunion round a camp fire. The evening meal was inedible, but no matter – we were glad that everyone was safe. Marigold Verity, who had brought her harp to South America (it is Paraguay's national instrument) soothed our nerves with a moonlit recital.

Lady Coleridge, with Marigold Verity, Pedro Cartwright, Les Winterburn and Roger Godfrey, had flown into Asunción a few days earlier and had joined us at Vallemí. As some arrived, some went: Ben Cartwright would have to leave at Asunción and Les would take over the Avon inflatable. Luke Cox also had army duties which would call him home. For a brief time, then, we had six former Zaire River members together twenty-six years after that memorable expedition – and their sense of déjà vu was heightened when we came upon an island in the river called Isla Stanley. This surely cannot have been named for Henry Morton, Livingstone's discoverer, and the man whose route we had once followed down the old Congo?

CHAPTER SIXTEEN

FIRE AND STORM

We were now only 83 kilometres upstream of Concepción, the first place of any size since Corumbá. On our way there we had many excitements on the river, fortunately fairly minor. One day, searching for a good place to moor up, *KM2* was seduced by a beach clear of water hyacinth and motored over to it – and promptly ran aground on a sandbank. 'Lighten ship!' ordered Chris Brogan. Almost everyone obediently jumped in the river. Gerry Masters had the bow-line but could not move the 8 ton boat single-handed. Nathan, Tarquin, Ed and Jim all heaved. To no avail. Eventually, the Avon, pushing amidships, did it. Afterwards, we had some fun hauling the seventy-year-old Admiral into the Avon and helping to decant him from it on to *KM2*.

On more than one occasion a broad wall of metal presented itself as we rounded a corner in the river. This would be a block of barges, three by four or four by four and all lashed together, being pushed upstream by a powerful *empujador*. There was sometimes little room to manoeuvre. 'Steam must give way to sail,' said one hopeful crew member in the early days. 'That bugger will give way to nobody,' replied Jim. Enormously broad, enormously long, it was understandable that so unwieldy an object could not easily change direction in a river of such variable depths and such serpentine course. It was fortunate, then, that we had a steering motor to guide us past these floating football fields.

On another occasion one of the dentists inadvertently dropped overboard a plastic fuel-tank filler cap. As it floated back past *Viracocha*, under tow, there was a cry, 'Dive for it!' and Erik Catari, very courageously, did so. But our course and the river's current were not quite the same and he missed it. We then had to put in action our Man Overboard drill to fish him out – once again, fortunately, free of the attentions of piranha or caiman.

KM2, with no keel, was a difficult vessel to helm, and often when a strong wind was on the nose a tiny lapse in concentration by the steersmen could turn her to one side or the other, whereupon no amount of effort on the helm could bring her up into the wind again and she would execute a graceful 360° circle to get on track.

At Concepción the expedition entered a new phase. Here a large party would leave the support ship to carry out tasks in inland Paraguay, while the reed boats would, of course, carry on down-river for the remaining 312 kilometres to Asunción, followed by *PQ* with its attenuated complement.

We had a rousing reception at this city of 23,000 people, delivered by the band of the 2nd Division of cavalry of the Paraguayan Army drawn up on the quayside. And very tuneful and cheering they were, too, playing many Paraguayan favourites, including 'La Galopera' and 'Noches de Ypacara'. Ramiro Carrasco, the eccentric Bolivian canoeist, was equally well fêted here. It is a pleasant, friendly place with some fine 1920s and 1930s houses now being restored. Yet it is undeservedly neglected by the principal guide-books – with the honourable exception of the excellent *South American Handbook*. A woman from Fuerte Olimpo told Yoli that she had seen the boats and had now come to Concepción just for the day to see the team as well, grateful for the work that had been done in her community.

There was a chance to change money, send off postcards, have a haircut, eat ice cream. The best soup for many a mile was had at the Hotel Piscis: a *Crema de Pescado Blanco*. We all enjoyed the touch of good living a place like this affords – some of us a bit too well. Mary Stewart emerged late one morning scowling like Grandma in the Giles cartoons. She had rather over-eagerly seized the opportunity to live it up the previous night, and it had taken six of us to help her home and down the vertical ladder, into the hold and into her hammock.

Our stopover in Concepción also gave Noel Burrell the opportunity to take DNA samples from the local population. For some while the SES had been cooperating with Professor Moses at University College London in tracing the ancestry of tribal groups through DNA. A successful exercise had been carried out in Nepal, and another research team had shown that a small tribe in southern Africa had originated in Israel. By similar means we hoped to discover any links between present-day South Americans and African tribes. Mary Stewart had taken samples from the Chipaya earlier in the expedition, and as we progressed down-river, Noel took more. The procedure was simple and painless: a cotton swab was wiped on the inside of the cheek and preserved in spirit for DNA testing back in England. To be sure of valid results, we needed an indigenous population of at least 2,500 that could provide twenty men over twenty-five who were unrelated on the male side. Alas, it was proving extremely difficult to fulfil these conditions, even in a city like Concepción, and Noel had to be content with a rather inadequate number of samples. However, the results, which are still being worked out, may well throw some light on possible links between the peoples of the Old and New Worlds.

Thursday 7 September dawned fine. At 7.30 a.m. Jim gave the order to cast off and the reed boats pulled away, leaving *PQ* to follow later after it had disembarked an archaeological study team under John, who were to investigate tales of strange runic script, cave drawings and petroglyphs at Cerro Corá on the Brazilian border north-east of Concepción. As John lugged his kit up the rickety ship's ladder, Yoli appeared, looking worried.

'I have spoken to Capitán Martin Lugo, the Commandant of the Navy base here,' she said. 'There is a bad storm coming, it will be very dangerous for the reed boats. They should not sail.'

'Too late,' grunted John. 'They've gone.' Sure enough, at 8.15 a.m. the sky darkened and within minutes the most violent winds to hit us yet sent everyone in the little port scurrying for cover. By 9.30 a.m. it was reckoned to be Force 6–7. White-capped waves swept downriver and all craft made fast to the bank.

With concern showing on his still yellow face, John called Jim on the satellite phone. 'Are you OK? Have you tied up?' he asked.

'We're fine,' replied the Admiral. 'We're going like rockets –

be in Asunción in two–three days at this speed.' Thankfully the wind was from the north.

The archaeological team took shelter in a warehouse and awaited the arrival of James Wright's 4 × 4 vehicles, which had had mechanical problems. *PQ* could not sail until the gale subsided and a feeling of frustration descended on us.

John had other worries, too. He had learnt of terrorist activity on Paraguay's eastern border. Apparently a group linked to Peru's infamous Shining Path guerrillas was targeting travellers and foreigners close to the area we wished to explore. Yoli was seeking more information on this when at last the cars arrived, driven once more by James and Pablo.

The relationship between John and Pablo was already an uneasy one and was to get worse. Pablo was almost a figure of caricature. An able man in practical terms, he seemed almost to be acting the part of a stereotypically obstinate, opinionated Teuton. If it was an act, he did it very well.

'So we go first to Belén,' Richard said as the two-vehicle convoy was setting off for the interior.

'I no go to Belén. We do not go to Belén,' Pablo asserted.

Tomas Hughes explained our itinerary and Pablo got out of his 4 × 4 and trotted over to John's vehicle rather like a Spanish bull in its first moments in the arena.

He was soon back and engaging first gear furiously.

'*Buscando fantasmas,*' he said. '*¡Estúpido!* I no go to the Equator *buscando* penguin. I go to South Pole to find penguin.'

It was clear that he felt there was nothing of archaeological interest in Belén.

Later, Richard noticed an Israeli 9mm Jericho pistol tucked under Pablo's seat cushion.

'What's that for?' he asked. '*¿Bandidos?*'

'*No. Para el Coronel.*'

In fact, the 213 kilometres of Route 5, from Concepción to the town of Pedro Juan Caballero on the Brazilian border, is the most dangerous in Paraguay, with a record of frequent hold-ups. When a sinister-looking car with black glass windows overtook us, stopped ahead of us and came up behind us again Pablo reached quickly for his controversial weapon. It could have been a bad moment – but the sinister car passed us peacefully a second time.

'I like Pablo,' said Tomas. 'You know where you are with him. He doesn't like anybody.'

We reached Belén and entered into protracted discussions with various locals, but the only archaeological lead was to a site too far away. At a street corner Pablo said: 'Here you cross Tropic of Capricorn again.' He had measured it on his GPS.

We drove off eastwards again into a Force 8 gale, the wind whipping the palm trees into a frenzy. After some hours we came to an important T-junction at a place almost impossible to pronounce: Yby-Yaú, a Guaraní name meaning 'Eat Land' and sounding roughly like 'ee-VEE chya-OO'. Here we stopped for petrol and a snack – and a mishap that caused Charles Sturge great distress. Carelessly he had allowed his borrowed JVC digital video camera, worth over £1,000, to drop to the floor in the crowded back of the 4 × 4. When someone opened the door from the outside it fell into the road. This was the end, for now, of Charles's filming and, sorrowfully, he left the rest of us in order to take a bus to Asunción to set in train the procurement of another. It was to take him three weeks, and it cost the expedition a lot of unrepeatable photo-opportunities.

It was at Yby-Yaú that we resumed the practice of having exchanges by satellite telephone with British schools that we had begun on the Bolivian Altiplano in 1998. Then they had been with Brixham Community College; this time around we spoke to Clayesmore School in rural Dorset. We had not been able to organize a call before this because of the school holidays. Now we could begin a weekly exchange. Unfortunately it was bucketing down with rain, but a nearby car showroom had a projecting canvas porch under which we could place the phone with its antenna pointing up at the right angle. There were no school-children here, so the Dorset pupils had to be content with a resumé of our journey from Richard and John.

Afterwards we followed the good road up into the Cordillera de Amambaí, Paraguay's highest mountains, never much more than 1,500 feet above the sea but older than the Andes, and not breathtaking but scenic: fertile agricultural land dotted with enormous chunky sandstone outcrops, many of which contained caves adorned with the petroglyphs which we sought. We turned off into the Cerro Corá National Park and made for the park headquarters, a smart new complex of brick buildings behind a high wire fence. This was not only a wildlife reserve – there was a delightful tame Brocket's deer wandering about between the buildings – but the park contained a national shrine. Close by is the spot where President Francisco Solano López died at the tragic end of the War of the Triple Alliance in April 1870.

The presentation of information for visitors by the French at the battlefield of Waterloo is a well-known example of how a thumping defeat can be turned into a glorious victory. Here at Cerro Corá the dictator of Paraguay between 1954 and 1989, President Alfredo Stroessner, had achieved another.

Marshal-President Francisco Solano López, weak and spoilt, was by most accounts a preposterous head of state. He has had apologists who have sought to see him in the context of his time and place and justify some of his more monstrous crimes. In his brief presidency (1862–70) he led his country steadily into disaster. The story of the pre-war machinations in the Río de la Plata area is complicated enough to make the eyes of dedicated historians glaze over. Suffice it to say that he allowed a quarrel with one political party in Uruguay to become a war also with Brazil and Argentina. He had inherited from his father, President Carlos Antonio López, a considerable army of 28,000 men with some 40,000 reserves, but the 'Napoleon of South America' could not hope to prevail against a coalition of three such neighbours. The war dragged on, with frequent lengthy intermissions, from 1865 to 1870, by which time Paraguay had lost a quarter of its population – in battle and from cholera and hunger.

Enlisting women, children and old men into the ranks, once his male soldiery had been sacrificed, like Hitler later, he and his remnant army of just 409 retreated at the end into the hills at Cerro Corá where, after his final defiant refusal to surrender, a Brazilian cavalryman gunned him down with a Spencer carbine. In the preceding days he had had his mother and two sisters caged and occasionally flogged, and their death warrants signed. He had ordered the execution of his two brothers, his childhood sweetheart and numerous ladies at court who had snubbed his Irish mistress, Elisa Lynch. He spent the few days before the *dénouement* amusing himself by designing a victory medal and ribbon for 'the campaign of Amambaí'.

His faithful mistress scratched a grave for him on the river bank where he had fallen and went off back to the Parisian *demi-monde* from which he had originally plucked her. After the President's death and the war's immediate end it was said that only women, children and donkeys were left – there were just 28,000 men in a population of 194,000, a minority of one in seven. '*Muero con mi patria*,' he had shouted before his death, 'I die with my country': and it is true that he took Paraguay with him.

As we were able that evening to see at Cerro Corá, Stroessner had done a thorough job of undeserved rehabilitation on his flawed predecessor. Tall hardwood trees surround an amphitheatre. Monkeys and three-toed sloths hang in their branches. In the evening gloom the landscape, far from habitation, had a sort of wild beauty. A giant cross stands where López fell; there are avenues of busts of his general officers, many of whom he himself had shot before the last battle. Irrationally cruel, vain, talentless, unprepossessing, he must have been one of the most unpleasant men ever to have been transmogrified into a national hero.

After glimpsing Stroessner's ludicrous manipulation of history we returned to park headquarters to find a bush fire raging dangerously close to the wire fence. It was as well the park authorities, fearing the wind could change, had refused us permission to camp in the forest but instead offered accommodation in an office building. The fierce northerly fanned the flames and things were made worse by the fact that there had been no rain for seventy days, despite its being the so-called wet season – an anomaly which apparently occurs every four or five years.

As the roaring, crackling fire swept towards our quarters, clouds of sparks wafted over the buildings. Ash fell everywhere and small animals scampered out of the bush. The local volunteer fire brigade arrived and did remarkably well in keeping the flames at bay, but John nevertheless decided to sleep on the verandah with an eye on developments. Twice during the night the sound of agitated voices woke him; the clouds of wind-blown embers passing over the full petrol cans on Pablo's roof rack were causing concern. However, by dawn the fire had burnt itself out and, as it turned out, there was not long to wait for rain to dampen any remaining embers.

Adelina Pusineri in Asunción had given John and Yoli details of the rock inscriptions to be found in the area and, after we had looked at the excellent museum in the visitors' centre, with its exhibits from the battle of Cerro Corá in 1870 as well as much on the region's natural history and ethnography, we set off to investigate them. The first site was Tuja-Og ('The house of the old man'), where an overhang at the front of a sandstone cliff sported a range of carvings. Some looked like rhea footprints; others were long parallel lines of dots which may have been a form of map. Andy Miller carefully measured and photographed them all. The next site, Cerro Acua, was much bigger and seemed full of depictions of male and female genitalia, the latter possibly giving an indication of how many children a woman had borne. Jim Woodman in Asunción and Frenchman Jacques de Mahieu believe that the Vikings were in Paraguay in the thirteenth century and had left runic inscriptions. Guided by an American seventeen-year-old, Jesse Weaver, we saw many rows of vertical lines and one rock face littered with squiggles. 'Perhaps they are crude maps,' suggested Richard. There were letters that might have been Greek. While John photographed them and Richard sketched, Andy studied the inscriptions thoughtfully. 'There are no ceramics here,' Jesse pointed out. Indeed, it was Jesse, the American living nearby, who had discovered some of the sites. 'I get the impression this was a ritual site,' said Pamela, who was helping to measure the inscriptions. Andy, however, remained totally sceptical; certainly these looked nothing like the runes that Richard had once seen in Sweden. 'Early indigenous peoples' was all we would say about their provenance.

Ironically, after the previous day's fire had burnt down outbuildings and laid waste to much of the park, heavy rain began to fall in the night and by 5 a.m. on 9 September it had become a deluge. The entire night sky had been lit by sheet and fork lightning in the most Wagnerian display any of us had ever seen. This seemed to clear the air and for the first time in several weeks lifted the *humo* which had blanketed Paraguay and almost obscured the sun.

We left Cerro Corá and headed south through fertile country, past ranches said to be owned by Evander Holyfield and Muhammad Ali: fine *estancias* with Friesian cows producing milk and cheese, all very European in appearance. As the sun broke through, dazzling now and sharp, we headed for Nueva Germania. This town had been founded in 1886 near the banks of the Río Aguaray Guazú in the remote Paraguayan hinterland by Elisabeth, the sister of the German philosopher Friedrich Nietzsche, her husband Bernhard Förster and fourteen German families – all united by a hatred of Jews. More families had joined them, but the colony had not really taken off: some settlers had returned, others married into Paraguayan families, others just dispersed to more easily cultivable farms. Nietzsche's complex philosophies were later to be hijacked by the Nazis, even though they were mostly at variance with National Socialist thinking, and his sister Elisabeth, who returned to Germany in 1893, found herself lionized in later life by Hitler, Goebbels, Frick and the rest of the pack.

What did we expect to find in this quiet settlement? Thick-thighed Aryans striding about in *Lederhosen*? Nueva Germania seemed quite unexceptionably Paraguayan. From the police station (no gauleiters; just friendly, laid-back locals) where we announced ourselves we went to the school for a long briefing from a master which contained almost no reference to the town's German origins. Ben Macintyre, who visited the town in 1991 to research his enthralling book *Forgotten Fatherland*, found some signs of these beginnings and met a few obviously German descendants of the first settlers. He stood in the ruins of Försterhof, the home of Elisabeth and Friedrich, of which now no trace remains. We were shown its site and the first street, and saw the Lutheran church which now holds an annual ecumenical service with Catholics. Juan Vauklo, a second-generation German, is still alive at ninety, and in the school we met Andrés Flascam, a very blond, Germanic sixteen-year-old. German is not taught at the school but is still spoken in the district. Of 310 pupils in the school, just twenty-five have German names.

Pablo, no happier than usual, said, '*Schnell* means . . .' and he chopped his hand up and down to indicate speed, 'and here is always waiting.' Yoli had to take every opportunity to make important phone calls to our forward destinations, and the rest of us spent a lot of time waiting outside the ANTELCO phone shops. Soon, however, we were again heading south on Route 3, towards James Wright's ranch, to which he had invited us all for a meal and a night under a roof. His extensive property, probably about the size of Rutland, owes its strange name, RI 3 Corrales, to the presence there in the Triple Alliance War of Regiment of Infantry Number 3, under General Corrales.

Pablo seemed unsure of the route and drove up and down the narrow dirt roads, stopping here and there to ask the way. John was just about to set up camp and get a meal cooked when the entrance to the ranch appeared. The five-bar gate was securely padlocked but Pablo demolished the lock in his usual style and we drove up to a scattering of low brick and stone buildings from which a sleepy James emerged to make us welcome in his somewhat laid-back manner. Once inside, Tomas Hughes soon had the Batchelor's Beanfeast heating up while Peter Hutchison and John set up the satellite phone link in the garden. Pablo proceeded to serve some extremely strong spirits to those unwise enough to take them on an empty stomach. Pamela, acting as the team's medic, then had to deal with a couple of very sick explorers, which she did with extraordinary good humour.

The phone calls at Nueva Germania and at our next port of call, Villarrica, were not all to do with practical forward planning. Many were difficult and protracted, and to do with Adrian Giménez Hutton. An urgent e-mail from friends in Buenos Aires, still almost 2,000 kilometres away, had brought disturbing news. In spite of what he had told John on his departure, Adrian had not enjoyed his visit and on returning home had advised several of our established supporters in Argentina not to continue backing us. Fortunately our main friends, the Prefectura Naval, were still on side, but others were wavering. The stories being bandied about were pretty wild and off the target, but with nobody in Buenos Aires to refute them they were damaging our cause, and could even harm the very Anglo-Argentine relations we had been trying to enhance. An election was due in Argentina on 24 October, President Menem had openly criticized Britain for its handling of the Pinochet case, and, although flights from Argentina to the Falkland Islands were about to recommence for the first time since the conflict of 1982, the Malvinas question was still a hot potato. Clearly it was no time for the Kota Mama expedition to become an issue. Still mystified by the reasons behind Adrian's action, John sought the advice of the British Embassy and decided with some reluctance to send in Stuart Seymour, whose linguistic and diplomatic skills fitted him for this task, to bat for us in Buenos Aires. He would leave as soon as the fleet reached Asunción and hand over the important job of adjutant to Nathan Arnison.

Villarrica is an attractive town on the gridiron pattern with a plaza given over to display boards describing all the battles of the 1932–5 Chaco War against Bolivia. We spent some time 30 kilometres away at Ybytruzu inspecting and recording two more petroglyph sites on Cerro Pelado. One rock face was completely filled with scratchings and lines, many similar to those we had found at Cerro Corá. Some had been chipped out, probably by souvenir hunters, and an elongated crucifix carved over the petroglyphs may have been added by Jesuits.

Near the summit of a forest-covered hill was a cave – which we should not have found without the help of the landowner's wife – which contained the best-preserved petroglyphs. Footprints, arrows and vertical incisions appeared as before; but again there was no pottery nor any other evidence of human habitation. 'It's very difficult to attach a date or any specific meaning to the patterns,' said Andy, who was also worried by the lack of conservation of these fascinating sites. However, he took details to study on return to Britain.

After weeks of shipboard life it was good to have to hack up a mountain through virgin forest. It was good, too, to be in camp again making hot drinks out of a Volcano kettle. This superb piece of camping kit, made by Kelly's of Daventry, works on the principle that a cylindrical sleeve containing water offers more surface area to the heat of a fire lit inside it than the bottom of a pan. It is very simple to use in wooded country or scrub – and saves cutting down trees for firewood. First, you light a small fire of dry grass and twigs in the metal pedestal on which the cylinder stands. Then you turn the air-hole in the side of the pedestal towards the wind. Then you fill the cylinder sleeve with water and place on the pedestal. (NB: Remove bung; injuries might result if this is overlooked!) Feed the fire from above with larger twigs – like dropping fuel into the crater of a volcano. Wait a few moments and you will have a good rolling boil in the sleeve, enough for three or four hot drinks. Richard was a well practised hand by the end of the expedition.

Meanwhile, back on the Paraguay river, the fleet seemed to be managing well enough without the full attentions of the Support Group. It might even be said that Jim and his men enjoyed the days when they could sail or motor down the river out of radio range of *PQ* and the media team. Three days out of Concepción they had covered the 153 kilometres to Villa del Rosario, passing on the way the mouth of the tributary up which the Germans had painfully made their way to Nueva Germania. Day followed day in a way which had by now become routine. The crew was divided into two watches. Two men were constantly on the steering oars; one, often Stuart McCallion, manned the outboard engine. Others kept watch ahead or worked the sails and the lee-board when necessary. If the following wind veered from the starboard quarter to the port quarter, a complicated manoeuvre entailed the realignment of the cruising sail – just as on the old Portuguese lateen-rigged caravels, many of which would once have plied up and down this river.

Pat Troy, often helped by John Teague, kept a close watch on the frequent navigation marks on the banks, many of which showed the distance in kilometres to Asunción. H directed shipping to hold to the centre of the river, a square meant 'Keep to the side the sign is on' and X was an instruction to cross to the other side.

The two or three crew in *Viracocha* were left pretty much to their own devices and were able to sail much more than those on *KM2*. To relieve the monotony of pushing *KM2* into a southerly wind (which sadly was almost constant downriver from Concepción) the crew of the Avon inflatable was brought on board the flagship from time to time, giving Ben Cartwright (later Les Winterburn) and Ed Ledsam a chance to dry off, warm up, relax, apply sun-cream or whatever, while two other crew members drove the Avon. There was a covered after-cabin in which off-duty crew could rest.

Gerry Masters took great care to keep everyone supplied with food. Towards the end of the morning he would start preparing sandwiches for lunch, and these were first passed down to the Avon and *Viracocha*. In hot weather he maintained a constant provision of fruit-flavoured drinks. Nobody need become dehydrated.

Jim usually invited a visitor or two on board for a day from among the many ancillary members on *PQ*. They were carefully briefed on safety drills. When both sails were up the helmsmen could see nothing of the river ahead, so there had to be a man in the fore-peak keeping a good lookout. This was often a visitor's job.

Erik was constantly checking the condition of the boats, tightening the cords that bound the reeds, replacing worn fittings and measuring the draught to see how much water was being absorbed. Knowing the success of the expedition depended on the craft reaching Buenos Aires, John was anxious about all this. Indeed, although he did not mention it to the crew, several 'boat experts' had prophesied that the craft would become completely waterlogged within two months and that the reeds would rot or be consumed by river creatures. Erik, too, had heard such predictions, but stoutly displayed confidence in his handicraft. As time went by and the rate of absorption was found to be slower than anticipated John felt easier, but he knew the real test would come when we reached the Río Paraná. Stories of violent storms and a current said by some to reach 12 kph were not thought to be exaggerations.

There were, inevitably, *longueurs*. Many of the crew, inured by now to the hot sun, took part in vigorous keep-fit sessions, vying with one another in the number of squats, sit-ups, push- or pull-ups that they could achieve. Some very tough men arrived in Asunción on Friday 10 September.

CHAPTER SEVENTEEN

La Ciudad de Nuestra Señora Santa María de la Asunción

Below the park, where the ground falls steeply to the river, are the shacks of the poor. By every falling stream-trickle squat women and girls washing clothes . . . In the distance the government palace describes an indifferent antithesis to this squalor, although the shack area concludes its boundaries almost at the Palace walls, like a scene of feudal Europe.

GORDON MEYER,
The River and the People, 1965

In his briefing on Friday 10 September, John said, 'When you get to A-Sun-Shone' – he always eschewed the Spanish pronunciation of the capital city – 'I want you all to be especially smart as the First Lady will be coming aboard.' Whether it was repercussions of the caiman incident, social constraints or just Paraguayan insouciance (probably the last), the President's beautiful wife did not join us several kilometres upriver and travel down on the flagship as originally hoped, but was to pay us a visit one morning when we were tied up at the port.

At all events, *PQ* and the reed boats did not proceed immediately there but paused at Los Remansos, a northern suburb of Asunción where a graceful and imposing road bridge carries traffic high over the river to the Gran Chaco. When the petroglyph hunters came in from Ybytruzu and Villarrica to Los Remansos they had a hard time finding the boats, which were moored on the outside of three massive, white, spookily redundant river cruisers.

A wasteland lay between the bridge approach and these once noble liners. A *marinero* led us down a rutted, overgrown track to a ruined house. Could this be the *Base Naval*? With a caving helmet on his head, a fishing rod in one hand and a large bunch of bananas in the other, Richard, with John and Yoli differently laden, climbed a rail-less gangplank leading up to the bows of the *Bahía Negra*. Closer inspection in the light of morning showed that this 5,000 or 6,000 tonne ship had once been the *Presidente Stroessner* but that the hated Alfredo had been painted out. We then climbed over various deck rails to get on board an identical vessel, the *Presidente Carlos Antonio López*. Finally we climbed on to the *Olimpo*, a cargo boat with deep, empty holds, built at Bilbao in Spain in 1961. 'There are plans to restore all three,' John said. It was a fine notion – these elegant relics of the 1950s and 1960s carving a gracious way up the river once more, with passengers bound for Alto Paraguay.

At Asunción John wrote in his log: 'Admiral Ocampos is our guardian angel, who in an unassuming way has ensured that our passage along the river has been without let or hindrance.' Only John and Yoli had so far met the Commander of the Paraguayan Navy. Many of us were still a bit surprised that land-locked Paraguay actually *had* a navy – for, unlike Bolivia, Paraguay has never had a sea coast. There was quite an air of expectation when, just before 7 a.m. on Monday 13 September, a nice, neatly moustachioed man in his mid-sixties came climbing over the rails of the derelict ships, ten minutes ahead of schedule. He cut a somewhat un-Admiral-like figure, in a light anorak and jaunty baseball cap, a cigarette in one hand and in the other his *poro* of *yerba mate*. John introduced him first to Captain Martin and the Bolivian Navy crew and then to Surgeon-Lieutenant (D) Melissa Wingfield, our only serving representative of the Royal Navy. The assembled company then sang 'Happy Birthday, Dear Admiral,' for such it was. Tomas Galeano interpreted while Jim and Chris Brogan explained the intricacies of the great flagship in which he was shortly to sail down to the port of Asunción. Erik Catari talked of how the reed boats were made and Pat Troy how they were navigated, and at 7.30 precisely they cast off under blue skies into an obligingly northerly wind. Our Paraguayan godfather had had to stub out his cigarette (one of Jim's most rigorously applied rules on this floating tinder box), but he had occasional sips of *yerba mate* as he took the helm and steered us downstream.

PQ followed at a respectful distance. Soon the high-rise buildings of Asunción came into view and in front, outshining them all, the big white wedding cake which was the Palacio de Gobierno or Government Palace, once the closely guarded home of presidents. Minutes later *PQ* seemed to be running past the capital when suddenly she turned into the broad backwater of the Río Paraguay which must have attracted Domingo de Irala when he founded the Spanish settlement here in 1537.

We had decided to arrive in the capital city singing a British song, but accompanied by Paraguay's favourite instrument, the harp. Marigold Verity brought her half-size version on to the deck. What could she play that we could sing? After some discussion we had settled on 'The Skye Boat Song'. The wind was freshening and made singing difficult. Ranged in a long line, we were hesitantly ploughing through the first verse with the usual British lack of fervour and clear evidence of under-rehearsal when some of us noticed that our own bonny boat was speeding over the sea far too fast. The stout wooden timbers of the quayside were quickly drawing close and Captain Martin seemed reluctant to order 'Full Astern!' Furthermore, we had competition: there was a full-scale military band up on the quay belting out the same rousing Paraguayan airs with which we had been regaled at Concepción. The less confident singers lost the thread of the Skye Boat Song as the trumpets and drums grew more audible, and the high wall loomed.

Suddenly it was all very chaotic. *PQ*'s bows struck the wooden uprights a formidable blow and the chorus line was pitched forwards, almost into the harbour. What a way to arrive! Of all the well-conducted landings we had made in the last month, we had to produce a real lulu under the watchful gaze of the Paraguayan top brass. Luckily Admiral Ocampos was still achieving a first for a Paraguayan Navy commander on his steering oar out in the river. *KM2* had to spend an hour running up and down the harbour practising sail-changing near a splendidly old river defence vessel, No. C2, *Humaitá*. Built in Genoa in 1931, this handsome Prussian blue ship lay permanently at anchor, ready, it was said, to evacuate fleeing presidents and fire on their pursuers with its 4.7 inch guns. The Admiral, having done his stint, was dropped off on board her.

There was time to tidy up ready for *La Primera Dama* – who was, conventionally and predictably, late in arriving; 'held up' was the ambiguous explanation. Richard's tape, recording the military band, had run out by the time Señora Susana Galli de Gonzalez Macchi came sweeping into the port precincts in a black limo almost as long as her name. But her smile and personality instantly charmed us all. In a powder-blue trouser-suit and high heels she skilfully negotiated *PQ*'s steep companionways, inspected a guard of honour and went on board *KM2*. There was much photography, Charles Sturge leaping from hatch cover to hatch cover like a nimble vicuña. Stuart, Billy and Tomas – all members of the Queen's Dragoon Guards – managed to get her to pose with them: one for the regimental album. John later said that she was the nearest to royalty that he had ever met in South America. Perhaps we went a bit overboard about her, but we had been a long time on the river. (There were, indeed, other people present who had a claim on our attention: Gerry Evans, Chargé d'Affaires at the British Embassy, Stuart Duncan of Lloyds Bank, the Bolivian Ambassador to Paraguay and, in attendance on the First Lady, the Bolivian Naval Attaché, Cesar Filartiga.)

The Señora's last kindness was to take part in the schools broadcast which was rigged up by Owain Davies on the quayside. Some of the pre-arranged questions came up, but there was too much ambient noise for her to hear the Clayesmore children clearly for very long. Some of us never ceased to marvel that this sort of link-up was achievable at all.

Asunción was bigger, more modern than we had thought. It had a nineteenth-century heart near the port and beyond it wide *avenidas* dotted with parks and the mansions of the rich. The Government Palace on the waterfront used to be off limits. President Stroessner lived there and it is said that an eight-year-old American girl was once shot when leaving the palace after a semi-official visit. A close approach and photography were at that paranoiac time forbidden. The worst that happened to Richard and Peter Hutchison was to be whistled at by a guard for walking on the grass.

The palace was an early symptom of President Francisco Solano López's *folie de grandeur*. Envisioned as a suitable monument to the future Napoleon of South America, it was begun in the early 1860s to the design of an English architect, Alonso Taylor. The lower parts are freestone, the upper of brick covered by whitened stucco. A tower that would grace any Gothic church stands at the centre. Today, a gigantic tricolour hangs lazily in the forecourt. The sculptural work was by an Irishman, John Moynihan, but the young President didn't like it and put it all in the basement – along with Alonso Taylor, whom he fell out with and had tortured, a fate that befell many other hired expatriates.

The War of the Triple Alliance halted its construction (mainly carried out by gangs of children) and the Brazilian fleet bombarded it, demolishing one corner. Richard Burton, British Consul in São Paulo, was twice in Asunción during the war and called it 'an utter absurdity'. Yachtsman E. F. Knight in 1881 thought it 'a haughty structure', but, on closer inspection, 'a mere wreck with broken windows, gutted as by a fire, a mere empty shell within . . . torn and pierced by many a shot'. It was just being completed when Elisabeth Nietzsche left in 1893, and she missed the inaugural ceremonies. Gordon Meyer approved of it in 1965, and it still dominates the river approaches to the city, to which we all thought it lent much dignity and grace.

The old heart of the city also contains a classic Palace of Justice, an independence column, a rather dull-sounding cathedral (almost always locked, so few of us saw it) and a grandiose equestrian statue on a high plinth – of Marshal-President Francisco Solano López.

Uphill and slightly inland Stroessner built a Pantheon de los Héroes, a small replica of Les Invalides in Paris. Here two stony-faced young Paraguayan soldiers in nineteenth-century garb stand guard over an urn containing what remains of El Supremo, Rodríguez de Francia, and the tombs of the Lópezes, father and son, together with Estigarríbia, the Marshal who lived for a while in Puerto Casado, and two unknown soldiers. Behind the Pantheon in the Plaza de los Héroes is a new piece of statuary put up for *los desaparecidos* – those who disappeared in the time of President Stroessner (1954–89). Though the man himself is still alive in Brazil, most vestiges of him in his former country have now themselves disappeared: the city which was once Puerto Presidente Stroessner is now rather prosaically Ciudad del Este (Eastern City), his international airport is now named for Silvio Pettirossi and the ship we walked over at Los Remansos is the *Bahía Negra*.

Sadly, Asunción's Belgian-made trams have gone now, but a

seven-minute taxi ride from the centre takes one to another relic of Paraguay's 1860s glory days. Built in 1868 as the residence of – you've guessed it: President Francisco Solano López, the Gran Hotel del Paraguay retains a faded grandeur, much as did the old Raffles Hotel in Singapore. It is a family concern now, run by the Weilers like an old provincial German hotel with dogs sprawling all over the place. The stage for Elisa Lynch's theatre is still there, in a dining room with painted wood on walls and ceiling where the portly President habitually appeared at his mistress's *bals masqués* as Napoleon.

There is a downside to Asunción, of course. The *lujo* mansions of the rich are largely the homes of big *contrabandistas*, drug barons and hoodlums of various stripes. Everyone is trying to sell something, illegally imported, pirated or stolen, to someone else. Hucksters will leap on to a bus and pass round samples of their wares, headache potions, trouser presses and the like. *Cambios* abound and outside the Pantheon de los Héroes is the main pitch of the street money-changers, who will take anything in return for their wads of grubby guaraníes. Old copies of *Playboy* (and worse) paper the walls of street kiosks, and the shops are full of counterfeit CDs, locally made Reebok trainers, slit-crotch knickers. Asunción has 27,000 registered prostitutes, according to James Wright.

It also has a wonderful neo-Gothic railway terminus. In 1856 President Carlos Antonio López (1844–62) began to lay the first line in South America, to start with for 5 kilometres from Asunción to Trinidad (now within the city). His son continued it, using stock acquired from the Crimea. President Juan Batista Gill raised £6 million in London to develop it and in 1872 tried unsuccessfully to induce an army of Lincolnshire farmers to come out and build it, settle on farms around it and repopulate the country, denuded of its menfolk by the Triple Alliance War. In the end nearly a thousand Londoners came out as navvies and were subsequently given grants of land.

The team enjoyed a welcome respite in Asunción. Almost all of us travelled in a coach, generously arranged by *La Primera Dama*, to visit the stupendous hydro-electric power plant and dam at Itaipú and the amazing falls, longest in the world and immortalized in the film *The Mission*, at Iguazú, just outside Paraguay on the Brazil–Argentina border. A few of us were shown something of the interior by James Wright in his 4 × 4 and were able to see the pottery of the renowned Rosa Britez at Ita, the beautifully restored Franciscan church at Yaguarón, built in 1775, and the little-known locomotive workshops at Sapucai, run until nationalization in 1961 by a colony of over a hundred British engineers and their families and still (just) in business under local management. These experiences gave us all a greater understanding of and love for Paraguay, a rarely visited land of immense charm.

Unhappily, we missed the chance to travel on the railway from Asunción to Aregua, a little way out of town. This steam-hauled trip leaves at 9 a.m. on Saturdays and Sundays only, and it was now midweek. The rail service through the country to Encarnación has not operated fully since 1993, but there are still steam locomotives dotted about the system: four at Asunción, nine at the Sapucai workshops (six out of action, three *en reparación*), two at Villarrica, two or three at Encarnación, one each at Tebicuary and Ypacarai – a grand total of nineteen or twenty. This is a part of Paraguay's heritage that must be preserved, and the growing army of enthusiasts who now travel the world for steam will no doubt descend on Paraguay in greater numbers and boost its embryonic tourist industry.

The future of Rocket, our fast-growing ginger piglet, became an increasingly urgent topic at Asunción. Stringent Argentinian regulations decreed that we could not take him from his Paraguayan homeland, which we should be leaving about 240 kilometres downstream. But he was becoming more and more attached to us all and often roamed the decks freely. In the early hours of one morning John, in his bunk under the chart table in the *sala de operaciones*, was aware of something breathing heavily and snuffling at his feet. Nathan, John's adjutant, in the next bunk was surely above suspicion. 'Such attachment will not improve your promotion prospects,' John murmured sleepily, and then realized that it must have been Rocket.

On the same night Les Winterburn, returning late from one of the many bars close to the port, picked Rocket up and carried him down into the hold. Whenever Rocket's feet left the ground he would emit prolonged and painful squeals. These now inevitably woke the entire hold. 'Take that pig out!' shouted Noel, but Les put him in Ben Cartwright's bed, with explosive results, and then let him roam about until 3 a.m. when, to the accompaniment of more piercing squeals, he carried him up on deck again.

Around this time John was becoming concerned about negative reports on the expedition which had reached Julia Linsley in Motcombe. He asked Richard to sound out the views of some of his old expedition colleagues to see if anything was amiss, and perhaps to get them to write a letter of rebuttal to Julia.

'John has asked me to have a word with you,' Richard said to Les. When he had outlined the problem Les, with a sigh of relief, said: 'Ee, I thowt it were about t'pig.'

In the end, a home was found for the piglet on a farm outside Asunción, thanks to Andrea Machain, the BBC stringer in Paraguay who had come on board to record some of us for the World Service and fallen under Rocket's spell. He was later reported to be surrounded by attractive sows and having a great time.

As for the expedition itself – 'There's nowt wrong wi' it,' had been Les's view, and in truth all was broadly well. Most of us felt that it was a grand concept, being very competently executed, within budget and up to time. Some of the tasks had not proved so fruitful, but by and large we were delivering the goods and doing a very good job for British relations with this part of the world.

CHAPTER EIGHTEEN

INTO THE
PARANÁ

*It was two days later that we came to Formosa . . . We had turned off
the great Paraná the night before near Corrientes and now we were on
the Paraguay. Fifty yards across the water from the Argentinian Formosa
the other country lay sodden and empty. It certainly seemed an ideal
town for smugglers with only a river to cross. In Paraguay I could see
only a crumbling hut, a pig and a small girl.*

GRAHAM GREENE,
Travels with my Aunt, 1969

Peter Hutchison and Richard had the fun of being interviewed
live one evening on Paraguayan television by an engagingly
jovial, bearded character called Humberto Rubín. It was another
opportunity to outline our theories about the possible use of reed
boats on the Paraguay river by ancient traders – and a chance
to say how welcoming the people here had been and how
intriguing we had found the country. Marigold Verity played her
harp while Peter and Richard sipped the generous helpings of
whisky and water provided by Paraguay's Channel Four.

One important part of Paraguay's national heritage which we
had yet to see was the assemblage of ruined Jesuit missions in
the south of the country. Andy Miller, Shaun Linsley and Marie
Peralta were now despatched to have a look round some of them
and make a report.

In the sixteenth century the Guaraní Indians proved to be exceptionally docile, pliant and ready to do the bidding of their Spanish
overlords. So the Society of Jesus decided to bring groups of

215•

families into specially built communities or Reductions, where they could be kept secure and taught not only Christianity but farming, arts and crafts. Between 1609 and 1768 some eighty missions were established by the Jesuits on both sides of the upper Paraná, across an area that now spans Brazil, Argentina and Paraguay. Of these, thirty remain and some of the best preserved are among the eight in Paraguay, two having been designated World Heritage Sites. They are of obvious importance to the Paraguayan Minister of Tourism, Hugo Galli, the First Lady's brother, who came to visit us; he was interested in our work and very generously said, 'You have awoken us to our potential.'

After several bouts of shopping, communal and personal – because food in Argentina, where we were headed, was believed to be so much more expensive – the reed boats left Asunción at 7.45 a.m. on 16 September, followed the next day by *PQ*. We all felt relaxed and well fed, having discovered the *comida por kilo* system of eating out. This Brazilian concept, sensibly imported by the Paraguayans, is simple and attractive. Go to some Asunción *churrasquería* like Rodízio or Zanzanie, pick what you want from the excellent buffet, take it to be weighed, pay, eat. Can it have been the good food that caused someone, as we rejoined the main stream of the Paraguay, to say: 'Funny thing is, there's no cannelloni floating down the river here'?

Leaving naval installations and refineries to port, we soon passed the easily missed mouth of the Pilcomayo to starboard. Since Argentina gained the Chaco Central in 1862 (Bolivia and Paraguay together have less of the Chaco than their southern neighbour) this river has marked Argentina's northern border. Now we would have Paraguay to our left and Argentina to the right. The previous day *KM2* had been accorded a tremendous welcome by the Argentinian Prefectura Naval, the vast and power-fully equipped body which controls Argentina's rivers and coasts. Already apprised of our arrival, they waved us in to a small station called Puerto Pilcomayo. Jim warily sent the Avon ashore. Peter Hutchison came back out with a small boat carrying a film crew, who invited our people for a party. The badges everyone was given showed the Falklands as Argentinian.

Our wariness was natural, and based on the somewhat chequered relations between our two countries since 1982. These had been complicated by the Lino Oviedo affair. The Vice-President of Paraguay, Luis María Argaña, had been assassinated in Asunción on 23 March 1999; the Paraguayan ex-Army chief

General Lino Oviedo, thought to be implicated in the killing, had fled and had subsequently been granted asylum by Argentina. A row had brewed between Paraguay, which demanded that General Oviedo be extradited for trial, and Argentina, whose President, Carlos Menem, declined to send his old friend back. The papers were now full of the stories of the stand-off between the two nations. The general's return might precipitate more riots, even civil war between factions of the ruling Colorado party.

We hoped it would not be widely known that, to thank General Oviedo for his help in the 1996 recce of the Chaco, John had bought him a beautiful replica of Sir Walter Raleigh's poniard, specially made by Wilkinson's, the swordmakers. Yoli was visiting Paraguay with an expedition of young people led by SES Development Director, John Hunt, so she took it with her. Hardly had she left when Graham Pirnie, British Ambassador in Asunción, faxed HQ in Motcombe to say that the general was under house arrest for trying to launch a *coup d'état*. By then it was too late to intercept Yoli; however, though Paraguayan customs raised their eyebrows at the ceremonial weapon inscribed 'To General Oviedo, with sincere thanks and best wishes', they let it through, and somehow Yoli managed to get to the general and present it. President Menem later compromised and sent Oviedo into exile in Tierra del Fuego.

Politics and diplomacy were far from our minds as *PQ* caught up the reed boats at Estancia San Geronimo, 155 kilometres south of Asunción. A glance at the map will show that we still had a very considerable distance to go to reach Buenos Aires, and ominously *PQ* began to have more trouble with her engine. This led to a very close shave.

PQ had pulled her bows in to the forested bank while Joselino Benites, the Brazilian engineer, sorted out the latest problem. *KM2* and *Viracocha* came slowly past her stern with a few derisive cries of 'Want a tow?' Suddenly the support ship's engines sprang into life and, to our consternation, she started moving backwards into the oncoming reed boats. Captain Martin, alerted to the danger, flung his engines to full ahead to stop her. Stuart McCallion, manning *Kota Mama 2*'s steering motor, opened the throttle and Les Winterburn drove the Avon hard into her ample backside. What might have happened if *PQ* had run down the flagship is unthinkable – but, with engines roaring, they missed each other by 3 metres. We did not then have direct communications from *KM2* to *PQ*'s bridge, but Owain soon fitted a Motorola UHF set.

The mechanical difficulties with *PQ* were a constant worry. Yoli had called the Brazilian–Lebanese owner, Dr Michel Chaim, several times to ask for proper maintenance to be done in Asunción, before we reached the hazardous Río Paraná. His replies were not encouraging and John spent many hours agonizing over the problem of the unreliable vessel. There were now plenty of boats that could support us and provide safety cover – at a price. But our budget was already stretched, and it was unlikely that *PQ*'s owners would agree to a refund. After long deliberations in the operations room, it was decided to go on with *PQ* – and pray!

That afternoon we noticed on the skyline two contrasting building profiles. On the right were smart Argentinian office blocks and towers, tree-lined riverside avenues down which cars sped. This was Formosa. On the Paraguayan side was the small township of Puerto Alberdi: a rubbish-strewn landing, peeling paintwork and low-rise shacks with clumps of bougainvillaea and rambling roses round the doors. It was at Formosa that the elderly canoeist, Ramiro Carrasco Quiroga, had given up his mission to underscore Bolivia's rights of river navigation.

Another 53 kilometres on Sunday 19 September, brought us to Pilar, the last good-sized Paraguayan town on our journey. There isn't much passenger traffic by river any more, but Pilar had a set of comfortable waiting rooms on a substantial floating jetty – one of which Noel was able to use as a consulting room. The town's main feature of historical interest was a *cabildo* or town hall, built in 1817 and now a museum. It was full of relics of the War of the Triple Alliance, during which Pilar was taken and looted by Brazilian and Argentinian forces. Richard Burton recounts an odd story of two English sailors with the invading armies who appeared at the river bank arm in arm with a drunken comrade in blue jacket and trousers. Closer inspection by an officer revealed that they had stolen, and dressed, a valuable wooden crucifix.

The two-storey *cabildo* had been the headquarters of the Marshal-President during the war, and a silvery bust of him, with protrusive lips, heavily lidded eyes and full beard, now stands outside. It was at Pilar that Francisco Solano López swore on the Paraguayan flag, and a priest told him: 'You will taint it with much blood.' He was to do so, and for his candour the priest was the first to shed some. Rosanna Carrasco, the Governor's secretary whom we met by chance and who showed us the town, explained that among Pilar's 21,000 population women still outnumbered men by three to one. It was hard to believe that this could still be the effect of the 1865–70 war, at the end of which there were said to be twenty-five women to every Paraguayan man.

It was here that one of John's recurring characteristics again manifested itself: in the middle of one expedition he will find time to begin work on the next. On the Blue Nile in 1968 he had drawn up plans for another river journey; on the Zaire River he had formulated the idea behind Operation Drake. Now he seemed to be postponing the notion of proving the theory of west–east Atlantic trade routes by sailing to Africa, and proposing first of all another inland journey along rivers which could have been alternative routes for Altiplano dwellers from the Andes to the Atlantic – by the Río Grande, the Mamoré and the Madeira to the Amazon. He had been prompted by Bolivian archaeologists in this, and Oswaldo Rivera had long thought it the more likely route to the ocean.

Others of us had more mundane concerns on our minds. The next day, Monday 20 September, saw Pamela Coleridge, Noel and Richard on cooking duty. What to have? Porridge or eggs in some form were our staple breakfasts; the most popular way to start the day in the field had been H.L.'s Boil-in-the-Bag meals, but they had now all gone. Lunch was a self-help snack, sometimes fortified with McDougall's Lentil Soup (but today it was 98°F in the shade, so perhaps not). The evening meal required the greatest resourcefulness, the most finesse. We had discovered the sweet potato, and now we all fell to and peeled the afternoon away. Even the tasty Batchelor's Beanfeast was beginning to pall: this is a vegetarian dish which even carnivores enjoyed for a while, but which eventually excited groans, as most foods will after so much repetition. McDougall's Sweet and Sour Chicken had its advocates, too, but by and large Billy shopped in the local markets when he could, and we had as much fresh food as possible. Plans to lose weight on this expedition were thwarted – except in the case of John, whose prescribed diet seemed to be entirely jam, bread, glucose and water.

In the middle of the day the seemingly endless palm forest was interrupted by a truly unusual sight on the Paraguayan side: a tall red stone ruin, a shell of a church, rather like a wing of Fountains Abbey translated to the tropics. This was the little town of Humaitá, whose name resonates in Paraguayan history as Masada does in Jewish history or the Alamo in American. Placed as it is in Paraguay's bottom corner, it was bound to be in the first line of defence against Argentinians and Brazilians coming upriver or by land from the south. President Carlos Antonio López began to fortify it in 1855 and linked it to Asunción by telegraph. A Hungarian Colonel of Engineers, Franz Wisner de Morgenstein, built 15,000 metres of trenches around the little town and erected batteries to defend the U-bend in the relatively narrow river here which Humaitá controls. Richard Burton reckoned there were 195 artillery pieces protecting it, though only sixty were serviceable. These preparations were timely but inadequate: in 1867 and 1868 the Brazilian ironclads came up the Paraguay river and with their 70 lb Whitworths in revolving turrets pasted the town and the church of San Carlos at will.

On both sides in the Triple Alliance War Humaitá had a greater reputation for impregnability than it merited. Burton scorns the idea of its being the Sebastopol of the South, but it took the Allies, who showed it exaggerated respect, two and a half years and 80,000 men to overrun it. Paraguayan Colonel Martínez with his 3,000 strong garrison were finally starved out and in July 1868 they retreated across the river to the Chaco – the last to leave, *Titanic*-fashion, being the military band. The shell-pocked church ruin which we examined is a moving tribute to the tenacity and bravado of the Paraguayan soldiers who, outflanked on the river, surrounded by land and outgunned, held on there for so long.

Melissa Wingfield, appropriately for a naval officer, led a small team to try to find a sunken Paraguayan gunboat, the 448 tonne *Tacuarí*. It had been built and armed by John and Alfred Blyth in London, and the Royal Navy was interested in trying to trace it. After ferrying Paraguayan forces across the river in 1868 it had been intentionally sunk. But where? Local knowledge proved elusive and contradictory. A naval officer said he knew where it was and guided the party upriver, but there was nothing to be seen – and his real aim seemed to be to enjoy a free day's fishing.

Below Humaitá the last miles of Paraguay seemed desolate. The deck plates baked in the sun. Washing, quickly dried, flapped listlessly on the lines. Richard idly read his horoscope in a copy of *Tatler*. A certain Debbi Kempton-Smith forecast he would be 'Making hot jungle love on the Aubusson.' 'Mine says that I should get out more,' said Graham. Richard glanced up at *PQ*'s bridge: there seemed to be nobody at the helm. In fact it was Jenny Sambrook driving the boat, her diminutive form barely rising over the top of the wheel.

We made a last Paraguay river camp and at 8 a.m. on Tuesday morning passed the Isla Cerrito and entered the even vaster Paraná river, upstream of the big city of Corrientes. As Paraguay fell away on our port quarter we seemed to be in an inland sea dotted with islands and small boats going in all directions. Like the M1 below Watford Gap, the Paraná would have even more traffic for us to contend with.

This was all Argentina now, a country with plenty of doctors and dentists where there was bound to be less that we could do to help. We did have an assignment given us by the Argentinian Wildlife Department to carry out a survey of marsh deer in a fascinating area of wetland called the Esteros del Iberá in the northern part of Corrientes province; otherwise our main task was to see if the totora reed could weather the expected rough water on the long stretch of river to Buenos Aires and actually reach the Atlantic.

Our arrival in Corrientes was not auspicious. More highly developed countries generally have swifter immigration procedures, but Argentinian formalities gave us the hardest time yet. The Port Director said his officers were going mad because they had told him that Vikings were arriving in straw boats. Our passports had been taken in, but because Stuart Seymour's name was on the list and he was already in the country we had a three-hour wait, pinned on board in the burning sun. Our boats fell into no known category, so time was wasted while they called Buenos Aires for advice. Pamela had just thrown a pear core into the river when we learnt that there was a hefty fine for throwing anything, including food, overboard. Nor could rubbish now be burnt: everything had to be taken ashore.

When we were finally released, however, Corrientes more than made it up to us in the warmth of its welcome and the rich quality of its facilities. It was a well-ordered city of 430,000 with fine parks, churches, restaurants and clubs. Three of us enjoyed a wonderfully serendipitous moment when we came upon the early twentieth-century Teatro Oficial Juan de Vera. Curious, we went in. A manager invited us to look into the auditorium. We did so, and found the Sinfonía de Corrientes rehearsing Schubert's Unfinished Symphony on the stage. Three-quarters of an hour of rare pleasure followed as we sat, listened and looked at the four tiers and the eight boxes of this 1913 gem with its ornate brasswork and plasterwork. Everywhere in the city were signs of former opulence: the Spanish Club and the Italian Club boasted fine classical facades. Corrientes had clearly boomed in the first quarter of the last century.

Another new phase opened here, much as it had done at Concepción: a land party would leave for the interior and the boats would continue down the river with reduced support. *KM2*, with *Viracocha*, set off at 7 a.m. on 22 September and *PQ* two hours afterwards. Yoli's little Inca face looked on anxiously as John, hung about with all his camera bags, came cautiously up the long blue ladder – many times buckled and many times repaired. Assembled on the stone quayside, we were gathered up into a big white people-carrier and were soon bowling eastwards across the pampas on good roads.

At Ita Ibaté the following day we made another good schools link-up by satellite telephone. The children of Escuela No. 415 'Coronel Martín Jacobo Thompson' (founded 1906) spoke to the children at Clayesmore School, Iwerne Minster, Dorset (founded 1896). Charles Sturge, equipped now with a new JVC digital video camera, recorded it all, but Owain had forgotten to bring a crucial piece of wiring and so we could not send pictures of the children back to Dorset, nor for the time being receive e-mail. He, Peter and Marigold went off to the nearby town of Ituzaingó for a replacement.

We had time here to read our press notices. The many newspapers of Corrientes had shown great interest in our venture, and some of us had been interviewed. *El Litoral* did a good job, but *El Libertador* said that we were a team composed of Bolivians, Paraguayans, Argentinians and Bahamians with no reference to the British! Of course, newspapers the world over get things wrong. *La Nación* gave us a double-page spread which was very accurate, except that they had a picture of Jennifer Sambrook in the galley where she almost never was, and the *KM2* crew picture included Marigold, our harpist, and Richard, whose only contribution was twice stuffing sails into their bags.

We had our own media element always with us. Shaun Linsley was making copious tape recordings for BBC Radio Four and regularly thrust his muffed microphone under our noses. Charles Sturge leapt about cheerfully and nobody found his tiny JVC camera an intrusion. Indeed, the fact that what he had filmed could instantly be watched on the camera's little fold-out screen was an added bonus. Tarquin Cooper was quietly observing everything for his three *Daily Telegraph* travel section pieces – though some of our service and ex-service members, John particularly, were wary when talking to him. John wrote in his log: 'It is as if some of the media boys are praying for an accident or a disaster that they can play up. Their presence in our midst is somewhat intimidating. I have never felt this before but as a result I avoid even the slightest excitement when they are around.' Tarquin and Charles both complained to Richard that they could never penetrate John's curtain of reserve. Tarquin defended himself by saying that the editor of the travel section had briefed him to look into every aspect of the expedition, not just the travel.

John was not alone in his concern: a number of the more experienced expedition members were not very happy about journalistic priorities holding sway. Yoli, a South American and an anglophile, was anxious too. 'You are from a different culture and continent. We are guests here and must respect local sensitivities,' she told Tarquin. Perhaps it was impossible for so ambitious and varied an expedition entirely to avoid a degree of tension among its disparate elements; there is always a tug of war between an expedition's PR hopes and journalists' quest for the gritty truth. On the whole, we did very well.

CHAPTER NINETEEN

THE PAMPERO STRIKES

There is a mystery and a loneliness that pervades the scenery of the Paraná, that agreeably affects the imagination; a mystery – for are not its shores unexplored forests, its sources indefinite, in an unknown region that is still a sort of fairy-land of fable and romance, even as it was when the first Spaniards came and sought the Eldorado?

E. F. KNIGHT,
The Cruise of the 'Falcon', 1883

On our way to the deer hunt the land team stopped at San Juan Poriahu, a 13,000 hectare *estancia* owned by Marcos García, darkly handsome and Argentinian to the core. Joined by a large, wonderfully loud, cheerful expatriate called Judy Hutton, we set off by boat into the wetlands of the Esteros y Lagunas del Iberá. Judy is ornithologically immensely knowledgeable, and in the Carambola marsh alone twenty-eight species of bird were seen and identified as well as many young spectacled caiman basking in the sun on wet tussocks. From here we moved on to Rincón del Monte, near the town of Gobernador Ingeniero Valentin Virasoro (Argentinians love names like this: their capital is after all Santisima Trinidad y Nuestra Señora de Buenos Aires). This was the home of another expatriate, Charles Pettit, who lives with his wife, Dolores Navajas Artaza de Pettit, on the site of an old Jesuit mission whose ancient bell stands in their sitting-room. Charles had been introduced to John by Barney Miller of the Anglo-Argentine Society and became an energetic and unstinting supporter of the expedition. Having set up camp in

BIRDS SEEN IN THE CARAMBOLA MARSH,
ESTEROS DEL IBERÁ
Friday 24 September 1999

Limpkin	Cormorant
Southern screamer	Picazuro pigeon
Cattle tyrant	Black vulture
Black-chested buzzard eagle	White-winged gallinule (coot)
Bare-faced ibis	Anhinga
White-necked heron	Yellow-throated spinetail
Great egret	Crested caracara
Jacana	Chimango caracara
Jabirú	Ashy-throated crake
Brazilian teal	Pinnated bittern
Everglades kite/Snail kite	Long-winged harrier
Muscovy duck	Ringed kingfisher
Apolomado falcon	Black-crowned night heron
Southern lapwing	White-faced ibis

Identified by Mrs Judy Hutton of Buenos Aires

Charles's spacious garden, we embarked on a series of game counts.

The marsh deer (*Blastocerus dichotomus*) is one of the largest in South America. Its combined head and body length can reach almost 2 metres and a stag may be 1.2 metres at the shoulder. An adult can weigh up to 150 kilos. In summer it has a chestnut coat but in winter it takes on a paler colour. As the name suggests, these deer are found in marshes and humid savannahs from the Amazon to the north of Argentina. Alas, being handsome beasts they have been poached by trophy hunters. Recently, disease, probably transmitted from domestic animals, has taken a toll and the population is declining. John had learnt that fewer than 1,000 were thought to live in Corrientes province and thus a survey was considered important. The marsh deer's russet coat and preference for open habitat make it conspicuous from the air, and thus it is one of the few South American mammals that can be counted from a plane. However, it might also be possible to see some from boats or on horseback. Our task was to do a brief survey using all these means.

First we all set off together through Charles's estate; then Shaun, Tarquin, Melissa and Bahamian Geoff Tomlinson took an inflatable to navigate the Río Aguapey. They saw capybara, caiman and myriad birds, but it proved difficult to see marsh deer from water level. Jenny Sambrook took another group to Colonia Carlos Pellegrini to catalogue the wildlife there; heavy rain and high vegetation hid the deer once again, but they too saw a lot of caiman and birds.

Luckily, Charles Pettit owned a microlight and enjoyed flying it. His friend Titi Bruni had a more Rolls-Royce amphibious version, fitted with floats and wheels. Boats and horses were also available, but by now we had found that the tall reeds concealed the deer, and it was only the airborne spotters who could locate them. Cruising over La Luna at around 60 mph with camera in hand, Yoli scanned the lakeshore. An alarmed capybara and a caiman or two splashed in – and then suddenly a deer broke cover right beneath them. Titi swung the little aircraft round in a tight turn. Sixty yards away a beautiful young buck turned to stare as Yoli's camera clicked, and she noted its sex and size on her pad. John's overflight was also productive. Spotting a group of females, he gesticulated to Titi who brought the floatplane down on the water. When they hit the black surface with a gentle thud a large caiman reared up right in front of them and a sounder of peccary plunged through the shallows. As the microlight came to a stop a cloud of mosquitoes descended on the crew. 'A wildlife paradise, pity about the bugs,' wrote John in his log that night.

In all we counted fifty-seven marsh deer, as well as seeing many caiman and numerous fat capybaras. These great rodents fascinated our leader and, catching sight of a herd with babies browsing by the lake near the *yerba mate* factory, he decided to stalk them. Clutching his faithful Nikon, John set out on a long, uncomfortable crawl down a muddy slope. After half an hour he was within 20 yards and shot off a whole film. The capybaras eyed him arrogantly but did not move. The prospect of retreating by the same method lacked appeal, so John stood up, mud dripping from his clothes. The giant rats ignored him and went on feeding. A former estate worker, who had watched his activities, met him as he walked back to camp. 'Señor,' he said, 'please be careful, last week the capybara kill two big dogs who chase their little ones.' Having seen the powerful jaws at close range, John could see what he meant.

During his crawl in the mud there had been time to study the local reeds, called pirí. They looked similar to the totora, if somewhat slimmer, and John took samples to show Erik. It seemed possible that these could have been used to construct boats in a similar fashion to those built on Lake Titicaca. However, Charles Pettit felt it more likely that a light, strong wood known as timbor would have been used. There were, indeed, accounts of Brazilian fishermen venturing far out into the Atlantic. 'If the combined Brazilian and Falkland currents caught them they could well have ended up in South Africa,' remarked Richard. John's logs and notebooks were filling up with clues to be followed up in our quest to see if ancient trans-oceanic trading would have been possible.

Although primarily involved with wildlife studies for a few days, we continued to seek historical evidence; later, Yoli heard of interesting discoveries on the Río Uruguay where some petrified wood covered in a black lacquer-like substance had been found. The wood carried a strange carving of what appeared to be an eagle and a map that looked a little like South America. There was also a map which was similar to one of Africa drawn by Herodotus in 500 BC. A line linked the continents, the 'South American' end being in the vicinity of the Río de la Plata. John noted it for further investigation.

Meanwhile, Andy was leading a small archaeological team to examine the Jesuit missions in southern Paraguay and northern Argentina, and was pleased to find that there was some serious conservation in hand. Three of us were taken to see some of these sites, which are concentrated in a province of Argentina that sticks up like a coat-hook between Brazil and Paraguay, actually called Misiones. We visited Loreto and Santa Ana, not far from the upper Paraná river. Both are more ruined than most of those in Paraguay, and here there has been no attempt at restoration: fully grown trees sprout from the top of crumbled walls. But there were fine displays in small museums at each.

The youngsters at a school near the Pettits, Vuelta Del Ombó, seemed to be the most sophisticated we had come across yet, and they talked to their Dorset counterparts in English – a tribute to their headmaster, Alfredo Poenitz, himself author of an excellent coffee-table book on the missionary heritage. Most of the parents of these children worked on the surrounding *estancias* or in the *yerba mate* and tea processing plants in the area. Each

Argentinian in the north consumes about 5 kilos of *yerba mate* per year as well as tea, and there are 1,500 employees at the nearby Las Marías factory, bagging and boxing various blends of these refreshing drinks.

The Pettits' hospitality was overwhelming and in spite of the cool weather, thunderstorms and rain, the team relished their stay under the tall trees in the garden. Sadly, John's hepatitis prevented his enjoying the great red wines the family produced, and he seemed a little withdrawn. In fact, in addition to local worries, he had other thoughts on his mind: his younger daughter, Victoria, was about to have a baby. Jack Beresford Matthews' arrival on 27 September was every bit as difficult as John's had been sixty-two years before; but after several terse e-mails and consultations with his ex-PA, now our nurse, Pam, he seemed more relaxed. Few knew, however, that he now had a grandson.

Soon it was time to rejoin the boats on the river. On the evening before the land party left Rincón del Monte, Richard sat in the garden smiling beatifically: 'I feel a bit like the man who danced with a girl who'd danced with the Prince of Wales. Charles Pettit has just given me a cigar which he gets from a man who still supplies Che Guevara's brother.'

The boats had left Corrientes on 22 September, motoring through choppy water on a very wide river, after the great bridge which links Corrientes with Resistencia, and then on south, still seventeen days from Buenos Aires. Intense media interest was displayed at Bella Vista, when a TV crew came on board. There was more at Goya, where visitors came on board all evening, some even after midnight, and there would be more still at Paraná. Bystanders regularly waved from the banks. Everywhere the Prefectura Naval looked after the boats wonderfully well, warning all oncoming vessels of their approach which, as sailing was often possible, was a welcome safeguard. At times, too, the boats' crews lived well: at Goya steaks were bought and cooked; at Hernanderias they were for one glorious night billeted in bunk rooms with a hot shower. Evenings ashore were uniformly jolly. But there were also storms and rain and the consequent discomfort – and for Gerry Masters the difficulty of storing dry wood for the next day's fire. It was getting colder, too, so after supper most went to bed early – so early, in fact, that Gerry once got up at 11.30 p.m. thinking it was breakfast time.

It was hoped that the fleet would get to Paraná in good time, and indeed, having already covered 105 kilometres on the first day out of Corrientes, the expedition record was broken on 26 September when the boats ran 117 kilometres.

At Paraná, the land party rejoined the boats. (Many of us combed our brains, but we could not think of another city named after the river it is on.) We had to buy drinking water here as Paraná's was polluted and tasted bad. At the quayside there was an astonishing press of people: a three-deep queue 50 metres long, which was being filtered by Prefectura Naval officers on to the deck of the *PQ* in groups of twenty. Apparently, after three days of newspaper publicity the queue had maintained its length all day and Erik Catari, whose voice was never very strong, was now giving commentaries almost inaudibly. Jim said he appreciated what it was like to be an animal in a zoo, and reckoned that some 3,000 people had visited the fleet.

The American Captain Thomas Page in 1853 had much the same experience on board *Water Witch*, a steam-powered paddle steamer with sails: 'People from a long distance in the interior flocked to see the wonderful bark. Men, women and children crowded on board and would sit for hours under the awning of the deck.'

The day we were to leave Paraná the first visitor came on board at 6.45 a.m. – a hospital doctor who was on duty at seven. After the doctor came an entire school. *KM2* cast off at 10 a.m. leaving, for the only time in the whole journey, two of the boats' crew ashore – Roger Godfrey and Ed Ledsam had mistimed it. Luckily *PQ* could bring them on; and in any event we did not go far on 30 September, turning in to Diamante, a city with a fine church on a hill and port below. There is a story that it had been called Punta Gorda (Fat Point) until in 1852 General Urquiza, Governor of the province of Entre Ríos, preparing to lead an army to Buenos Aires to unseat the dictator Juan Manuel de Rosas, chose this place to cross the river. He did so without losing man or animal and, some say, renamed the place Diamante: 'Diamond'.

It holds different connotations for the Kota Mama expedition, however, based upon what happened the following day, Friday 1 October. It began badly for Jim, Gerry and Nathan, who were rained on at 4 a.m. and so got up at 4.45, made coffee and began cooking potatoes and onions. Richard, officially on breakfast duty, only had to fry thirty eggs while Shaun kept the coffee pot filled. John woke to find the maximum–minimum thermometer had broken and the barometer was dropping fast. It was a cold, grey morning and the boats left at the usual half-hour interval, *KM2* at 7 a.m. and *PQ* at 7.30 a.m., heading into low, dark cloud. Within an hour it was very rough indeed: a howling pampero wind hit the fleet right on the nose. *PQ*'s bows thwacked into the choppy waves; *KM2* rolled and wallowed, pushing a big bow wave ahead of her; little *Viracocha* pitched and tossed. It felt like a bad day in the English Channel.

We had passed through the narrows below Diamante and the river here was several hundred metres wide. On the distant banks trees bent low and beds of reeds were blown almost flat. Cattle huddled together for shelter in the fields and horses galloped in panic as dust and sand clouds swirled off the shore.

Then it seemed to become even worse. Pamela, Richard and Shaun could not produce the planned lentil soup for lunch, so they retreated down to the hold and made tuna rolls. On deck Billy Huxter's large jar of cooking oil broke loose, spilling over the steel deck and turning it into a dangerous skid pan. In the operations room John and Nathan fought to secure their precious maps, but several were torn from the walls and disappeared into the roaring storm.

The crew ran out safety lines along the length of *PQ* and life-jackets became compulsory wear for all on deck. The tops were now being blown off the grey-brown waves. It must have been Force 7. There was a rattle of chains as the crew of *PQ* secured the metal hatch covers. John climbed up to the bridge for a better view of the reed boats and met Gustavo Gallardo, the Argentinian pilot who was giving his services free to the expedition. 'Is only moderate for the Paraná,' he grinned.

It was interesting to read that Knight in his *Falcon* in 1881 endured much the same near Rosario: 'It blew a strong gale from the SSW – a pampero . . . the rain fell in blinding torrents and the lightning and thunder were more terrible than I think I have ever experienced.' In our case there was no rain, just a bitter wind. Astern of the support ship, *KM2* under bare poles and with *Viracocha* in tow bashed through 6 foot high waves, the great jaguar figurehead rising and falling in the tumult of water. John felt very uneasy.

'How are you doing?' he radioed to Jim.

'No problem. This is what she was built to do,' came his reply. In fact, at one point *KM2*'s mast was nearly unstepped.

As the great troughs and crests rolled under *PQ* her bows slammed into them, sending all the stanchions in the hold a-quivering and all the planks on its floor shuddering. The steel plates squeaked and groaned. All hands not working the ship were in their hammocks.

At 3.45 p.m. a radio announcement was picked up: the Prefectura Naval had closed the river to shipping but had warned vessels that the Bolivian Army had an expedition coming down the river!

The banks closed in again and white-horsed waves came rolling upstream like the Severn Bore. Poor old *PQ*'s deck seemed to twist and corkscrew even more. It was bizarre to recall that just a day or two before this Marigold Verity had been sunbathing in her deckchair with her feet cooling in a bucket, while Noel, in the shade, was whittling away at his next little wooden netsuke.

John called Jim again. The Admiral came back, with a touch of asperity in his voice: 'Don't bother yourself about us so much. We're doing fine.' Indeed, Erik Catari could feel proud of his and his father's work on this dramatic day.

In the narrows near Puerto Martin *PQ* had difficulty steering. 'Not a good spot to lose power,' yelled Graham McElhinney, looking for places on the chart that might offer shelter. But this time it was not *PQ* that failed: suddenly the steering engine on *KM2* packed up. Drenched to the skin and shivering with cold, Les Winterburn and young Ed Ledsam gunned the Avon's Suzuki outboard and, with waves breaking over them abeam, pushed the great reed boat into the bank for repairs.

Further downstream Captain Martin responded skilfully, spinning *PQ* round and round in midriver, holding position until he could select a landing place on the east bank and drive his vessel straight at it. Her bows clove the soft earth with a shudder.

'Get a fire going on shore,' shouted Billy, 'They'll be frozen stiff when they get here.' But they never did. A fire was going well when Jim called up, 'We can't make headway. Can you come back to us?' With astonishing good humour the team doused the fire, the crew unloosed the mooring lines and *PQ* let the pampero push her back upstream. Four kilometres away they found the battered reed boats and all tied up together.

A human shield around the galley kept the gas flame in and some Beanfeast was cooked. Another fire now blazed on shore and we made rice on it. A very basic meal; but a very welcome one.

By nightfall the wind had dropped a little, though it was still only 54°F and cold enough. Erik inspected *KM2*'s bows which looked as if some sea monster had taken a bite out of them. 'She has lost one skin of totora,' he said, 'but there's plenty more behind that.'

It was a raw night. Some of us recalled those days in northern Paraguay when we had said, 'Do you think it'll get any cooler as we go south?' At the evening briefing Jim said, 'You came here, some of you, for a bit of adventure. Now you've had it, and let's hope it's the last on this trip.'

A curious phenomenon met the early risers next morning: a thick mist on the river was swirling across it and up and over the bank. As we headed towards the big city of Rosario we looked out for Gaboto's Tower. Sebastian Cabot, the first recorded European up the Paraná, built the Sancti Spiritu fort in 1526, and its tower is said to be 30 miles north of Rosario. Sadly, we did not see it.

Rosario is the city of the flag. A grandiose monument in the Plaza de la Bandera on the waterfront commemorates General Manuel Belgrano, who devised the Argentinian flag. We were always punctilious in paying it the due courtesies. E. F. Knight described what used to happen: 'The passenger-steamer *Inca*, of the Brazilian River Company, was steaming down the Paraná, flying the Brazilian flag; there happened to be a small Argentine gunboat hidden in the jungle under the bank, the captain of which, observing that the steamer did not dip on passing, snatched up a rifle and deliberately commenced to fire shot after shot at the Brazilian captain as he stood on the bridge . . .'

Today we enjoyed the wholehearted support of the Prefectura Naval, who at Corrientes had seconded to the expedition the thirty-year-old Fabio Stricci, a shaven-headed coastguard officer built on generous lines – an Argentinian Kojak. Fabio was appreciated by all of us for the dedication and humour he brought to his task of seeing us safely down his country's rivers and canals.

Rosario, the birthplace of Che Guevara, is said to be a very nationalistic city. For the first time since we began our journey there were no crowds to greet our arrival, and none subsequently came. There was little press interest and no coverage – and this was certainly not because of any failure on the part of Peter Hutchison, our efficient PR king. The city adulates General Belgrano, and in 1982 Britain had sunk the battle cruiser that carried his name. Could it in some small way have contributed to the first coolness that we had experienced?

No Rosarians witnessed our early start. On another bitterly raw morning we had sent every spare piece of warm clothing to the crews of the reed boats. Once more, soup for lunch was going to be tricky, but Pamela and Marigold struggled on in the galley as *PQ* butted into the waves. When we reached San Nicolas in the early afternoon the wind had moderated somewhat. An ostensibly suitable wharf was turned down: a Prefectura Naval patrol boat came up and directed *PQ* back upriver to another mooring in a narrower channel that the reed boats had taken. We shall never know whether Captain Martin gave the Prefectura the wrong draught for *PQ* or whether the river was shallower than believed. In any event, as *PQ* moved into the narrow channel she ran on to a sandbank and ground to a halt. Captain Martin, Fabio, the patrol boat and Gustavo the pilot all had different ideas as to what should be done. For some time nothing was. The patrol boat pushed *PQ*'s flanks until the bows pointed directly towards the nearby shore where, under a 100-foot sheer cliff, a dredger was busy trying to salvage the *Río de la Plata*, a partially submerged tug. *PQ* was on full power when suddenly she broke free, shot forward and headed straight for the dredger, whose crew dropped their tools and ran for it. The inevitable happened. With a sickening thud, she struck the wreck. Out came the notebooks, video cameras and radio microphones of our media section. Rather like an elderly driver in a crowded car park, Captain Martin backed his vessel on to the sandbank again. Her bows swung round and she sideswiped the dredger. Executing a laborious three-point turn, *PQ* next rammed the cliff, bringing down a shower of small rocks. But we were free. Nathan, the adjutant, who had been clutching the expedition's cash box, now put it safely back in the ops room.

Ironically, *PQ* was now led back to the wharf which had been disdained in the first instance. Some of us went on shore to assess the damage to her bows. It rather resembled a prizefighter's nose, the recent scars difficult to distinguish from the ancient.

John decided to miss out Ramallo, the next projected port of call. There was tension in the town following a mishandled police rescue of hostages taken by robbers of the Banco Nación. Police had shot at an escaping car and killed one robber, but also the bank manager and his wife. Another thief was wounded, a third not yet caught. Best give it a wide berth.

We were now in the wide estuary of the Paraná, and it was over 100 kilometres from San Nicolas across it to the northern shore – the province of Entre Ríos, still Argentina, not yet Uruguay. Ocean-going ships abounded, taking on soya at San Lorenzo or natural gas at Puerto General San Martín. A very great many wore flags of convenience: Panama, Malta, Bahamas, Cyprus, Liberia. *PQ* passed one wonderfully rare bird, the Georgian *General Merkviladze*, registered in Batumi at the far end of the Black Sea. How many times in maritime history, if ever, Richard wondered, has a Bolivian boat passed a Georgian? It was a very busy waterway and required skilful navigation.

The fleet headed for a point known unromantically as Kilometre 240. At 6.30 a.m. on Monday 4 October the deck temperature was –3°C, and it didn't get much warmer. Thankfully, there was a good porridge breakfast. Then those who were not employed took refuge in the hold. Graham McElhinney found a shaft of sunlight and bathed in it; Tarquin and Charles played endless noisy games of Beggar My Neighbour; Owain missed breakfast and, like a spaniel under its blanket, remained asleep in his hammock; Noel read Norman Davies's monumental *Europe: A History* – for the second time on this journey; Rabia attended to her face in a mirror; Billy lay behind a screen listening to bagpipe music on his portable CD player.

In the evening it warmed up a little and, for what we thought might be the last time, *PQ* ran into the bank and tied up to a stout tree while the reed boats came alongside. In this final bit of countryside we lit a fire and cooked supper on it. It was what we had done for the last two months; but soon it would not be happening again. Time for nostalgic thoughts. Of the upper Paraguay and the choking, smoggy heat and the mosquitoes and the Japanese sport fishermen zooming past; of bemused, broad-faced Indians whose smiles revealed teeth so rotten that Mel or Graham would later have to extract them (a total of 1,450 in Bolivia and Paraguay, with 150 pieces of restorative work); of broken jetties, ancient warehouses, derelict railway lines and, beyond, the flat, endless, unforgiving Chaco with its 8 inch thorns; of jolly Paraguayan brass bands and the astonishing warmth of the welcomes we had at every landfall.

The southern summer was coming on apace and it stayed light for quite a while on this magical evening by the broad Paraná as we remembered, with a glass of *caña* in the hand, all the days since we had left La Paz in mid-July.

CHAPTER TWENTY

PROVING
HISTORY

*The Paraná river is possibly the most treacherous in the world . . . its
foundations are of sand, shifting and restless, a bank one day, a deep
pool the next, a silent obedient slave to the whims of the muddy water.*

JULIAN DUGUID,
Green Hell, 1931

Tuesday 5 October got off to an uncertain start after the
previous night's jollifications round the fire (and in some
cases into it). *KM2* ran straight into a tree. But there followed a
good day's run and by mid-afternoon the fleet had arrived at the
Prefectura Naval academy at Zárate, with its impressive bridge
– the only one across the Paraná estuary, carrying traffic from
Buenos Aires to Entre Rios province – and its wonderful hot
showers. *KM2* tried to go into a boating lake so that some PR
pictures could be taken, but fouled three small dinghies and had
to come out. A contretemps ensued between Jim and Shaun, whom
Jim thought was intrusively interviewing *KM2*'s skipper, Chris
Brogan, while Chris was supervising the arrival at the Zárate
quayside.

This was a smart town and only about 100 kilometres from
Buenos Aires. We had already been able to go ashore in Argentina
once or twice and enjoy its excellent steaks, and we knew that
in the vast conurbation of the capital that lay ahead of us before
journey's end in its suburb of Tigre there would be no more
opportunities for on-shore cooking; the compensation was the

increasing number of opportunities to indulge ourselves in the evening in well-conducted restaurants. Here at Zárate, La Pentola (19 de Marzo 242) was one of the best.

The night was bitter, 8°C, and those slaving away in the operations room piled on their warmest clothes. John was determined to have the expedition report drafted before everyone dispersed, so the two Sight and Sound laptops were in constant use by Marie and others, working hard to record all our findings. Thanks to the versatility of these machines, the engineers were able to illustrate their project proposals with splendid graphics and colour photos taken with the Olympus digital camera. To ensure maximum output, Nathan drew up a programme for the use of these vital computers and e-mailed Stuart Seymour in Buenos Aires asking him to have more ink cartridges and paper ready for our arrival. It was a far cry from the Zaire River expedition twenty-five years previously, when one rusty typewriter had been our sole item of office machinery. Even the IT experts among us were impressed by the reliability and robustness of the laptops and the digital camera, which still functioned well after three months of hard use under adverse conditions.

Perched on the bar stool Gerry had made for him, John edited far into the night. As his log was to show, something strange would often occur at times like this. John would fall asleep as he wrote, his pen trailing across the page; then the writing would start again. A reasonably legible description of a subject quite unconnected with the events of the day followed – written while he was asleep with his eyes open! It was as if his mind worked on two tracks . . . still, having moved across South America for 1,000 miles overland and 1,800 miles by river, nothing seemed very strange any more.

The next day we took some final pictures of the reed boats under sail before proceeding to Campana, where John and Yoli talked to our agent about shipping *KM2* back home – not to the Boat Show, as had been hoped, but to Lowestoft, where she would be on permanent exhibition.

That evening, like all good organizations, we had our final office party and entertainment. Everybody devoted the day to preparing a sketch: at one point Pamela and Peter Hutchison were fashioning bikinis from Beanfeast packets. It was hoped to celebrate *al fresco*, but the falling evening temperature, the wind chill factor and an unsuitable bit of bank drove us into the hold. Here we sang lustily, drank immoderately, took our forfeits manfully, enjoyed ourselves hugely. It was a very funny evening in which some hidden talents emerged, among them Pat Troy's firm control as compère and Rabia's accurate impersonations . . .

Odd as it may seem, some of us had been talking about homeward travel arrangements as long ago as mid-August. This was not always a sign of yearning to be back in dear ole Blighty, more often just a change from talking about sleep patterns and bowel movements. Now we were all talking about going home – and about being back there.

'What are you looking forward to most?' Rabia asked Charles.

'Not having to put the used loo paper into a plastic basket because it won't go down their narrow pipes.'

'I'm looking forward to not having to empty the basket,' said Noel.

Our last day of actual running took us down the Rio Paraná de las Palmas, into the Canal Gobernador Arias and through a confusing maze of now tidal waterways finally to the Río Lucan and Tigre.

As we neared the end Peter Hutchison prepared press handouts in Spanish. The Argentinian media had been eagerly following the story and John was keen that those members of the team with South American connections, as well as the unsung heroes and heroines, should be featured. Alas, disasters at home like the terrible train crash at Paddington had left little room in the British news for an account of a bunch of reasonably happy people achieving reasonably good results in a distant continent. The safe attainment of an objective is not necessarily gripping reading, and it seems that many newspapers prefer stories of scandal and cock-ups, which we had been able to avoid.

We had ten nationalities in the team, working in four countries with four languages (English, Spanish, Portuguese, Guaraní), as well as local dialects. Although John and Jim had selected as many Spanish-speakers as possible, there were only eight who spoke it well enough to interpret for the doctor and dentists. This task frequently fell on the same people. Stuart Seymour, Peter Hutchison, Tomas Hughes, Marie Peralta and Mary Stewart, who was coordinating community aid, were constantly on interpreting duty while Billy Huxter, our only German-speaker, was sometimes brought in too. Stuart Seymour and Peter Hutchison did much of the liaison work as well, but the heaviest responsibility in this field had been Yoli's.

During the final days Yoli spent much of her time sitting

cross-legged in the hold surrounded by receipts and invoices as she valiantly converted our accounts into a single currency. Having run for three months with British pounds, US dollars, Bolivian bolivianos, Brazilian reals, Paraguayan guaraníes and Argentinian pesos, this was a real challenge – even for a Colombian economics professor!

Yoli had been on most of the recces and both phases of the expedition itself, and she knew everyone involved. She understood the hierarchy and the culture of the countries through which we passed, just as Pamela Coleridge had done on the 1974–5 Zaire River expedition. She was John's *alter ego*. A tireless worker, no matter how long she laboured Yoli always found time to help others, whether it was washing clothes for the reed boats' crews, helping John cure his hepatitis or buying Richard a replacement pipe. One moment she would be sorting out problems with Captain Martin, the next she would be rushing off, dressed in the most immaculately pressed outfit, to charm some VIP ashore. She lived on the phone, preparing the way ahead, ensuring the owners of *PQ* kept to their agreement, bargaining for fuel and keeping our South American backers in the picture. A fiercely loyal person, she was determined that the Kota Mama expedition should succeed and enhance Anglo-Latin American relations. Somehow she managed all this with humour, politeness and a twinkling eye which melted the most macho of officials. Without her efforts it is hard to see how we would ever have got to Tigre.

So, on that final afternoon as the rain fell over the Paraná delta, Yoli stood proudly in the bows of *KM2*. She nearly never made it, though: as she and John, Carlos Cespedes and Marigold with her harp were being transferred in the tin boat from *PQ* to *KM2* the helmsman set off with the stern line still tied to *PQ*'s deck. The support ship was under way, and as they were dragged along water poured over the tin boat's side. 'Mind my harp,' cried Marigold as Captain Martin released the line.

We had been warned: 'Accidents often happen in the last few days of an expedition,' Jim had reminded us at the previous night's briefing. Ironically, one was to happen to him on the very last day. His arm was squashed between *KM2* and the stone quayside when the wash of a passing tug hit the boat. At first it seemed broken, but luckily this proved not to be the case. However, he was in pain and now one-handed. Yoli and the Prefectura's medics dressed the tough old soldier's wounds and he carried on without complaint.

John had wanted the fleet to arrive at its final destination on the dot of 4 p.m., but with the weather deteriorating and the traffic heavy in the narrow channel, Fabio Stricci was keen to press on. Certainly there was little room for two vessels the size of *PQ* to pass. As the procession neared Tigre, bystanders looked on in amazement; there were some muted cheers and clapping, pleasure boats braved the rain and some came out to photograph. Aware of *KM2*'s sluggish steering, the Prefectura Naval tried to clear the way. We reached the Prefectura HQ thirty minutes ahead of time and, after some confusion, got all the vessels moored up. Thanks to the Prefectura the formalities were completed quickly. Fabio and Gustavo came ashore to well-deserved congratulations, for it was they who had guided us along the perilous Paraná and its congested delta.

Yoli went off to telephone Dr Michel Chaim at Cinco Bacia in Corumbá about some funds he owed us which the expedition now needed. She came back fuming: 'He's gone to Spain, but they have promised the money is on its way.' Five days later it had still not arrived; five months later she was still pressing him. It still hasn't turned up.

Some of the rest of us did not quite know what to do. We had reached our objective. We were at Tigre. What now? For a while we lived on the ship, eating up the last of our fresh rations. There was an air of bewilderment. A slight tetchiness crept in, compounded perhaps by Seasonal Affective Disorder – the weeping rain and heavy, grey skies were not what we had expected.

Pat Troy pottered about complaining about the lack of salt, putting people right and not quite agreeing with anyone.

'You're a miserable old git!' Marigold told him, 'but I love you.'

As we had arrived a day ahead of schedule it was agreed that all who wished to could move into an inexpensive hotel in the middle of Buenos Aires and spend a few final days sightseeing and shopping. So most of the team headed off, leaving Jim, Gerry, Pedro Cartwright and Erik to strip down *KM2* and prepare her for the voyage to England while Billy concentrated on packing up his stores and distributing the last of the Beanfeast to unsuspecting Argentinians.

Erik found that *KM2* had only sunk down about 20 centimetres in the seventy-eight days afloat, which he reckoned meant that she had absorbed around 1,000 litres of water into her hull and could have sailed on for at least another seventy-eight days. Apart from the ripped sails and the damaged steering transom, both of which we had repaired, the only problem was the loss of the outer skin of reeds along the bow waterline. *Viracocha* had far less wear and tear. The performance of these boats was quite remarkable, and a great credit to Máximo and Erik. We had no doubt that, although they would certainly have taken longer, ancient mariners could have reached the Atlantic.

On Friday 8 October the sun came out at last, and Tigre port filled with pleasure craft. The weary Kota Mama team tidied themselves up for the official welcoming ceremony that the Prefectura Naval had arranged. *Viracocha Spirit of Bahamas* was lifted out of the water and on to a trailer, her red ensign still flying proudly on her stern post. Placed in front of the Prefectura HQ she looked in surprisingly good condition, but the pong of putrefying reeds was pretty bad. (It took several days to disappear.) Assuming 'Spirit of Bahamas' referred to a brand of liquor, the Prefectura objected to the banner that Don Tomlinson, Geoff's father, had sent from Nassau, until Yoli explained its significance.

At noon the smartly dressed Prefectura officers lined up on the quay. Our great supporter, Prefecto Mayor Luis Oscar Zunino, was there, as was the Bolivian Naval Attaché. His Excellency William Marsden, the British Ambassador, arrived with Andrés Feldman and other members of the Embassy, along with cases of champagne and neatly cut sandwiches; American Airlines representative Martin Cucchi and other sponsors were also present. Speeches followed; then came the official handing over of *Viracocha* to the Prefectura as a symbol of our gratitude and for exhibition in their museum. The Prefectura presented a fine plaque to the Ambassador and a beautifully inscribed plate to the expedition. To Yoli, this display of Anglo-South American friendship meant a great deal.

Across the river at the Tigre Sailing Club, Pamela, Rabia, Marigold and Melissa had prepared a great buffet of Beanfeast and other delights for those guests who could stay on. By mid-afternoon the party was over and the tedious job of packing up got under way.

A good many Argentinians came to look at the boats. Richard even stood on the pavement in a somewhat belated attempt to recoup expedition expenses by selling them postcards and brochures. Many spoke excellent English and some had British connections which they seemed proud to air. According to a well-known adage, an Argentinian is an Italian who speaks Spanish, thinks he's French and would like to be English.

John and the ever helpful Pedro Cartwright were pushing papers and maps into the office box when a teacher of English arrived with half a dozen pupils. 'Please may we come aboard?' he asked. 'Our school is in the Delta and I want the children to see the boats, for you have made history.'

'Not really,' smiled John, 'but perhaps we've proved it'.

Perhaps the most important remaining task was to get *KM2* to England, where the International Sailing Craft Association Maritime Museum at Lowestoft had agreed to house her permanently. Their famous collection of craft from all over the world would be fitting company for our flagship. Thanks to Mike Hodgkinson of Freight Agencies Ltd and their principals Norsul, *KM2* had free passage as deck cargo on the *Mascot*, due into Campana in November. Unfortunately, Norsul were appointing a new agent at Campana and we had no one to deal with before we left the country. In addition, all South America was that weekend celebrating the arrival of Columbus in the New World and not so bothered about getting boats back to the old.

A knight in shining armour turned up in the form of Frans Rogaar of the J. P. Knight Group Ltd, together with Capitán Eduardo San Miguel and Capitán Daniel Duran Costa of Consultora del Plata, their agents in Buenos Aires. As sponsors of *KM2* J. P. Knight knew the boat well, and, after a quick examination to determine her weight with the absorbed water, Frans said, 'I guess she's now about fourteen tonnes. Let's see what we can do to help.'

Captain Martin was keen to take *PQ* back to Bolivia as quickly as possible, so the rear party team moved into a friendly lodging to await developments, bidding farewell to the captain, his Bolivian sailors and the Brazilian engineer. They had done well to get *PQ* this far and, although no great beauty, she had fulfilled her role. However, we were not surprised to learn that she only reached Zárate on her way home before breaking down again.

Frans, our smiling Danish knight, soon came back to us. 'All is fixed,' he said. 'Our agents will take the boat to a secure mooring downriver, hold her there and tow her back up to Campana when *Mascot* arrives.' Yoli kissed him. It was the best news for a long time.

So it was that, quite fittingly, the Admiral of the Fleet, Jim Masters and his indefatigable brother Gerry were the only two of us who actually reached the centre of Buenos Aires by boat – on *Kota Mama 2* herself, towed down offshore to a safe haven.

Today, one of the Cataris' boats is in a children's park in La Paz, another at its journey's end in Tigre and a third in an exhibition hall in Lowestoft. Richard and John did not imagine when they arrived on the Bolivian Altiplano in March 1998 that the story would end on the windy coast of Suffolk. We had set sail from Bolivia's easternmost port, and the flagship was now at Britain's.

KOTA MAMA 3?

The first two phases of the Kota Mama project were now complete. The archaeological discoveries were pleasing and the rest of the scientific programme had been completed satisfactorily; only the DNA sampling had not been fully successful, but the medical and dental programme had been a real winner. We hoped that the engineers' reports on the Paraguayan schools, clinics, churches, wildlife reserve buildings and the Puerto Casado railway would be of value to the people who had shown us such kindness. Carlos Cespedes' work was to be published by the Bolivian Navy as the first hydrographic report on the rivers. Thanks to British Telecom, the linking of children across the Atlantic had gone well. Asked by the press how he felt about the expedition, John said, 'We've completed almost all the projects, on time, within our budget and without any serious casualties – I could not ask for more,' and added: 'This has been a most valuable reconnaissance in force and we have identified a huge number of tasks for the future.'

The reed boats, which had been the theme of the entire enterprise, had come through with flying colours. 'Solid as oak!' said Jim, stamping his foot on *Kota Mama 2*'s deck. 'Do you think you can build one to tackle the ocean?' he asked Erik. '*Sí*,' grinned the Aymará as he headed back to Bolivia to complete another reed boat in which an American sailor, Phil Buck, was planning to sail to Easter Island. Indeed, reed boat voyages were proving increasingly popular. In February 1999 a Spanish-led team had embarked in a massive three-sailed vessel on a journey of 5,000 miles from Arica in Chile to the Marquesas Islands, taking three months. The boat had, however, come apart in the final stages of the voyage. This was blamed on molluscs eating away the fabric, but Erik thought it more likely a design problem or the constant flexing of the reeds.

The plan for our own next phase had been to cross the Atlantic, and for this our Argentinian friends recommended constructing a boat using a light, strong wood called timbor. Having studied Thor Heyerdahl's reports of his epic Ra expedition, neither Jim nor John was convinced that even a robust reed craft would cross 5,000 miles of stormy ocean from the Río de la Plata to southern Africa, but Brazilian fishermen were known to venture far out into the Atlantic in hand-built boats. Back in Britain Roy Jarvis, an enthusiastic sailing member of the Scientific Exploration Society, was already working on a design, Jim Allen had produced a study plan with detailed drawings, and yachtsman Frank Esson was examining the best route and timings. However, historians and hydrographers in Bolivia believed that the ancient people might have used another route to the ocean.

The Río Grande rises near Potosí, the legendary silver mountain, curves around Santa Cruz, joins the Río Mamoré, heads north through the Beni country and eventually joins the Amazon. Depending on where one starts a voyage along this route it is around 2,900 miles to the Atlantic. There is one problem: 300 miles of cataracts obstruct the Mamoré and Madeira in Bolivia and Brazil. 'If they went this way,' said Jim, 'they must have had reed boats capable of shooting rapids.' 'Perhaps they had,' mused John, who was so impressed by the performance of *KM2* that he had already discussed the possibilities with Erik Catari.

Now it was back to La Paz for Erik, John and Yoli to report to our Patron, the President of Bolivia, the Navy and the National Academy of Science, and to thank our sponsors. At the Sucre Palace Hotel Lita Kushner was waving a copy of the *Bolivian Times*, the English-language paper of La Paz. 'See,' she cried, 'your friend has found Atlantis!' While we had been proving the early navigation theory with our trip to Argentina, Jim Allen had been busy in Bolivia, and his painstaking study of aerial photographs had located a new site for investigation just south of Lake Poopó. Indeed, Jim's latest discovery was the talk of the town; although many were sceptical, the undaunted enthusiast was still searching the Altiplano for possible sites which would fit Plato's description.

The philosopher had said that the City of Atlantis was on a small island surrounded by three rings of water and two of land, with a perimeter 'sea' wall at a distance of 50 stades or 5 miles. There were several possibilities, but Jim's most promising site was a volcanic crater on the edge of Lake Poopó which fitted Plato's description well. It was in the centre of a plain at the required distance of 50 stades from the lake, and was a perfectly circular gently sloping cone of the required diameter of 21 stades with a low mound in the centre, flanked to the north and south by two peaks – possibly, Jim thought, dating back to the Tertiary Period and thus of considerable antiquity on the geological timescale. The original crater ring had been destroyed, either in some violent blast that vaporized everything on the site or possibly by earthquakes such as Plato described. No rings of land could be seen within the area, although when the lake flooded the site became an island surrounded by a ring of water.

Ever optimistic, Jim – still in Bolivia – wrote to John:

From the highest peak on the southern side, an outstanding view of the perfectly level surrounding plain can be had with Lake Poopó in the distance. It is easy to imagine how a canal could be dug from the inland sea to a circular canal surrounding the site, allowing the passage of ships for transportation of goods and metals. It is also conceivable that a sea wall could be constructed at a radius of fifty stades to prevent flooding of the site at the times when the water rises.

All the metals Plato spoke of exist only a short distance away and the famous mines of silver and tin at Potosí are only 80 miles away, making the site an ideal place for the shipment of goods arriving by land and lake via the Desaguadero River and far-away Lake Titicaca.

The mound in the centre of the site supports an existing village supplied by water from a spring beneath, and hot springs and baths are also found in the mountains nearby. Red and black rock is abundant and even the pillars of the church in the centre of the village are constructed of red and black stones with white mortar, similar to the buildings of the lost Atlantis.

In the Aymará language the name of the site means 'broken ash', whereas in the Quechua of the Incas it means 'the volcano with something missing'. It seems then fair and likely that this site should be considered the 'Thira' of Bolivia, which offers a direct challenge to the notion that Atlantis was ever lost beneath the Atlantic Ocean or should have existed on the Mediterranean island of Thira. Every single detail of Plato's history exists only here, and nowhere else.

John felt it would need a team of archaeologists, geologists and volcanologists to give a sensible opinion, but promised he would look into it. We all admired Jim Allen's enthusiasm, and indeed, even if the quest proves futile, he deserves credit for his moral courage in putting forward ideas unpopular with contemporary archaeologists. 'Look what they said about Darwin and Galileo,' commented Yoli. It was, after all, Jim's suggestions that had done much to fire us up to undertake the Kota Mama project in the first place.

Oswaldo was doubtful about Jim's claim but did not dismiss it out of hand. He knew, as he had said to us long ago, that if we did not seek we would not find, and there were still plenty of archaeological sites awaiting discovery in Bolivia. All that was needed was the funding; and the Kota Mama expeditions had managed to attract sufficient to support Bolivian archaeologists on several useful projects. 'If you are turning your attention to the northern part of my country,' he said, 'I believe there is an important site near the Beni river that has yet to be examined. However, I have not seen it myself and am only judging by what Indians say.' For several hours John, Yoli and Oswaldo pored over maps and reports. They talked of the ancient Beni culture, whose people had lived in north-eastern Bolivia on circular mounds connected by canals and raised tracks. In this way they survived floods and developed an advanced form of intensive agriculture. Today little but the mounds remain. Another mystery!

At the Navy's Hydrographic Department, Capitán Angel Valdivia Nuñoz produced *mate de coca* and reams of charts. 'We are still mapping many of our rivers,' he said, 'especially in the north and west. Your help would be most welcome.'

'How about the Mamoré rapids?' asked John.

'Some are very dangerous but there may be ways to navigate them,' said Carlos Cespedes. 'They are the blockage that prevents river traffic sailing all the way from Bolivia to the Amazon and the Atlantic.' The photographs produced reminded John of the mighty Congo that the Scientific Exploration Society team had navigated twenty-five years before.

By the time John flew out of La Paz all concerned in Bolivia had agreed on the essential elements of a new expedition.

Fortunately American Airlines upgraded him and while most passengers slept through the Atlantic crossing he sat festooned with maps and papers. By the time the wheels touched down at Heathrow on 18 October the outline plan was complete.

Back home, the wintry weather was brightened by the knowledge that we had made a positive contribution to Anglo-South American relations. Three expedition members were in love with ladies they had met on the voyage, and on his return to the UK John Teague became engaged to Ilia Hayes of Buenos Aires.

It was a chilly, damp January morning at Sheerness when Jim Masters, John, Chrysoulla Kyprianou and a bevy of press arrived to welcome *Kota Mama 2* to Britain. Mike Hodgkinson of Freight Agencies Ltd had already offloaded her from MV *Mascot* and the great reed boat sat proudly, if somewhat incongruously, with her boggle-eyed jaguar figurehead looking out over the dock. Apart from some damage caused by the crane strops when lifting her out of the water in Argentina, she was in good order. Neil Hunt of the ISCA Maritime Museum was there with his low-loader ready to take her off for refurbishment and exhibition at Lowestoft. This was quite a lift as she now weighed over 21 tonnes: if Erik's estimate of 8 tonnes at the start was correct, *Kota Mama 2* had absorbed 13 tonnes of water since we had launched her in July. 'It will take a while to dry out,' admitted Neil. Still as there were already thirteen reed craft in the museum, he was well qualified to handle this.

A few days later the Scientific Exploration Society council approved the plan for a recce expedition to examine the Mamoré rapids and Oswaldo's suspected archaeological site with a view to a full-scale voyage from the Andes to the Atlantic via the Amazon in 2001. John phoned the news to Yoli in Bogotá. 'Here we go again,' she said. 'It is as well I have kept my jungle boots.'

In March Dr Thor Heyerdahl received a photo of *Kota Mama 2* and said how delighted he was that the Indians who had helped him in the past were involved with the Kota Mama Expedition, as it seems to show that their ancestors were the real pioneers striving for world unity which he so admired and respected. Dr Heyerdahl stressed that man's survival depends on international collaboration.

Jim Allen, now well into the writing of a new book, sent word of the identification of a terracotta bust, scientifically proved to be of Roman origin, that had been buried in Mexico in 1510, a decade before the arrival of the conquistadors. When we added this to the reports of Mediterranean amphorae found off the Brazilian coast, New World pineapples drawn on ancient walls in Italy and traces of cocaine and nicotine in Egyptian mummies, as well as the new fossil discoveries in Argentina, there seemed all the more reason for us to continue the quest.

THE KOTA MAMA EXPEDITION

ACKNOWLEDGEMENTS

The Kota Mama Expedition wishes to thank the following organizations and individuals for their invaluable support.

PATRONS

General Hugo Banzer Suárez, President of Bolivia
Señora Susana Galli de Gonzalez Macchi, First Lady of Paraguay

HONORARY VICE PRESIDENTS

HE Señor Rogelio Pfirter
Ambassador of The Republic of Argentina
HE Señor Raul Dos Santos
Ambassador of The Republic of Paraguay
HE Señor Jaime Quiroga Matos
Ambassador of The Republic of Bolivia
HE William Marsden CMG
HM Ambassador to The Republic of Argentina
HE Andrew George
HM Ambassador to The Republic of Paraguay
HE Graham Pirnie
Formerly HM Ambassador to the Republic of Paraguay
HE Graham Minter
HM Ambassador to The Republic of Bolivia
IIE David Ridgway OBE
Formerly HM Ambassador to the Republic of Bolivia
HE Edgar Gutierrez Mercado
Ambassador of The Republic of Bolivia in Spain
Ing. Julio Sanjínes Goytia
Ing. Roberto Capriles G.
Almte Jorge Zabala Ossio

Almte José Ramon Ocampos Alfaro
Prefecto Mayor Luis Oscar Zuniño
Senador Ruben Poma Rojas
Dr Carlos Aguirre B.
Prof. Jorge Asin Capriles
Dr Jaime Ponce García
Arq. Oswaldo Rivera Sundt
Sra Lita Kushner López
Lic. Adrian Giménez Hutton
Lic. Carlos Olea
Sr Ricardo Paz Soldán
Mrs Elodie C. Sandford
Peter R. E. Monson

The expeditions owe much of their success to many kind people and organizations. Barry Moss, Robert and Faanya Rose, John Warburton Lee, Dr Frank Dawson, Mr and Mrs Ron Rosner, Stephen Rumsey and members of the British Chapter of the Explorers' Club were most helpful in organizing the venture. We are also grateful to the Council of the Scientific Exploration Society for its backing and the staff of the map room at The Royal Geographical Society.

Support was generously provided by:
Adlam Building Supplies, Jim Allen, American Airlines, Carolyn Amhurst, Arthur Anderson, Ashton and Waverley (for IT support), Avon Cosmetics, Avon Inflatables, E. P. Barrus (for a great Mariner outboard), Barts Spices, The Bechtel Foundation, Edward and Wendy Bentall, Marta Bosacoma, Brasher Boots, British Forces Post Office, Brixham Community College, Lt Col Clem Brown, BT Mobique (for their superb satellite phones used in 1999), Burton McCall (for invaluable Swiss Army knives), Canning House, Casella London, Cellhire Global Phone Rental, Cigna (for standing by to rescue us), Clayesmore School, Dr David Coates, Coleman UK (for their fine stoves), Cotswold Camping, Barry Cooke, Ken Crowe (for his video editing), CMI (for help with the schools satellite phone link), the *Daily Telegraph,* DHL (for carrying important loads to and from South America), Discovery Initiatives, Dorling Kindersley, Eyedon Kettle Co. (for the outstanding Kelly volcano kettles), Sarah Farquharson, Roddie Fleming, Freight Agencies Limited, Freud Communications, Furnace Hosiery, Timothy Glazier, HarperCollins, Headline Book Publishing, Henri Lloyd (for protective clothing that made life bearable under extreme conditions), Dr Mark Horton, HSBC Insurance (for covering us so well), John Hunt,

Nick Hunt (for help with maps), Norma Jacobsen, Jaguar Cars, Journey Latin America, Justerini and Brooks, JVC (whose video camera did so well on Phase II), J. P. Knight (Paranam) (for sponsoring the flagship *Kota Mama 2*), Kodak, Henkel/Loctite (whose super glue solved many a problem), Julia Linsley, John and Suzanne Lobel, James Lock (for hats), London Clubs International, London Communications (whose VHF radios gave outstanding service), Lord Maclaurin, Magic of Bolivia, Makro (for robust folding tables), Manby International Sportswear (whose trek poles got our leader up mountains!), Sqn. Ldr Nigel Marix, Vince Martinelli, G. Masters and Sons (for special packing boxes), Mercedes Arenas, The Millennium Britannia Hotel (who gave us a great send off for Phase II), Ruth Mindel, Mosimann's Dining Club, Motorola (their UHF radios were invaluable on Phase II), Anna Nicholas and the team at ANA Communications, Nikon UK, Nomad Travellers Stores, Cia De Navegacao Norsul, Norton & Sons of Savile Row, O'Gara Satellite Networks (for their superb satellite phone in 1998), The Oil Industries Club, Olympus Cameras (whose digital camera was so useful in 1999), Jaime Ortiz Patiño, John Perrett, Col. John Pocock, Porvair International, Jonathan Potter (for ancient maps), QM Services (for tasty, easy to use, boil-in-the-bag meals), Raleigh International, Redwood Stone, Alan Rind, Roxton Sporting, Elodie Sandford (who brought in the Bahamas team), Schroder Charity Trust, Scouts Shop, Seven Seas (whose vitamins helped to keep us fit), Michael Sheppard, Sight and Sound Ltd (for the superb laptops), Shakespeare Co. (UK), Sheraton Park Tower Hotel (for a wonderful launching), Silva UK (for the vital navigation equipment), Colin Smythe, Sowester, Stahly Foods, Storm Watches, Suzuki GB (their incredible outboard and generators achieved wonders on Phase II), Tastefully Yours, Tractel UK (whose superb Tirfor jack was greatly appreciated), Major General Tim Toyne-Sewell, Don Tomlinson (who sponsored *Viracocha*), Carol Turner, Vicki Unwin, Van den Bergh Foods (whose Beanfeast we marched on in 1999), Varta (for excellent batteries), J. J. Vickers (for tremendous binoculars), Roy Ward and the Institute of the Motor Industry, John West Foods, Wilde Sapte, Andy Whiting, Julia Williams, General Sir John Wilsey.

The support of the Ministry of Defence with Royal Navy and Army personnel was most valuable. The Foreign and Commonwealth Office was extremely helpful, and we are especially grateful to Greg Faulkner, Henry Hogger, John Ashton, Ian Orr, Stephen Durrant and Alex Curtis. Throughout the expedition the advice and assistance of the British Embassies in Argentina, Bolivia, Brazil and Paraguay was much appreciated.

BOLIVIA

Aby's Rent Car, Lic. Pedro Avejara Belarte, AeroSur, Academia
Nacional de Ciencias, Lic. Hugo Boero Rojo, Bill Brady, H. of
Central Aguirre Portuaria SA Zona Franca, 'Tito' Barron Robles,
Chris Brain, María Angelica de Calvo of Ecco Publicidad, Canal 7
de Bolivia, DHL, DINAAR, Dirección Nacional de Patrimonio
Empresa Ferroviaria Oriental SA, ENTEL, Lic. Blanca Soria de
España, Fuerza Naval Boliviana, Gravetal Bolivia, Hotel Bibosi,
Hotel Felimar, Hotel Inka Utama, General Juan Hurtado Rosales
Jefe de la Casa Militar, IMBEX Rent car, Internacional Park Hotel,
Lic. Francisco Javier Iturralde, Instituto Geográfico Militar, Dr
Luis Kushner of Clinica Alemana, Lic. Paola Mackenzie de
American Airlines, Dra Martha Duenas del Mercado from the Vice-
Ministry of Tourism, Dr Franz Michel from the Instituto de
Documentación y apoyo Guaraní, Ing. Darius Morgan de Crillon
Tours, Museo de Etnografía y Folklore de La Paz, Museo de
Samaipata, Sra Marcia Paz Campero, Sapesa, Dra Mirtha Quevedo
Acalinovic formerly Prefect of Oruro, Alan Raven, Martin Murghan
of Shamrock Irish Pub in Santa Cruz, Servicio Nacional de Defensa
Civil, Servicio Nacional de Hidrografía Naval, Servicio Nacional
de Meteorología e Hidrología (SENAMHI), Eng. Jorge Schmidt,
SHELL–Bolivia, Raul Alfredo Schenone F., Simón Bolívar School,
Calacoto, Sucre Palace Hotel, Don Rolando (Toto) Valdivia, Vice-
Ministry of Culture of Bolivia, Lic. Juan Quesada Valda, formerly
Vice-Minister of Tourism.

PARAGUAY

ANDE, Fuerzas Armadas Paraguayas, Padre Arminto Barrios, Lt
Raul Berdejo, Fundación Moises Bertoni, Miss Susan Butcher, Dr
Martin Antonio Chiola V. Minister of Public Health and Social
Wellbeing, Lic. Alejandro de Urrioste, Technical Advisor for the
Nature Conservancy, Sr Felix Diaz Barrios, Chief of Protocol of
the First Lady's Office, Dirección de Parques Nacionales y Vida
Silvestre, Mr Stuart Duncan, Managing Director Lloyds Bank
Asunción, Mr Scott Donald, formerly Director of Lloyds Bank in
Paraguay, Gral. Guillermo Escobar, Robert and Gracie Elsam, Mrs
Diane Espinosa and Dr Antonio Espinosa, Gerry Evans, Sr Cesar
Filartiga, Assistant for the First Lady's Office, Fundación Guyra,
Fundación Tierra Viva, Fuerza Naval Paraguaya and all the
Commandants along the river, Lic. Hugo Galli R., Minister of

Tourism, Lic. Raul Gauto, Wilfred Giesbrecht, Executive Director for the Fundación para el Desarrollo Sustentable del Chaco (Des del Chaco), Col. Hugo Gomez, Sgt Gonzalez, Hotel Pioneros, Hotel Sagaro, Industria Nacional de Cemento, Ministry of Education and Culture, Ministry of Environment, Ministry of Foreign Affairs, Ministry of Public Works and Communications, Col. Osorio, Prof. Carlos Pusineri Scala, Curator of the Museum Casa de la Independencia, Lic. Adelina Pusineri, Curator of Ethnographic Museum 'Andrés Barbero', Senator Heinrich Ratzlaff, Lic. Dip. Cornelius Sawatzky, Dr Segovia, General Oscar Shultz, TAM MERCOSUR Airline, General Eligio Torres Hein, Lic. Jorge Vera of San Lorenzo Museum, Roberto Villagra, Padre Zislao.

ARGENTINA

Oswaldo Aguilar from Agencia Maritima, Ashoka, Hon. Dominic Asquith, Bed and Breakfast Familia Escauriza, Titi Bruni, Lucio Contigiani, Martin Cuchi of American Airlines, María Cristina Diaz, Daniel Alberto Duran of Consultora del Plata, Horacio Ezcurra, Dr Peter Fiaccadori, Marcos Garcia, Alimentos Genzer, Lic. Victor Gonzalez Prandi of the Ministry of Culture and Education, Adrian Giménez Hutton, Grupo Las Marias, Hotel Luey, Mrs Judith Hutton, Lic. Enrique Lipps, Sr Jorge A. Mozatti, Vice-President of Río Paraná Company in Corrientes, Don Pablo Navajas, Roberto Navajas, Marcos Oliva Day, Charles and Dolores Pettit, Prefectura Naval de Argentina in Buenos Aires and all the Commandants of ports along the river, Lic. Maurice Rumboll, Eduardo San Miguel of Consultora del Plata, Jorge Trabuchi, Universidad del Litoral, Prefecto Mayor Luis Oscar Zunino, Chief of the Department of Nautic Sports.

COLOMBIA

Dra Monika Hartmann, Consul of the Republic of Bolivia, HE Nelson Alcides Mora Rodas, Ambassador of the Republic of Paraguay, Lic. Marcelo Escapini, Norma de Escapini.

Dramatis Personae

ALLEN, Jim, former RAF photographic interpreter, amateur archaeologist and Atlantis author: Atlantis adviser

ALVAREZ, Adrian, Bolivian archaeologist: 1998

ARNISON, Capt. Nathan, RE, BA, Cumbrian bomb disposal expert: engineer leader, *KM2* crew member, 2nd phase 1999

ASIN, Capriles, Prof Jorge, Bolivian economist at La Paz University: liaison officer in Bolivia, 1998 and 1999

BEALE, Christopher, Bournemouth computer expert: website co-ordinator 1998

BLASHFORD-SNELL, Col. (Retd) John, OBE, DSc (Hon) D Eng (hc), FRSGS, Chairman Scientific Exploration Society, leader Blue Nile and Zaire River expeditions, Director Operations Drake and Raleigh: expedition leader, 1998 and 1999

BOERO, Rojo Hugo, Bolivian historian (deceased): author of *Discovering Tiwanaku*

BROGAN, Lieut. Chris, RE, BEng. Nordic skier: skipper *KM2*, 1999

BURRELL, Dr Noel, MA, BA, BChir., retired GP and woodcarver: expedition medical officer, 1998 and 1999

CARTWRIGHT, Ben, aircraft engineer and computer lecturer: Avon boat crew and technician, 1998 and 1st phase 1999

CARTWRIGHT, Pedro A., Bahamian student: *KM2* crew member, 1999

CATARI, Erik G., Bolivian Aymará, industrial engineering student at University of La Paz, designer and builder of reed boats on Lake Titicaca: boats crew, 1998 and 1999

CATARI, Máximo C., Bolivian Aymará, father of Erik, designer and builder of reed boats at Huatajata, Lake Titicaca: boats crew, 1998

CÉSPEDES, Carlos, Teniente de Navio, Bolivian navy hydrographer: chief of department, liaison officer and hydrographer, 1999

CHAIM, Dr Michel, owner of support vessel *Puerto Quijarro*

CHAMBI, Rene S., Nissan driver, 1998

CHAMORRO, Captain Angel, Paraguayan Naval commander of Bahía Negra, 1999

CIPAGAUTA, Prof. Yolima R., lecturer in economics at the Colombian Military University: PA to expedition leader and chief liaison officer, 1998 and 1999

COLERIDGE, Lady (Pamela), PA to leader on Zaire River expedition: nurse, 2nd phase 1999

COOPER, Tarquin, ex-Ampleforth and Newcastle University trainee journalist: *Daily Telegraph* travel section reporter, 1999

COX, Lieut. Luke, RE, BA, Yorkshire rock-climber: skipper *Viracocha*, 1998 and 1st phase 1999

DAVIES, Owain, ex-Clayesmore School: IT and computer expert, 1999

DAWSON, Dr Frank, American amateur archaeologist and explorer, adviser in UK

ESTEBAN, Eduardo, writer, mountain rescue leader, Warden in Aconcagua Provincial Park, member of Argentine chapter of Explorers' Club: liaison in Argentina, 2nd phase 1999

EVANS, Gerry, Chargé d'Affaires at British Embassy in Paraguay

GALEANO, Teniente Tomas, Paraguayan naval liaison officer, 1999

GALLARDO, Gustavo, Argentinian river pilot, 1999

GALLI DE GONZALEZ MACCHI, Señora Susana, First Lady of Paraguay, 1999

GIMÉNEZ, Adrian H., Explorers' Club Argentine Chapter, 1999

GODFREY, Roger, Yorkshire company director: boats crew, 2nd phase 1999

GUERRA, Dr Luis G., Bolivian archaeologist, 1998

GUILLEN, Tejada, Almirante Luis Adolfo, Bolivian Navy Chief

HUAÑAPACO, Alexander, Bolivian Aymará student, Máximo's cousin: boats crew, 1998

HUGHES, Tpr Tomas D., QDG, keen Spanish-Welsh sportsman, Spanish speaker: radio operator and boats crew, 1999

HUNT, John, formerly SES Development Director

HUTCHISON, Peter, BA, writer, mountaineer, South American enthusiast, Spanish speaker, ex-Editor *Bolivian Times*: information officer, 1999

HUXTER, Sgt Billy, QDG, Scots footballer and bob-sleigher: quartermaster, 1999

JOYCE, L/Cpl Jason, RLC, postal officer and boats crew, 1998

KIRCHHOFER, Pablo, Paraguayan of German-Swiss extraction: driver, 1999

KUSHNER, Lita, Executive President of Hotel Sucre Palace in La Paz, expedition vice-president

KYPRIANOU, Chrysoulla, BA, British Cypriot South American enthusiast: sponsorship coordinator, video recording, boats crew and recce officer, 1998

LEDSAM, Edmund, BSc, Rugby player, ex-Operation Raleigh: Avon boat crew, 2nd phase 1999

LINSLEY, Julia, PA to JBS in Dorset; wife of Shaun

LINSLEY, Shaun, BA, Dorset fishing-rod maker: radio recording, anthropologist and ornithologist, 1999

LIPPS, Enrique, caving expert, Explorers' Club Argentine Chapter, 1999

LOBEL, Mark, ex-St Paul's School: boats crew, video cameraman, 1998

LYONS, John, American international business consultant and engineer: IT expert, 1998

McCALLION, Lieut. Stuart, RE, BEng (Hons), canoeist: engineer and *KM2* crew, 1999

McELHINNEY, Capt. Graham, RADC, BChD, skier, scouter, kayak instructor, navigator: dental team, 1999

MARRINER, Capt. Toby, RE, engineer and reconnaissance, 1998 and 1999

MASTERS, Gerry, brother of Jim, specialist restorer of old churches and construction engineer: quartermaster 1998 and engineer/cook 1999

MASTERS, Major (Retd) Jim, MBE, experienced Somerset white-water expert, ex-Blue Nile and Zaire River expeditions: deputy leader 1999; fleet commander, 1998 and 1999

MILLER, Andrew, MA, BSc, archaeologist specializing in burials and paleopathology: archaeologist, 1999

MINTER, HE Graham, British Ambassador to Bolivia

MINTER, Peter, wife of British Ambassador to Bolivia, photographer: liaison in Bolivia, 1st phase 1999

MOSS, Barry, FRGS, director of HSBC Gibbs, ex-Operation Raleigh leader, SES Council member, Secretary to British Chapter of Explorers' Club: deputy leader and treasurer, 1998

OCAMPOS ALFARO, Almirante José Ramon, Paraguayan navy chief, later Chief of Armed Forces

PERALTA, Marie, BA, LlB, Gibraltarian barrister, TA officer cadet, Spanish speaker: scientific assistant, 1999

PIRNIE, HE Graham, British Ambassador to Paraguay during preparation

PONCE, Dr Carlos S., a Bolivian authority on Tiwanaku culture

PUSINERI, Adelina, head of the Andrés Barbero ethnographic museum, Asunción

QUELCA, Ricardo, Headmaster Simón Bolívar School, Calacoto

QUISPE, Rodolfo C., Bolivian navy civilian employee: driver, 1998

RAE, Andrew, American Airlines Business Development Manager: 1st phase 1999

RAMOS, Sgt Freddie R. Bolivian Navy topographer: hydrologist and boats crew, 1998

RIDGWAY, HE David, British Ambassador to Bolivia, 1998

RIVERA, Oswaldo S., one time Bolivian director of national archaeology; archaeological director of Kota Mama project

ROCA, Commandante Ernesto, officer in charge of naval base at Puerto Quijarro, 1999

ROCA, Hugo, Commandant of Navy Base, Santa Cruz

ROSE, Faanya, BA, company treasurer, wife of Robert: 1998

ROSE, Robert, BA, widely travelled American, former chairman life insurance company, photographer, 1998

RUBÉN, Castedo, Bolivian driver, 1998

SAMBROOK, Jennifer, BSc, Bolivian-Canadian postgraduate student of genetics and molecular biology and occasional lecturer at Bangor University: zoologist, 1999

SEYMOUR, Capt. Stuart, QDG, BA, Spanish speaker: adjutant, treasurer, 1999

SHEPPARD, Sebastian, MBA, pilot training coordinator for Lockheed Martin, Operation Raleigh, former navy helicopter pilot, Spanish speaker: boats crew, interpreter, 1998

SIDDIQUE, Rabia, BA, LlB, Australian solicitor and barrister: sponsorship coordinator, assistant anthropologist, 1999

SMART, Capt. Lee, BSc, Royal Signals, PR and liaison officer Bosnia, Italian speaker: boats crew, artist, 1998

SNAILHAM, Richard, MA, FRGS, Hon. Vice-President SES, ex-Blue Nile and Zaire River expeditions: author, 1998 and 1999

STEVENSON-HAMILTON, Andrew, BA, independent financial adviser, round-the-world yachtsman, marathon runner: boats crew, artist, 1999

STEWART, Mary, widely travelled senior nursing officer and administrator Bahrain, Thailand, Belize: community aid coordinator, photographer, nurse, 1999

STRICCI, Fabio, Argentinian coastguard officer in Prefectura Naval: Argentinian liaison, 2nd phase 1999

STURGE, Charles, former computer engineer, now freelance photographer, ex-Operation Raleigh: photographer, 1999

TEAGUE, John, operation theatre technician, ex-TA Sergeant medic in Gulf War, motorcycle racer and mountaineer: nurse, 1999

TERRAZAS, Vladimir M., Teniente de Navio, head of security at the Bolivian Navy hydrographic school: liaison in Bolivia, 1998

TOMLINSON, Don, supporter from Nassau, Bahamas

TOMLINSON, Geoffrey, Canadian living in the Bahamas: reconnaissance and boats crew, 1999

TROY, Major (Retd) Pat, RM, widely travelled Jersey-based ex-Royal Marine, formerly in oil and gas industry in south-east Asia, keen yachtsman: fleet navigator, 1999

TURNBULL, Elsbeth, BA, read archaeology/anthropology at St Peter's, Oxford: assistant archaeologist, 1998

USNAYO, Antonio, Bolivian driver, 1998

VACA, Martin V., Teniente de Fragata, Bolivian Navy: captain of *Puerto Quijarro*, 1999

VALDIVIA, Capt. Angel, Director of National Hydrographic Service, Bolivian Navy

VERITY, Marigold, widely travelled freelance harpist: ethno-musicologist, 2nd phase 1999

VILLAMOR, W. Danilo E., University of La Paz postgraduate student of paleopathology: anthropologist, 1998 and 1999

VILLARROEL, German A., Bolivian Navy: driver, 1998

WEATHERHEAD, Patricia, DipM, MCIM, DMS, CDipAF., chartered marketer, widely travelled SES member: recorder, 1999

WILLSON, Liz, American Airlines National Account Manager: 1st phase 1999

WINGFIELD, Surg.-Lieut (D) Melissa, RN, BDS, widely travelled Derbyshire dentist, Tall Ships racer: dental team, 1999

WINTERBURN, Les, senior NCO in British and Omani armies, now HM Prison Officer at Wakefield, member Zaire River expedition: Avon boat crew and mechanic, 2nd phase 1999

WRIGHT, James, Paraguayan rancher originally from Zimbabwe: driver and liaison in Paraguay, 1999

ZABALA, Almirante Jorge O., chief of Bolivian armed forces

BIBLIOGRAPHY

Allen, J. M., *Atlantis: The Andes Solution* (Windrush Press, 1998)

Anstee, Margaret Joan, *Gate of the Sun: A Prospect of Bolivia* (Longman, 1970)

Attenborough, David, *Zoo Quest in Paraguay* (Lutterworth, 1959)

Boero, Hugo Rojo, *Discovering Tiwanaku* (Los Amigos de Libro, La Paz, 1980)

Box, Ben, ed., *South American Handbook* (Trade and Travel, 1999)

Brennan, Herbie, *The Atlantis Enigma* (BCA, 1999)

Caccia, Angela, *Beyond Lake Titicaca* (Hodder & Stoughton, 1969)

Castaneda, Jorge, *Compañero: The Life and Death of Che Guevara* (Bloomsbury, 1997)

Cattebeke, Carolina, *Karcha Balhut* (UNA, 1998)

Collins, Andrew, *Gateway to Atlantis: The Search for the Source of a Lost Civilisation* (Headline, 2000)

Crewe, Quentin, *In the Realms of Gold* (Michael Joseph, 1989)

Daniels, Anthony, *Coups and Cocaine* (John Murray, 1986)

Davies, Peter, *Woman on Horseback: the Biography of Francisco López and Eliza Lynch* (London, 1938; Stokes, New York, 1938)

Duguid, Julian, *Green Hell* (Jonathan Cape, 1931)

Durrell, Gerald, *The Drunken Forest* (Rupert Hart Davis, 1956)

Fawcett, Lt.-Col. P. H., *Exploration Fawcett* (Century, 1988)

Fifer, J. Valerie, *Bolivia: Land, Location and Politics since 1825* (Cambridge University Press, 1972)

Flem-Ath, Rand and Rose, *When the Sky Fell: In Search of Atlantis* (Weidenfeld and Nicolson, 1995)

Fleming, Peter, *Brazilian Adventure* (Jonathan Cape, 1933)

France, Miranda, *Bad Times in Buenos Aires* (Weidenfeld & Nicolson, 1998)

Furlong, Guillermo, SJ, *Misiones y sus Pueblos de Guaranies 1610–1813* (Buenos Aires, 1962)

Gibson, Sir Christopher, *Enchanted Trails* (London Museum Press, 1948)

Gott, Richard, *Land without Evil* (Verso, 1993)

Greene, Graham, *Travels with my Aunt* (Penguin Classic, 1969)

Greenfield, Oliver, *In Quest of the Unicorn Bird* (Michael Joseph, 1992)

Grey, Henry, *The Land of Tomorrow: A Mule-back Trek through the Swamps and Forests of Eastern Bolivia* (H. F. & G. Witherby, 1927)

Grubb, W. Barbrooke, *An Unknown People in an Unknown Land* (Seeley & Co., 1911)

Guise, A. V. L., *Six Years in Bolivia: The Adventures of a Mining Engineer* (T. Fisher Unwin Ltd, 1922)

Hanbury-Tenison, Robin, *The Rough with the Smooth* (Robert Hale, 1969)

Hancock, Graham, *Fingerprints of the Gods* (William Heinemann, 1995)
    Heaven's Mirror: Quest for the Lost Civilisation (Michael Joseph, 1998)

Harvey, Robert, *Liberators: Latin America's Struggle for Independence, 1810–1830* (John Murray, 2000)

Hemming, John, *The Conquest of the Incas* (Macmillan, 1970)

Heyerdahl, Thor, *The Ra Expedition* (George Allen & Unwin, 1971)

Hicks, J. W. and Dunbar, I. M., *The Golden River* (Philip Allen & Co., 1922)

Isherwood, Christopher, *The Condor and the Cows* (Methuen, 1949)

Iyer, Pico, *Falling off the Map* (Black Swan, 1994)

Jones, Tristan, *The Incredible Voyage* (Futura, 1984)

Kandell, Jonathan, *Passage through El Dorado* (Allison & Busby, 1984)

Klein, Herbert S., *Bolivia: The Evolution of a Multi-ethnic Society* (Oxford University Press, 1982)

Knight, E. F., *The Cruise of the 'Falcon': A Voyage to South America in a 30-ton Yacht* (Thomas Nelson & Sons, 1883)

Lewis, Norman, *A View of the World* (1987)

Lindert, Paul van and Verkoren, Otto, *Bolivia: A Guide to the People, Politics and Culture* (Latin American Bureau, 1994)

Mahieu, Jacques de, *El Rey Vikingo de Paraguay* (Hachette, 1979)
    L'Agonie du Dieu-Soleil: Les Vikings en Paraguay (Paris, 1974)

Markham, Clements R., *The War between Peru and Chile 1879–82* (Sampson, Low, Marston)

Macintyre, Ben, *Forgotten Fatherland: The Search for Elisabeth Nietzsche* (Macmillan, 1992)

Métraux, Alfred, *Ethnography of the Chaco*

Meyer, Gordon, *The River and the People* (Methuen, 1965)
    Summer at High Altitude (Allen Ross, 1968)

Morris, Arthur, 'The Agricultural Base of the Pre-Inca Andean Civilisations', *Geographical Journal* 165, 3, November 1999

Mulhall, Marion, *From Europe to Mato Grosso* (London, 1877)

Murphy, Alan, *Bolivia Handbook* (Footprint Handbooks, 1997)

Page, R. I., *Runes* (British Museum)

Parris, Matthew, *Inca Cola* (Weidenfeld & Nicolson, 1990)

Pendle, George, *A History of Latin America* (Pelican, 1992)

Phelps, Gilbert, *Tragedy of Paraguay* (Charles Knight, 1975)

Poenitz, Alfredo and Esteban Snihur, *La Herencia Misionera* (El Territorio, 1999)

Roosevelt, Theodore, *Through the Brazilian Wilderness* (London, 1914)

Salmon, Ross, *My Quest for El Dorado* (Hodder & Stoughton, 1979)

Shukman, Henry, *Sons of the Moon* (Fontana, 1991)

Swaney, Deanna, *Bolivia* (Lonely Planet, 1988)

Theroux, Paul, *The Old Patagonian Express: By Train through the Americas* (Hamish Hamilton, 1979)

Williamson, Edwin, *The Penguin History of Latin America* (Penguin, 1992)

Young, Henry Lyon, *Eliza Lynch, Regent of Paraguay* (Anthony Blond, 1966)

GLOSSARY

adelantado	Governor
alcalde	Mayor
alcaldía	Mayor's office
alojamiento	lodging house
arroyo	stream
asfaltado	hardtop road
autopista	motorway
autovía	railcar
baños	loo
barrio	suburb
boliviano	monetary unit of Bolivia
cabildo	town hall
cacique	village headman
caliente	hot
camelote	clump of floating water hyacinth
campesino(a)	country person, peasant
caña	drink distilled from sugar cane
cantina	bar
caramelos	sweets
chachapuma	stone effigy, Man-puma
chicha	corn drink
chico(a)	child
chulpa	funerary tower
churrasquería	steakhouse
contrabandista	smuggler
cordillera	mountain range
Corregidor	local government official
descarrilamiento	derailment
empanada	pastry filled with cheese, etc.
empresa	business, company
empujador	vessel pushing barges
empurrador	vessel pushing barges (Portuguese)
estación	station
estancia	farmstead, ranch
ferrocarril	railway
gasoducto	gas pipeline

gobierno municipal	town hall
guaraní, pl. *guaranies*	monetary unit of Paraguay
guardafauna	wildlife warden
hamburguesa	hamburger
lapacho	tree
limpiabota	bootblack
lujo	luxurious
marinero	able seaman
mate de coca	hot drink made from coca
máximo autoridad	highest authority
mesa	tableland
No Adelantar	No Overtaking
norte	north
oleoducto	oil pipeline
los Paceños	the people of La Paz
pescador	fisherman
pollo	chicken
los Porteños	inhabitants of Buenos Aires
quebracho	'axe-breaker': a very hard wood
red	system
responsables	those in authority
sala de operaciones	operations room
seroche	altitude sickness
supermercado	supermarket
sur	south
teniente	lieutenant
tola	brushwood
vaquero	Paraguayan cowboy
viuda negra	black widow fly
yerba mate	Paraguayan green tea (*Ilex paraguayensis*)

Index

The Kota Mama Expedition was backed by the Scientific Exploration Society. The Society organizes challenging and worthwhile expeditions in remote regions of the world for people of all ages. For further details of these two- to three-week projects, or if you are interested in joining us, please contact:

Expedition Manager
Scientific Exploration Society
Expedition Base
Motcombe
Shaftesbury
Dorset
UK
SP7 9PB

Tel: 01747 854898 Fax: 01747 851351
base@ses-explore.org
www.ses-explore.org

An interactive CD ROM by Charles Sturge: Photographer is available. The web interactive CD slide show of the Kota Mama Expedition is menu-driven and includes over 50 images, soundtracks, background information and reports from the experts on the trip. *Requirements: Multi media, Pentium PC with web and e-mail connectivity.*

For further information or to place an order, contact
charles@ccsreportage.cix.co.uk
or call +44 (0)20 7737 5509.

If you enjoyed this book here is a selection of other bestselling non-fiction titles from Headline